Tense in the Novel

An Investigation of Some Potentialities of Linguistic Criticism

Tense in the Novel

An Investigation of Some Potentialities of Linguistic Criticism

W. J. M. Bronzwaer

Wolters-Noordhoff Publishing Groningen 1970

ISBN 90 01 17020 X

Contents

Preface

This book deals with linguistic criticism, that is to say, with the practice of applying to literary texts techniques of description borrowed from structural and post-structural linguistics. Linguistic criticism came into vogue in the fifties and has since then been searching for a theoretical justification that would establish it as a branch of applied linguistics. Since linguistic criticism can be seen as rooted in the stylistic work of Spitzer and Vossler and the literary theory of I. A. Richards, even if the parentage is not always acknowledged, it has already become a historical phenomenon.

The first chapter of the present study tries to sketch one aspect of the historical background by suggesting how the linguistic criticism of fiction is a phase in a broader historical development, that of the criticism of fiction. The chapter is limited in scope and does not attempt a history of modern novel-criticism, to which a separate full-length study could well be devoted. It tries to make the point that there are natural links between linguistic criticism and the developments that have been taking place in literary criticism since, broadly, the rise of the New Criticism.

The second chapter is offered as an interim report on the efforts of linguists and critics, in the fifties and sixties, to provide linguistic criticism with theoretical foundations. This search for a useable theory has been inspired by the prevailing notion that criticism ought to be 'scientific' at least to the degree in which modern linguistics is, and that there can be no science without a well-defined theory and a rigid methodology. The picture that results from our report is not one of complete chaos; in emphasizing such concepts as 'norm' and 'deviation' linguistic criticism has, from the linguistic point of view, contributed to focusing the study of literary texts upon 'the words on the page'.

The third and fourth chapters, which are more closely related to each other than to the other two, concentrate on one particular problem in literary language that is felt to be of primary importance: the relation between the 'Aussagesubjekt' of a text and its 'Aussageobjekt' or, more simply, between the writer and his subject matter. The assumption that such a relationship exists in literary works is based on an even wider assumption that has become questionable in certain literary fashions, namely, that a literary text is an utterance of a human mind about something. Chapter 3 studies this relationship with reference to the use of the grammatical tenses in fiction, a subject that has been dealt with by Käte Hamburger and Harald Weinrich in particular, but about which it is felt that more can be said. Since the behaviour of the grammatical tenses lends itself to fairly exact linguistic analysis, it is hoped that the approach adopted in this chapter guarantees accuracy of description, while the fact that what is studied is the relationship - moral and emotional - between the writer and what he writes about should guarantee that the issues the chapter deals with are meaningful. One of the main points which this chapter makes is that in talking about the use of the tenses we are talking about free indirect style, and that free indirect style is one of the most important linguistic tools by which the writer expresses his attitude towards his subject matter.

Chapter 3 uses the first chapter of Iris Murdoch's *The Italian Girl* (reprinted in the Appendix) and Michael Frayn's *A Very Private Life* as illustrative material. These books have not been chosen for their literary merits - or lack of them - but because they use the grammatical tenses in highly pointed ways. Their simplicity and high degree of 'patterning' are an advantage rather than a disadvantage because they enable the linguistic analyst to acquire a certain degree of skill in dealing with tense in the novel before tackling more complex novels.

Chapter 4 offers an extensive analysis and explication of Iris Murdoch's novel. It is a practical application of the observations made in Chapter 3, and enables us to reject once and for all Käte Hamburger's thesis that free indirect style cannot occur in a first-person novel. In fact, a careful investigation of how free indirect style is used by Iris Murdoch, based on the evidence of the behaviour of the tenses, results in an explication of the whole novel. In order to ascertain whether the approach through the tenses has been valid, this explication is verified by means of external evidence about Miss Murdoch's literary intentions, derived from her non-fictional writings.

The concluding chapter tries to justify linguistic criticism as a useful if not exclusively privileged approach to literary works, suggesting that the behaviour of the grammatical tenses as an important indicator of the relationship between 'Aussagesubjekt' and 'Aussageobjekt' deserves study not only in fiction but in poetry as well.

I owe a special debt of gratitude to Professor Dr. G. Storms and Professor T. A. Birrell of the University of Nijmegen, whose contributions to the genesis of this book have not been restricted to supervising it as a doctoral thesis. Without Professor Storms's constant encouragement and stimulation the book might never have been written at all, while his searching and abiding interest in the expressiveness of language has strongly influenced my formulation of the problems dealt with. Although Professor Birrell was not confronted with the book until it was in an advanced stage of preparation, the enthusiasm with which he played the role of *advocatus diaboli,* together with his own peculiar brand of efficient helpfulness, have done a great deal to streamline my thoughts and to give the book its ultimate shape.

I also wish to thank my colleagues at the English Institute at Nijmegen for creating an atmosphere in which it is still possible to work and think at a time when most academics find themselves too frequently taken up with duties that bear little relevance to what they were appointed for. In particular I should mention Mr. Jan Aarts, with whom I have had many discussions on linguistic matters that were enjoyable as well as instructive, and Dr. F. Aarts, who spared no time in helping me to see the book through the press.

Acknowledgements

Acknowledgements are due to Iris Murdoch, Chatto and Windus Ltd. and The Viking Press Inc., New York, for permission to reprint the first chapter and additional passages from *The Italian Girl* (London 1964), and to Michael Frayn and Wm. Collins, Sons and Co. Ltd. for permission to quote from *A Very Private Life* (London 1968).

I am grateful to the Netherlands Organisation for the Advancement of Pure Research (Z.W.O.) for a grant which enabled me to do part of my research in England.

I Linguistic criticism and the novel - a preliminary sketch

When the history of the criticism of fiction comes to be written, the eighteen-eighties will probably be considered as an important watershed. In Miriam Allott's words, 'Until this century, "lay" criticism of the novel tended to concentrate on a limited number of elements, notably characterization, plot and, quite frequently, style' [1]. The researches of Richard Stang and Kenneth Graham have shown that Miriam Allott's dating of the change that came over the criticism of fiction is conservative; the process had already begun in the second half of the nineteenth century [2]. On the other hand, the kind of primitivism Allott alludes to was not characteristic of 'lay' critics only but affected the work of professional literary men and reviewers as well. In the mid-Victorian period the novel was under constant attack from moralists who regarded the influence that Charles Reade or Wilkie Collins could have on young minds as a 'subtle poison', while the reading of fiction was defended on grounds no less moralistic, such as its power to 'awaken heroism' or to teach young girls 'unselfishness, kindliness and courtesy'. In such a narrowly moralistic atmosphere the critic was not expected to discuss novels in the same terms in which one would discuss the acknowledged masterpieces of poetry or drama. The emancipation of the novel from the state of artistic immaturity in which the prevailing didactic and moralistic types of criticism had kept it swathed was achieved in the face of heavy odds. If it is true that the novel was brought into being by realistic, rationalistic and positivistic tendencies in the eighteenth century, and flourished during the moralistic and utilitarian Victorian age, it may be said that the very forces that created the new genre impeded its growth towards artistic maturity. We should not be too surprised that the emancipation of the novel did not begin to take place until about 1880, when Victorian standards were losing much of their force.

Vernon Lee's essay on 'The Aesthetics of the Novel', collected in *The Handling of Words* (1923) [3], but written some time earlier, may serve as an interesting example of the transitional stage through which the criticism of fiction went in her days. In this essay, the novel is undoubtedly taken seriously as an art-form, demanding from the literary critic the same seriousness and sophistication of response as any other genre; in fact, the first essay in her book, 'On Literary Construction', deals with the novel as the most important literary genre. The aesthetics of the novel, then, is worth serious consideration, but the novel does not *need* aesthetic attractions: 'But in the question of novels, as in all others, the most useful thing, perhaps, is to be at the same time very aesthetic and very capable of momentarily shelving our aestheticism, or rather of being able to see and understand dispassionately, while keeping the most passionate aversions and preferences'. [4]

By the time Henry James started to write the Prefaces for the New York edition of his novels, later collected in *The Art of the Novel* [5], a long struggle had come to a definitive end. It had been a struggle that in its very issue reflected the primitivism of current critical practice: the question, in its barest form, had been whether the novel could be considered as a serious art-form and a worthy product of the human mind. That question, at least, had been answered: the Novel had been emancipated from the Story, to use Middleton Murry's terminology [6]. Criticism of the novel could stretch its wings confidently once serious-minded people like George Eliot and G. H. Lewes had proved the novel's philosophical and moral significance, and creative writers like Henry James, Joseph Conrad and R. L. Stevenson had announced its aesthetic coming of age. It was not long until, in Percy Lubbock's *The Craft of Fiction* (1921), the new critical approaches to the novel found expression in a form that may be called monumental, both on account of the self-confidence with which the book pretended to be the definitive treatment of the genre, and of the immobilizing effect it had on the criticism of fiction for a not inconsiderable period of time. For if Henry James is the inspiring force behind Percy Lubbock, *The Craft of Fiction* lacks the flexibility and subtlety of James's critical insights, and freezes into prescriptions what are in themselves exact, intelligent and sensitive observations of James's novelistic practice. Percy Lubbock's book gave the critics of fiction a new hare to chase, and the words 'art', 'craft' and 'structure' occur again and again in the critical efforts of the period. Thus the book which marked the acceptance of novel criticism as a serious and valuable occupation at the same time tended to limit its scope to technical matters.

Structure was indeed a fashionable critical object for the generation of critics and readers that looked condescendingly upon the old moralists and entertainment-seekers for whom plot, characterization and 'style' were all that mattered in a novel. Although Edwin Muir's little study *The Structure of the Novel* does not fulfil the expectations raised by its title, his statement that '...the plot of the novel is as necessarily poetic or aesthetic as that of any other kind of imaginative creation... [7], shows how sophisticated his conception of *plot* is compared with that of Trollope, who in his *Autobiography* compares the novelist to a man who hurries out to tell to the first person he meets a story he has just heard [8], a description curiously echoed in our own time by Frank O'Connor: 'You have to have a theme, a story to tell. Here's a man at the other side of the table and I'm talking to him; I'm going to tell him something that will interest him'. [9]

The sophistication was, however, achieved at the cost of something that in particular F. R. Leavis's criticism has enabled us to apprehend as a uniquely English force: a critical concern with moral and traditional values as enacted within a society that is recognizably our own, even if it is removed from us in time. E. M. Forster's *Aspects of the Novel* (1927) and in particular the Chapter 'Prophecy' may be cited as illustrative of the loss. What is conspicuously absent from Forster's book is a chapter called 'Style' or 'Style and Language', and Forster's promise that in dealing with the theme of 'Prophecy' we may come 'nearer than elsewhere to the minutiae of style...' is never carried out. The greatest distinction of Leavis's criticism is that it combines a sensitive response to language and style, the 'words on the page', with a conception of literary art in which style represents a value only in so far as it shapes a moral vision. To call Leavis's criticism 'moral criticism' is just as misleading as to call it 'linguistic' or 'stylistic' criticism; yet, at its best, it exhibits both these emphases. The corrections which Leavis's novel-criticism brought about in a climate determined by such critics as Lubbock and Forster resulted from a return to a closer attention to style and language and a comparative loss of interest in 'structure' in Lubbock's sense of the term.

The reaction against the type of criticism exemplified by Percy Lubbock's book was in fact headed by Leavis, who in 1933 published an article 'Towards Standards of Criticism' [10] in which he discussed an essay by C. H. Rickword, entitled 'A Note on Fiction' [11]. Although Rickword's essay starts out as an attack on character-criticism, it constitutes, Leavis says, the perfect comment on the kind of novel-criticism Lubbock stands for. Rickword, endorsed by Leavis, stresses the fact that novels, like poems and plays, are made of words; therefore, the critic's duty of '...responding sensitively and with precise discrimination to the words on the page' [12] applies to the novel as well as to the poem or play. The question whether the novel is to be taken seriously as an art-form is no longer put; it had, as we have seen, been settled by James, Conrad and others and, for Leavis, not in the last place by D. H. Lawrence. What matters to Leavis is to stress the kinship the novel has with other literary types, and the way in which the novel uses the resources of the language, which have been refined and in part created by the literary tradition. The artistic emancipation of the novel had, in the hands of such writers as Flaubert and Joyce, led to a growing distance between the new art-form and the literary traditions of the language in which it was composed. 'La prose est née d'hier, voilà ce qu'il faut se dire. Le vers est la forme par excellence des littératures anciennes', Flaubert wrote in 1852 [13], thus suggesting that the novel was written in a linguistic medium of its own, a language fit to be employed by the novelist independently from content, implying a conception of style that could ignore subject-matter since the new style was in itself

'...une manière absolue de voir les choses' [14]. It is precisely on the grounds suggested by such a 'programme' that Leavis objected to Joyce's *Work in Progress;* the concentration on the medium, with all the resulting experiments that go under the name of 'internationalization of language', is the result of the absence of a '...commanding theme, animated by some impulsion from the inner life capable of maintaining a high pressure' [15]. The resulting sophistication of the language is, as Leavis suggests, in reality a debilitation, amounting to the loss of the characteristic strengths of English. It might be said that the kind of attention Leavis pays to the linguistic surface of the literary work is too serious to allow for any absolutist ideas of style to arise. Between the extremes of 'structure-criticism' and 'stylistic criticism' he strikes a balance inspired by a firm conviction of the moral function of literary criticism, insisting that the balance is a characteristic English virtue. Moreover, through Leavis's efforts the idea of style undergoes an important modification. What matters is not style as verbal embellishment of an epic idea, but style as the organization of language through which ideas find expression.

The way in which Leavis's ideas about the novel have been put into practice by many of his followers, and in particular also the influence of I. A. Richards, have opened the field for what may be called a 'close reading' criticism of fiction, a criticism that gave the novel the kind of attention awarded to poetry by those twentieth-century critics who called themselves and each other 'new'. Leavis's definition of the novel as a 'dramatic poem', which has been largely taken over by the 'practical criticism' industry, incorporates some of the James-Lubbock views on the novel as a self-contained structure but at the same time redirects interest to the language in which the novel is composed, and to the necessity of paying to the texture of a novel's language the same attention as is afforded the language of poetry [16]. There must be no misunderstanding, however, about the implications that the term 'poem' has in Leavis's phrase. It is striking that Leavis's call for a close textual criticism came at a time when the novel had definitely grown 'poetic', for could the poetic novel not be trusted to invite exactly that kind of criticism of its own accord? As Kenneth Graham has shown, the self-consciously 'poetic' novel had its roots well back in the nineteenth century, even in the works of such hard-boiled naturalist writers as Zola and George Moore [17], while it has been said of Meredith that '...the medium in which he paints his characters is always poetry' [18]. The question, so familar a cliché of examination papers, whether Chaucer's *Troilus and Criseyde,* Byron's *Don Juan* and Browning's *The Ring and the Book* could be considered as novels is, from this point of view, hardly an anomalous one. In fact, at least one typology of the English novel subsumes the works of such writers as D. H. Lawrence, Virginia Woolf and James Joyce under the heading 'lyric', thus giving official academic status to the poetic novel [19], while the Bloomsbury writers obtained popular recognition for the

4

concept. For instance, T. S. Eliot's praise of Djuna Barnes' *Nightwood* sounds distinctly Bloomsburian: '... it is so good a novel that only sensibilities trained on poetry can wholly appreciate it' [20].

To this kind of evaluation Lionel Trilling took exception in a famous essay, 'Art and Fortune', which, though it is at least doubtful whether Leavis would support its wording and most of its conclusions, helps to explain why Leavis objected to the prose of poetic novelists like Joyce and Virginia Woolf precisely because it had alienated itself from the common heritage of the language and the best poetic tradition. Joyce's experiments with traditional styles in *Ulysses* are pastiche and therefore not creative in any real sense of the term. There can be little doubt that Leavis would agree to at least these arguments of Trilling's: 'The loss of a natural prose, one which has at least a seeming affinity with good common speech, has often been noted... A prose which approaches poetry has no doubt its own value, but it cannot serve to repair the loss of a straightforward prose, rapid, masculine, and committed to events, making its effects not by the single word or by the phrase, but by words properly and naturally massed' [21]. And further on: 'The admitted weakness of the contemporary novel, the far greater strength of poetry, the current strong interest in the theory of poetry, have created a situation in which the canons of poetical perfection are quite naturally but too literally applied to the novel'[22]. 'Poetic', applied to the novel, has, to Leavis and Trilling, acquired much the same pejorative sense that the phrase 'poetic diction' had for Wordsworth or Byron. This is an important reservation, which Leavis's term *dramatic poem* can now be seen to imply.

It has been suggested by R. L. Drain that Trilling's essay has prophesied the development of the English novel since the Second World War, if not in fact partly determined it [23]. Other critics have pointed to the influence which C. P. Snow's journalistic writings have had on the contemporary English novel [24]; in fact, they have noted surprising and unexpected resemblances between Leavis's and Snow's views on the novel. The alleged similarities between Leavis and Snow will not, of course, bear a moment's serious consideration and can be attributed to the same kind of misunderstanding of Leavis's intentions that is so striking in the writings of those 'practical critics' who like to think of themselves as Leavis's followers but whose main achievement seems to be that they condition their students to give the right answer in examinations. The link between Snow and Trilling, however, is established much more smoothly: 'The novel achieves its best effects of art often when it has no concern with them, when it is fixed upon effects in morality, or when it is simply reporting what it conceives to be objective fact' [25]. This passage seems to hark back to Vernon Lee in its effort to save the novel from artistic demands and at the same time reflects faithfully Snow's ideas about the form and function of fiction in our modern society, ideas that go back to the nineteenth century's journalistic conception of fiction in many respects.

The rise of what is commonly called the New Criticism, with its emphasis on the necessity of studying the verbal surface of literary works, together with the descriptive techniques that modern linguistics has developed, have between them led to a renewed interest in stylistics during the past thirty or forty years. This *rapprochement* between linguistics and literature has been discussed by many authors; for our purpose it would be superfluous to go into the background and explanations of this development. We may use a current term, *linguistic criticism*, for the approach exemplified by such books as Sebeok's *Style in Language;* the term does not imply a statement of principles but simply serves as a useful name for certain developments in stylistic and literary studies resulting from the impact of modern linguistics. Broadly speaking, linguistic criticism refers to the application of the descriptive techniques of structural and post-structural linguistics to literary works for the purposes of analysis and interpretation [26].

The awareness of the possibility of a linguistic criticism broke through to critics of poetry first of all, as is evident from such a notorious fruit of the movement as the Indiana 1958 conference on Style in Language, whose proceedings have been recorded in the book edited by Sebeok [27]. The reasons for this are not difficult to understand. There is, on the one hand, simply the novel's unwieldy size while, on the other, the fact that novels use the literary effects of language is less obvious than this is in the case of poetry, for which a whole tradition of diction-criticism has long been available. This tradition had taught critics of poetry to pay close attention to the way in which the resources of language, and in particular the vocabulary, were used in the poems they studied. Novels were traditionally read for the story they told, the psychological interest of their characters, and the moral message they conveyed, while style was considered as a kind of embellishment the novel could very well do without.

The rise of a linguistic criticism of fiction, then, took place considerably more recently than was the case with poetry. A frequently reprinted call to action was Mark Schorer's 1948 essay 'Technique as Discovery' [28]. The resources of language, Schorer complained, are in the usual criticism of fiction never thought of as '...a part of the technique of fiction - language used to create a certain texture and tone which in themselves state and define themes and meanings'. Schorer's terminology as well as his critical assumptions owe a great deal to the critical writings of John Crowe Ransom, and his real interest in the language of fiction turned out to be rather one-sidedly centred on metaphor. Neither in the 1948 essay nor in an essay published in 1949, 'Fiction and the Analogical Matrix', does he ever really come down to linguistic analysis or observation; although he states that '...criticism of the novel must begin with the base of language, with the word, with figurative structures, with rhetoric as skeleton and style as body of meaning' [29], it is in the end quite obvious that to him, as to Ransom, texture means metaphor and language imagery [30]. There is no evidence in these essays that Schorer envisaged practical ways to execute his programme of linguistic criticism for the novel beyond the fields of metaphor and imagery.

In 1950 Martin Turnell, in a book on the French novel, restated in a more explicit manner than Schorer what had been Leavis's intention in his attack on Percy Lubbock. He did so in terms that pointed to the possibility of a linguistic criticism for fiction, thus illustrating one of the lines of development that can be drawn from Leavis's seminal work on the novel: 'A novel is essentially a verbal pattern in which the different "characters" are strands, and the reader's experience is the impact of the complete pattern on his sensibility' [31]. Turnell relates certain developments in French fiction to certain changes that took place in the French language itself, in particular focusing his attention on syntax [32]. The common New Criticism obsession with metaphor has, in his book, given way to an approach that is quite literally linguistic.

The correspondence, in 1951, between Emil Staiger and Martin Heidegger, together with Leo Spitzer's interference in the discussion, reflects the battle between 'metaphysical' and 'linguistic' criticism that was coming to an end at that time [33]. Spitzer accuses Heidegger of lack of philological discipline, and points to the English *'Kulturmilieu'* from which the critic has much to learn. It is true that the large amount of work done in 'linguistic' criticism since 1950 is to a great extent due to the efforts of English-speaking scholars, while they have in particular been devoting more and more studies to the work of novelists and prosewriters. The computer has facilitated statistical jobs and so helped to solve the problems imposed by sheer bulk and size, but a considerable number of critics have not waited for the computer before applying linguistic procedures to longer prose texts, trying to understand the impact these texts make on their artistic sensibilities [34]. In the 1958 English Institute Essays, *Style in Prose Fiction* [35], we come across places where technical linguistic observation is applied to the study of style, and the terminology employed serves as an index of the kind of approach followed: terms like *syntax, prepositional phrase, main clause, predicate, coordinate conjunction*, all occur in a single essay, 'Style in American Fiction', dealing with the syntax and vocabulary of classical American fiction. We have linguistic analyses of the language of individual authors, among whom Jane Austen and Charles Dickens seem to be favourites [36]; we have articles with titles like 'The Present Tense in Bunyan's *Pilgrim's Progress*' or 'The Present Tense in *Jane Eyre*' [37].

Apart from such cases, in which the linguistic critic concentrates on specific features of the novel's language, there has arisen an approach that works by analysing short, selected passages from novels. Jonathan Raban, who has

7

practised this approach himself, sounds a warning that criticism applied in this way can at best be descriptive, and that the critic must avoid turning the selection itself into a form of value judgement [38]. He recognizes in particular the usefulness of linguistic criticism in helping to define the register or registers which a novelist employs. He also illustrates, in the case of a passage from Margaret Drabble's *Jerusalem the Golden,* how the observation of syntactic features can help to identify the point of view from which a particular passage is presented. Raban's book is representative of what the application of linguistic criticism to the novel has so far achieved; his insistence on the purely descriptive character of such criticism sounds a note of modesty that is perhaps not heard often enough.

It may, then, be doubted whether Anthony Burgess was right when he wrote that the general view is that literature has nothing to do with linguistics [39]. Linguistic criticism has become a popular field of study through such books as Winifred Nowottny *The Language Poets Use* (London 1962), Christine Brooke-Rose *A Grammar of Metaphor* (London 1958), Francis Berry *Poet's Grammar* (London 1958), Donald Davie *Articulate Energy* (London 1955), Roger Fowler, ed. *Essays on Style and Language* (London 1966), William E. Baker *Syntax in English Poetry 1870 - 1930* (Berkeley 1967), Seymour Chatman and Samuel R. Levin, eds. *Essays on the Language of Literature* (Boston 1967), James D. Barry and William U. MacDonald Jr. eds., *Language into Literature* (Chicago 1965) and Geoffrey N. Leech, *A Linguistic Guide to English Poetry* (London 1969), while bibliographies of the subject are already available.

The title of the special issue which *A Review of English Literature* devoted to the new developments in linguistic criticism is significant: 'New Attitudes to Style'. The concept of style will have to be redefined when the means and methods by which it is studied have become so different [40]. Of course there are critics who demur at what they tend to think of as the new fashion; F. W. Bateson's polemic with Roger Fowler in *Essays in Criticism* (1966 - 1968) is a case in point. Bateson's reservations must be taken seriously, especially because they come from a scholar whose awareness of the rôle played by language in the history of English poetry has been expressed in many publications since *English Poetry and the English Language* (Oxford 1934). There is a very real danger, of course, that linguistic criticism, through the superficial impressiveness of its technical vocabulary, might assume an authority which it cannot sustain, since its methods remain essentially descriptive and analytical only. That linguistic criticism has already become a controversial issue is due to the fact that claims have been made for it beyond its proper descriptive sphere. Thus, if the rise of linguistic criticism can be seen as related to the influence of the New Criticism, it is no less exposed to the danger of hypertrophy than some of the other critical fashions that Leavis has opposed. Meanwhile, nothing can be gained from taking dogmatic *pro* or *contra* positions. We hope to show that linguistic criticism, whatever its theoretical justifications may be, can provide valid descriptive tools for literary analysis.

II The theory of linguistic criticism - an interim report

(1)

The theoretical issues involved in what has come to be known as linguistic criticism are inevitably related to the wider question of the relation between literary and non-literary language. Since the descriptive techniques of modern linguistics have mostly been developed from analyses of non-literary material [1] the question arises whether it is possible to apply them to the study of literary texts. The answer supplied to this question by the majority of modern linguists is affirmative. In Roger Fowler's words, 'It is unlikely that any formal feature, or set of features, can be found, the presence or absence of which will unequivocally identify literature. Put another way, there is probably no absolute formal distinction between literature and non-literature: neither of these two categories is formally homogeneous' [2]. Fowler's statement may be taken as characteristic of the theoretical assumptions of such writers on the theory of literature as Susanne K. Langer, Isabel Hungerland, many of the New Critics, Laurence Lerner and René Wellek and Austin Warren, as well as of the approach taken to literary language by such linguists as M. A. K. Halliday, Brian Lee, A. L. Binns, G. N. Leech and C. J. E. Ball [3]. Halliday formulates the position with a bluntness that is at least remarkable: 'The linguistic study of literature is textual description, and it is no different from any other textual description; it is not a new branch or a new level or a new kind of linguistics but the application of existing theories and methods. What the linguist does when faced with a literary text is the same as what he does when faced with any text that he is going to describe'. To Halliday, there is no difference between literary and non-literary texts discernible to the linguist. His conception of linguistic criticism is extremely restrictive and tends to minimalize literature to those features that the linguist can discover.

If this suggests how far the linguist can go, it certainly does not imply that the literary critic cannot and should not go any further. During the Language and Literature Seminar, held at the Linguistic Institute of Indiana University in 1953, it was also assumed that literary works cannot be studied unless the student is '...deeply versed in scientific linguistics', but there it was explicitly stated that although a piece of literature is a language act like other language acts, it is differentiated from them by characteristics of its own [4]. Whatever the exact relationship between linguistic and literary criticism will turn out to be, it seems obvious that assumptions of the latter sort underlie the approach to literary texts taken by statistical stylistics and by computational linguistics.

The view generally offered by these theorists and many of their colleagues is that the language is a *continuum* in which only differences of degree exist between various uses of languages or, in David Lodge's words, that all uses of language '...can be placed on a scale according to the extent to which each example *draws attention to the way it is manipulating language*' [5]. The view exemplified by this statement implies a definition of literature as '...discourse that calls attention to the ways general grammatical possibilities are worked out in combination' or 'discourse that calls the reader's attention to its own organization' [6]. Such a definition seems to be understood by most writers in the field of linguistic criticism, and its convenience from the viewpoint of analysis, as Karl D. Uitti has remarked, is obvious [7].

The term *continuum*, probably first used in this sense by Laurence Lerner [8], has become a household word among writers on the subject [9] and has even obtained a degree of popular currency, as its use in a popular magazine illustrates [10]. As David Lodge's book makes clear, the theory of a linguistic continuum is committed to certain philosophical presuppositions, which need not occupy us here. William E. Baker has used the word to describe a perception theory using a scale-model to which the linguistic continuum would run parallel: 'To summarize this discussion of the poetic process, we might imagine a linear continuum from perception through waking consciousness to the dream-world or frontier of the unconscious. At either end of this continuum occur largely visual images, or at least unverbalized sensations of one sort or another, while at the center there exists a structured body of knowledge or ideas and a corresponding body of grammatical utterances capable of communicating this information - if, indeed, the two are separable at all' [11]. Thus, the continuum-theory provides a linguistic as well as a perceptional model, and makes it possible to describe the linguistic message and its perception as proportionately related. To each degree of 'literariness' there would be a corresponding 'state of mind', in this kind of description.

There remain, however, dissidents to the idea of a linguistic continuum or, in other words, the idea of literature as being linguistically selfconscious to a higher degree than other forms of discourse. An oft-quoted phrase by Eliot, '...the poet must... dislocate... language' [12] is not relevant here, especially not in view of Eliot's other statements about the nature of poetic language and in view of his poetry itself. But there are linguists who still maintain a dichotomy between literary and non-literary language. In most cases their views can be traced back to a simplistic interpretation of I. A. Richards' time-honoured distinction between *symbolic* or *referential* and *emotive* use of language, and it is perhaps not unexpected that we should find most of these dissidents in America [13]. Thus Robert B. Heilman states quite unequivocally not only that '...poetry and prose are fundamentally different kinds of expression', but also that a distinction must be drawn between literary and non-literary uses of language. Although he admits that '...rigid distinctions waver', he repeats Valéry's metaphor '...prose is walking to a destination, poetry is a dance' [14]. Similar views are held by Cleanth Brooks and by Herbert Read, who has also repeatedly subscribed to Valéry's poetics: 'I agree with that great poet Mistral, whom Paul Valéry so greatly respected, that form alone exists - only form preserves the works of the mind'. For anyone who accepts the poetics of the French symbolist and imagist poets, the doctrine of the continuum must necessarily be heretical [15].

The simplified version of Richards' distinction which seems to underlie the theories of Heilman, and to which Read's poetics may perhaps be related, asserted itself quite clearly during the 1958 Conference on Style in Language at Indiana. The view that the study of poetic language falls within the realm of linguistics was questioned there by Edward Stankiewicz, John Hollander and, most forcibly, René Wellek: 'Literary analysis begins where linguistic analysis stops' [16]. Wellek's remark, like many of his contributions to the discussion, sounds dead-pan but very sensible, and quite pertinently shows up the confusion to which theoretical disputes on theoretical linguistic and critical issues may easily give rise.

Richards' dichotomy has left its traces in many critical works that do not as such deal with the theoretical question whether there are essential formal differences between literary and non-literary language. Thus, Ian Watt's remark 'It would appear, then, that the function of language is much more largely referential in the novel than in other literary forms...' [17] reflects the influence of Richards without committing the author to any theoretical position of the larger question. Similarly, modern linguists owe a debt to Richards, especially in their concern with emotive or subjective styles of discourse, without being obliged to accept all the theoretical implications to which Richards' views have given rise [18]. The fact is that Richards' dichotomy does in no way imply a set of different formal features for emotive and referential discourse. His distinction merely poses a different *semantics* for each of the two forms of discourse. Purely referential discourse occasions single interpretation; poetic language occasions multiple interpretation. As Jerome P. Schiller points out, mathematics and poetry are described as the extremes of a continuous scale by Richards himself [19]. In spite of the difficulty that Richards has not made it unambiguously clear what is to be understood by emotive language, there can be no doubt that poetry to him is a form of emotive discourse. Allowing for the fact that there seems to be some confusion here between intention and use of language, we can nevertheless say that a dichotomy between different functions of language, let alone different forms, is not implied in his views. That the terms 'emotive' and 'referential' have suggested such a dichotomy to Richards' readers is probably due to the fact that they have been used as catch-words by critics and linguists alike ever since *Principles of Literary Criticism* (1924) [20].

On the whole, the influence of Richards' terminology, however hard it dies, does not seriously affect the general conviction that the linguistic stratum of literary works is more than a vehicle or instrument, but that it is vitally involved in making literature what it is, and that the study of literature must at least begin with the linguistic stratum. From our appreciation of literature as a verbal art, the conviction that the tools and methods of descriptive linguistics are relevant to literary analysis must necessarily follow. A few exceptions must perhaps be mentioned that do not fit into the general critical climate of our day: the structuralism of the neo-Aristotelian school of the Chicago critics [21] and a number of experimental theories concerning the seman-tics of literature, which claim that literary language is a 'metalanguage' and that the semantics of literature must be studied '...without reference to external correlates...' [22]. Whether one likes to take such extreme views seriously or not, there can be little doubt that there is a consensus of opinion on the problem of literary language that might be paraphrased as follows: literature is composed in language, oral or written, that is, in the medium of all common forms of discourse, and not in a 'metalanguage' with a set of phonological, grammatical and semantic rules of its own. Nevertheless, literature is distinguished by the extent to which it uses language in a manner different from its use in non-literary texts. This extent is not fixed; therefore, if there is a poetic use of language recognizable as such, and peculiar in its effect on the reader or listener, it cannot be isolated from other forms of discourse by linguistic description. Therefore, linguistic description is relevant to literature at least to the extent to which it is relevant to other forms of discourse. But linguistic description can never exhaust literary analysis.

(2)

Various attempts have been made by modern linguists to define the different ways in which language is used in literary and non-literary texts. A well-known distinction, very popular in the nineteenth century, is that between subjective and objective language. Alexander Bain's standard work on rhetoric reflects this contrast in its division into two volumes, devoted to 'intellectual' and 'emotional' elements of style respectively [23]. The nineteenth-century use of the terms subjective and objective has been studied by Richard Stang [24], whose investigations show that subjective prose was supposed to be the right vehicle for the novelist by nineteenth-century critics, and for our purpose it is relevant that such prose was considered 'poetic'. A similar distinction is made in a twentieth-century handbook on prose by Marjorie Boulton [25], although here an important differentiation is added between stylistic and psychological subjectivity. Thus Miss Boulton shows that what is unpoetic in the nineteenth-century sense may well be subjective and so 'poetic' to a twentieth-century reader. It is precisely because the terms poetic and subjective cannot be defined in an exact manner, nor related to formal linguistic categories, that they are of little save impressionistic use for our purpose. Of the two 'subjective' passages Miss Boulton quotes on pp.96 and 97 of her book, one is characterized by the large number of descriptive adjectives, metaphors and similes it contains, while the other is characterized by their sparsity. Subjectivity, then, cannot be described as a linguistic category, not even if we ignore the extra complication of diachronic changes. It is true that the concept of *register* might help to differentiate between Miss Boulton's two passages, but this would ultimately necessitate assigning all registers to the categories subjective or objective. Such a classification would be heavily oversimplified, and to many registers quite irrelevant. One must conclude that the terms *subjective* and *objective* can only be of a very general use in conveying impressionalistically either a certain impression which a passage makes or a certain response that a passage evokes, but that they cannot serve as indicators of the 'degree of literariness' of a text.

Another concept that has been suggested as a means of explaining the difference between literary and non-literary language is *foregrounding* [26]. The idea of foregrounding was originally raised by the Prague school of linguists; their term is *aktualisace*. Basically the term denotes the extent to which, in a literary text, attention is drawn to the *way* in which the resources of language are used. Thus, in Tennyson's line

The wily Vivien stole from Arthur's Court [27],

there is metrical foregrounding (the alternation of stressed and unstressed syllabes is more regular than one would expect in ordinary discourse); phonetic foregrounding (the restriction to labial and liquid consonants in *wily Vivien;* the opposition of front vowels in the first half of the line and rounded back vowels in the second); and orthographic foregrounding (the recurrent *i* and the similar *v* and *w* in the same words); all these phenomena can be described in linguistic terms. We are entitled to say that the line foregrounds these features, and therefore that it places in the centre of our interest the way in which these features of the language are employed. Whereas the function of such features is purely communicative in non-literary discourse, they assume a symbolic function in poetic language; they are used autonomously. Thus we are able to recognize the line as being literary before we need even ask ourselves what the line means. Of course morphological, syntactic and semantic features also lend themselves to foregrounding, but the concept of foreground-

14

ing seems to enable us to recognize a literary text before these levels, at which meaning becomes a consideration, are reached. Theoretically this would mean that we can sooner recognize a text as being literary than we can recognize it as being linguistically meaningful; in other words, that we can sooner recognize *literature* than we can recognize *language*. Absurd though this may seem, anybody who allows typographical poetry, for instance, the status of literature, will have to concede the point.

From this an objection to the idea of defining literature on the basis of fore-grounded features becomes clear: criticism is minimized in favour of purely structural descriptions. There is a suggestion that the linguistic features exist-ing in a poetic text are interesting for their own sake, and have thus lost the nature of signs which point towards meanings transcending the purely struc-tural level. In fact, the view seems to imply that the linguistic features of a poetic text can be equated with what poetry is [28]. The linguistic philosophy underlying the concept of foregrounding is purely structuralistic and seems to reduce poetry to autonomous structure. Again, typographical poetry would seem to be the ideal to which poetry aspires in this line of thought.

If these implications are rejected, and the term 'foregrounding' is to be understood in a mitigated sense, merely denoting the occurrence of striking patterns, similarities, contrasts and the like, it is open to another objection. It is obvious that the recognition afforded by foregrounding can only be made with reference to a 'background'. That a certain feature is foregrounded can in the last analysis only be established by statistically referring to its occur-rence in ordinary or in any discourse. So the idea of foregrounding necessi-tates the availability of an inventory, a fully described or describable back-ground against which each feature can be measured. Thus foregrounding comes to mean much the same thing as deviation, as G. N. Leech noted. This in turn evokes the concept of the linguistic *norm*, a discussion of which will follow in due course.

The comparatively recent interest in the role played by grammar and syntax in literary language, emphasizes once more the fact that literary and non-literary language form part of the same continuum [29]. Yet, as the studies devoted to this subject make clear, in literary language, and in poetry first of all, the grammatical resources of the language are used much more con-sciously than in non-literary discourse; thus the study of grammar can help to enlarge our insight into what constitutes the literary quality of a text. More clearly even than by Levin's 'couplings', (paradigmatic resemblances arranged in parallel positions), this is illustrated by Roman Jakobson's theory of the linguistic fiction which is realized most fully in poetic language. The part of speech is an example of a linguistic fiction, but so are parallelisms; these phenomena have a 'formal meaning' of their own, independent of lexical meanings. As Jakobson points out, Hopkins was aware of these linguistic fictions and called them 'figures of grammar' [30]. These 'formal meanings', '...find their widest application in poetry as the most formalized application of language' [31]. We may speak, then, of 'figures of grammar', or even of 'figures of phonology' instead of the traditional 'figures of style' and 'rhetorical figures', thus creating the possibility of a purely linguistic description for all those phenomena that used to be the prerogative of that fascinating but elusive discipline called 'rhetoric'.

Another pair of terms frequently met with in modern writings on the nature of literary language is *casual* and *non-casual*. These terms go back to A. A. Hill's attempt to define literature as a formal category on the basis of stylistic features [32]. In Hill's system, non-casual literary texts are distinguished from casual or non-literary discourse. C. F. Voegelin, however, who used the terms with a much wider application than Hill, does not endorse this equation; casual and non-casual are for him merely a contrasting pair of descriptive terms, like *metric* and *non-metric* or *poetic* and *non-poetic* [33]. If *metric* should not be understood to mean *literary*, neither should *non-casual* so be understood; the concept merely offers an angle from which the definition of literary language can be approached. As Roman Jakobson pointed out, the equation of casual with non-literary and non-casual with literary uses of language is obviously erroneous in view of the fact that '...any verbal behaviour is goal-directed...' [34]. If the term *casual* is to be understood here in the sense which the word commonly has, it is useless for the purpose of characterizing non-literary discourse. An important step in the direction of a more concrete meaning of the term was undertaken by Sol Saporta during the Indiana Conference in 1958 [35]. Using Chomsky's notion of a hierarchical scale of grammaticalness, Saporta suggests that the linguistic traits distinguishing poetic language can be described as deviating from a norm constituted by perfect grammaticalness, the 'casual' grammaticalness of easily generated sentences. The kind of features of poetic language with which Saporta is mainly concerned might be called 'figures of grammar' again; thus Saporta has limited the original meaning of the term 'non-casual' to a purely structural level, and little has been left of the original intention to make the term serve as a denomination of poetic or literary discourse. An attempt to remedy this, and to give the terms a more comprehensive meaning, has been undertaken by Weinreich, who has called the use of language in conventional or casual discourse 'desemanticized', in contrast to the 'hypersemanticized' use of language in literature. These terms do not open any new perspectives either, since the degrees of semantic intensity need description in linguistic terms, such as foregrounding or ungrammaticalness, in order to be amenable to further analysis [36].

Another complication arose when Saporta went so far as to equate casual with 'prose' and non-casual with 'poetry'. This leads to a fundamental problem which underlies the whole question of literary and non-literary language: the problem of defining the difference between prose and poetry, and the results of their distinction for the problem of literary and non-literary language, and for the stylistic, linguistic and critical study of literary texts.

(3)

In the first edition of Herbert Read's *English Prose Style* (1928) the following two statements occur: 'Poetry alone is creative', and 'The art of prose is not creative, but constructive or logical' [37]. In the second edition of 1952 these sentences have been omitted. The dichotomy had obviously become untenable by 1952. It had, in fact, been untenable since, in the *Preface to the Second Edition of the Lyrical Ballads,* Wordsworth had written: 'It may be safely affirmed that there neither is, nor can be, any *essential* difference between the language of prose and metrical composition', or even since the days of Sidney and Jonson, behind whose distinction between 'verse' and 'poetry' lies the use of 'poetry' as an appreciative rather than a descriptive term [38]. That poetry and prose came to be regarded as essentially different uses of language for a period during the last quarter of the nineteenth and the first of the twentieth century, a period of which Herbert Read was in so many ways the legitimate heir, was due to the influence of the French symbolist poets, and in particular to Valéry's famous essay *Questions de Poésie* [39]. Of course, as F. W. Bateson has said, there have throughout the history of English poetry been periods, schools and individuals that considered poetry to be '...either the alternative or the antithesis...' of prose [40]. But eighteenth-century notions about poetic diction concerned the lexical aspect of language almost exclusively, and the Augustans, as Bateson himself observes, held that '...the condition of poetry's health and intelligibility is that those words that it does use - briefly, anything except archaisms, vulgarisms, and technical terms - shall derive from that common fund of language which it shares with prose' [41]. Even Thomas Gray's famous statement 'Our poetry ... has a language peculiar to itself...' [42] refers only to 'idioms', 'derivatives' and 'expressions', in one word, to vocabulary.

Coleridge's answer to Wordsworth's *Preface* in Ch. 18 of *Biographia Literaria* presents a more complex case. He begins by stating that, if Wordsworth is referring to vocabulary only, his observation that there is 'no essential difference between the language of prose and that of metrical composition' is merely trivial, thus solving the problem of 'poetic diction' at one stroke. There must be some sense then, in which prose and poetry differ - or do not differ - more significantly. Arguing from metre, Coleridge states that there are occasions that naturally - organically we might say - call for metrical composition while there are others that do not. The linguistic features that Coleridge mentions in order to specify the difference are order of words, figures of speech and amplifying adjectives. This is obviously not a complete linguistic description of the language of poetry, and Coleridge is not really interested in such a description. Poetry is defined to him not by its linguistic characteristics but by its effects. Now in rejecting Wordsworth's demand that poetry should be linguistically like prose (which, as he says, it hardly ever is even in Wordsworth's own compositions), Coleridge may seem to be verging towards a theory implying a different function for poetic language, a different semantics for poetry. That this is in fact not so is evident from his suggestion that some of Wordsworth's pieces might gain by being re-written in prose. What Coleridge is trying to do is to formulate an organic view of literary language. In the process he has unmasked Wordsworth's phrase as essentially *prescriptive*. It is obvious that Coleridge, whose influence on I. A. Richards has been so strong, is liable to the same sort of misunderstanding as is Richards himself. In terms suited to our purpose we might say that neither Coleridge nor Richards break the continuum, i.e. delegate poetic language to a position where it can no longer be described linguistically.

Against this native English background of a common-sense approach to the problem of poetry and poetic language, the insistence of the French symbolists that poetry is a kind of super-language, an 'autotelic' language with a reference system of its own, stands out as exotic [43]. Nevertheless, the revolution in the ideas about poetic language brought about by the French symbolists has left less isolated traces than in Herbert Read. We have already seen that the symbolist view of poetic language is in line with the simplified interpretation of I. A. Richards' dichotomy of symbolic and emotive use of language. Laurence Lerner, in 1960, was taken in by the Richards-Valéry parallel, and his comment suggests the incompatibility of the theory with Richards' educational and critical aims: 'If Richards' theory of the two kinds of language finds such unlooked-for support, we may feel confirmed that it is at odds with the main purport of its author's writings' [44], an incompatibility that has also been commented upon by Trevor Eaton [45].

Whether or not by way of Richards' unintentional influence, it is notable that the symbolist doctrine recurs in a number of American writers. We have already mentioned Robert B. Heilman, who quotes Valéry's famous comparison: 'Prose is walking to a destination, poetry is a dance', and to whom poetry and prose are '...fundamentally different kinds of expression' [46]. We meet similar ideas in Philip Rahv's call for a '...sharp distinction in principle between prosaic and poetic speech' and in his statement that the function of language in novels is *communicative* [47]. A novel, to Rahv, is in the final analysis not a verbal construction; it is the mock-reality the novel offers that we are ultimately interested in, not the words that compose it. Rahv, then, quite consistently objects against using style as a criterion for value in judging fiction, and he blames John Crowe Ransom for doing exactly that. Never-

18

theless, Ransom himself, in an essay entitled 'The Understanding of Fiction'. to which Rahv refers, never really breaks through the dichotomy, although he is constantly on the verge of doing so: 'Till I am persuaded otherwise I must assume that the stylization of language in prose fiction will have the same consequences for critics as the tricks of language upon which they are adept at pouncing in the poem' [48]. Ransom's definition of style also implies, unwittingly as it were, the concept of language as a continuum accommodating all degrees of poeticalness: 'A style is the aggregate of those characteristic turns of speech by which the author frees himself of the restrictions of logical prose; the latter being of course the strict prose of science or the common bread-and-butter prose of affairs: either way, the prose of utility' [49]. At the same time, the second half of the definition almost but, if taken literally, not quite, endorses what is known as Richards' dichotomy. The difficulty here seems to be that Ransom sees style as an extrinsic, additive quality of the literary work; at the one extreme there is poetic language, heavily ornamented and loaded with 'style', while at the other there are 'style-less' uses of language, which nevertheless do not essentially differ from the others precisely *because* their stylistic embellishment is merely an additive. Over against Ransom's extrinsic view of style may be put W. K. Wimsatt's and Monroe C. Beardsley's definitions of style as an intrinsic quality of discourse, closely related to its ultimate meaning. Their views have, in turn, been attacked by Seymour Chatman, who describes the opposition as a battle between Platonists and Aristotelians, claiming that the Aristotelian view is more useful for purposes of description, as does Richard Ohmann in another context [50]. Yet Wimsatt's distinction between *logical* and *counterlogical* figures of style retains a vague suggestion of being related to the symbolic/emotive, prose/ poetry dichotomy in its equation of the counterlogical figures with non-logical or poetic discourse [51]. Though style is recognized by Wimsatt to be an inherent feature of any text, yet the dichotomy is preserved by being simply lifted on to another level: the verbal. This has been made possible by including style in the conceptual dimension, where the dichotomy obtains. Thus, Wimsatt's theory of style has the advantage of bringing a time-honoured semantic distinction to bear on the linguistic level and has created a possibility for a semantics of style. The importance of such an attempt at a time when style tends to be equated with structural patterning will be obvious.

American linguists have reported cases where poetry operates in a linguistic system different from that of non-poetic language [52]. All European languages have, or have had at one or more periods of their history, a 'poetic' vocabulary, that is, a structured set of words and phrases set apart for use in poetry. Nevertheless, the conclusion that poetic language constitutes a system different from and independent of the system of the language as such, is not justified. 'It may therefore appear that the difference in the phonemic inventory, or more broadly in the linguistic system, constitutes one of the distinctive characteristics of poetic discourse. Such a conclusion would, however, be unwarranted, considering that some poetic works, or even entire literary traditions, show a strict adherence to the prevailing synchronic norm' [53]. This statement raises a number of vital questions, among which the problem of the *norm* and of deviation from that norm will have to be dealt with at some length. As we have seen before, the concept of the norm is also implied in Ransom's definition of style; there will be occasion to show that it is implied in most current definitions of style. Meanwhile, it is of some relevance to note that in the discussions evoked by the fact that the language of poetry can in some cases be shown to be consistently different from non-poetic language, the metrical question plays no role, so that in these cases poetry and poetic language are lumped together in opposition to non-poetic or non-literary language. Thus the question of the difference between poetry and prose may in these cases be replaced by the problem of literary versus non-literary language. The two questions are closely related, but they are not identical; confusion between them evokes the whole problem of 'poetic prose' for instance. Traditionally, the difficulty is partly solved by regarding metre as a condition of poetry but not of poetic language. Strictly speaking this view is incorrect, given such borderline-phenomena as 'rhythmical prose' and 'free verse'. Metre must therefore be regarded as irrelevant to the problem of poetic language as such, as in fact it was by D. H. Lawrence [54]. Metre is the distinctive characteristic only of *verse*, not of poetry, and therefore it cannot be a distinctive feature of poetic language. On the other hand, metre is so far the only reliable feature that distinguishes verse from all other uses of language [55]. Therefore, if metre is disregarded, the problem of poetry versus prose can be stated in terms of the alternative literary versus non-literary language, so that the term 'poetic language' comes to be equivalent to 'literary language'.

A statement like the following, quoted from an American textbook for High Schools, may at first sight seem confusing enough for the readers to whom it is addressed: 'As a matter of fact, many plotless "short stories" are in reality not narratives at all but lyrics in prose' [56]. When read against the background of what has been said, however, it makes perfect sense: the term *lyric* refers not to a poetic form, but to a poetic use of language. The word *plotless* is even more revealing: it suggests that fiction is defined not according to textural criteria, to use John Crowe Ransom's term, but according to structural criteria. If, then, we have stories that are plotless compared with other stories that do have a plot, and, on the other hand, stories that are 'lyrics' over against stories that are straightforward prose narratives, we can always, disregarding metre, set up a continuous scale that accommodates both the story and the lyric, both prose and poetry.

Similar views also emerge from modern European discussions of the subject. Käte Hamburger's *Die Logik der Dichtung*, one of the most important books in the field of the theory of literature to have appeared during the past twenty years, attempts to categorize literary works on an entirely different basis than the distinction between prose and poetry affords. The Eichendorff stanza, the Rilke letter and the passage from the C. F. Meyer novel which she quotes, cannot, she claims, be distinguished by any criterion derived from the 'poeticalness' of their language [57]. Hamburger's categories 'fictional' and 'lyrical' cut across the prose-poetry distinction squarely, and in support of this part of her theory - which, unlike most other parts, has not been challenged - she quotes Novalis: 'Die höchste eigentlichste Prosa ist das lyrische Gedicht' [58]. Käte Hamburger's book pays no attention to the problem of whether literary language is a kind of language different from non-literary language; her assumption is that the fictional genre (comprising prose-fiction and drama) on the one hand, and the lyrical genre on the other, employ language in different ways and make use of different 'Origos' or 'personae'. The distinction of genres is to her, however, exclusively a logical problem, and has nothing to do with the 'grammar' of their respective dialects. The different uses of language which she recognizes separate the fictional from the non-literary, but they also separate the fictional from the lyrical, while they do not separate the lyrical from the non-literary. Therefore, a possibility of distinguishing the literary from the non-literary uses of language does not emerge from her theory.

The well-known historical explanation which Owen Barfield offers for the distinction between poetry and verse once again calls up the problem of 'poetic prose'. In Barfield's view, 'prose' is a development out of the primeval poetry that was the beginning of language, and he quotes Emerson in support of his view: 'Language is fossil poetry' [59]. Obviously this theory, strongly influenced by Transcendentalist ideas as it is, poses the essential unity of all linguistic utterances in a common 'poetic' origin. 'Poeticalness' is the essence of all linguistic utterances, and the fact that this quality seems to belong naturally with verse at one time and comes more easily to prose at another, is accounted for by certain structural developments in the language: '...where a rigidly regular metrical framework has to be applied to a language in which grammar is itself growing strict concerning the order in which words may be placed, it must become harder and harder for verse and poetry to keep house together' [60]. To all intents and purposes, it may be said that Owen Barfield poses the same *continuum* as do most modern linguists and critics, even if he bases it on speculations concerning the origin of language and emphasizes the fact that the continuum may be broken.

In such a popular book as Middleton Murry's *The Problem of Style*, the presupposition that there is no essential difference between prose and poetry underlies the whole argument. The difference between the two is explained as a '...difference of tempo rather than structure, except, perhaps, in the case of that prose whose appeal is made directly to the rational faculty...' [61]. The term 'tempo' does not clarify the argument, but elsewhere Middleton Murry expresses himself more conventionally: 'Where thought predominates, the expression will be indifferently in prose or poetry, except that in the case of overwhelming immediate personal emotion the tendency is to find expression in poetry' [62]. Superficially this may sound very much like I. A. Richards, but there is an essential difference: whereas Richards maintains a different semantic function for language in either case, Murry is simply saying that the same medium is used with different emphasis *(tempo* is his own word) in the case of poetry and of prose. Like F. L. Lucas, however, whose position is nowhere essentially different from Murry's, the latter warns against the danger implied in the facile use of a 'poetic' prose style: '...there is nothing more dangerous to the formation of a prose style than the endeavour to make it poetic' [63]. Lucas recognizes the existence of poetic prose in a passage whose metaphors again evoke the idea of the linguistic continuum: 'Let us rather be grateful that both kinds of prose exist - that the Parnassus of prose has two summits; though for most of us, and for most subjects, the less lofty of those summits seems the safer' [64]. There are, in the opinions of these writers, no formal features dividing poetry from prose apart from metre. Even if Marjorie Boulton's questionable statement that '...metaphor is almost an essential of poetry; prose can be devoid of figures of speech...' is accepted, it does not affect the validity of the generalization. In Isabel Hungerland's terms, literalness and figurativeness are 'fluctuating properties of language', and her theory suggests that metaphors could be placed on a semantic scale ranging from extreme literalness to extreme figurativeness [65]. This scale could then be superposed on the continuum in which all linguistic features are ordered.

Middleton Murry's formulation that the difference between prose and poetry is merely one of *tempo* implies that the distinction should be considered as gradual and not as essential. It is easy to see why many of the theorists in whose eyes poetry and prose, or literary and non-literary language cannot be shown to be structurally different from a linguistic point of view, should still feel the need of some such concept as 'gradual difference' to describe the various effects that more or less literary uses of language produce. Winifred Nowottny, in her book *The Language Poets Use*, uses the term 'degree of patterning' (by which she understands the ordering of linguistic features in recognizable patterns such as parallelisms, oppositions, assonance, semantic rhymes, and so on) as a criterion to establish whether a given text is poetry or not: 'If there is not, in any respect at all, a recognizably higher degree of

22

patterning than ordinary language affords, there will not recognizably be a poem'[66]. Elsewhere she writes that it is the function of poetry to do 'at full stretch' what 'ordinary man does with his language'[67]. Most unequivocally this view of the matter has been formulated by Roland Barthes in *Writing Degree Zero*: '...poetry is always different from prose. But this difference is not one of essence, it is one of quantity'[68]. Although Barthes uses this statement, in his description of classical poetry, as a stick to beat the symbolists with, in whose hands the language of poetry had become entirely divorced from common discourse, the forceful wording nevertheless may betray a dissatisfaction not only with the practice of symbolist poetry but with certain concomitant theories of language as well.

To what extent those writers who use terms like 'degree' or 'quantity' or 'tempo' have anticipated what modern linguistic theory has come to establish as the common view may be seen from the following passage by Samuel R. Levin, in which the difference between poetic language and non-poetic language is shown to be one of degree in three different respects: 'If we now ask ourselves what intuitive responses to the language of poetry we might expect a theory of poetics to account for, there would seem to be at least these three: poetic language is more unified (or is unified in a different way) than the language of prose; poetic language is more highly compressed than the language of prose; and poetic language is more novel, that is, it contains more deviations than the language of prose'[69]. A similar notion of 'higher patterning' lies behind Stankiewicz' statement: 'The clearest distinction between poetic discourse and everyday casual language is in the periodic organization of the message'[70]. The same assumption seems to underlie Eaton's theory of the semantics of literature[71].

To sum up, we may say that prose and poetry can be regarded as two extreme positions on a continuous scale, just as is the case with the pair literary and non-literary language. Tentatively one might suggest the following model of language, in which any text could be placed according to the extent to which it is literary or non-literary, and shows the characteristics of poetry or of prose. The model does not accommodate the category of *verse*, which, as we have argued, is irrelevant to our discussion. To illustrate the model, we might place such works as Gray's *Elegy Written in a Country Churchyard*, Theodore Dreiser's *An American Tragedy*, T. E. Hulme's *Autumn* and Conrad's *Heart of Darkness* in those places where we expect that linguistic analysis, given the necessary descriptive tools, would put them. Of course this is not a critical model in the sense that any evaluative conclusions can be drawn from the assignments it permits; it merely enables us to classify literary works by means of linguistic criteria without committing us to any genre-theory and without falling into the danger of pigeon-holing. For linguistic criticism the usefulness of the model is immediately apparent, since its sophistication is precisely as high as the refinement of which linguistic description is able at any given stage. But it cannot pretend to be more than a tool for linguistic criticism.

	Non-literary	Literary
Poetry	HULME	GRAY
Prose	DREISER	CONRAD

(4)

If literary and non-literary language, or poetry and prose, do not differ in essence but only in quantity or degree from the linguistic point of view, it is nevertheless necessary to find criteria by means of which these gradual differences can be described. Such a criterion many modern writers now claim to possess in the concept of literary language as deviating from a norm. If a theoretical use of language is assumed that is entirely non-literary, this may be called the norm, and all other uses of language may be described according to the degree to which they deviate from that norm. Stylistically, then, literature may be defined as deviation from the ordinary language norm, and in fact such a definition has frequently been suggested [72]. Just as Buffon's famous dictum 'Le style, c'est l'homme même' [73] was the fashionable catch-phrase in discussions of style for a long time after 1753, the year in which it was coined, a current definition of style nowadays is: *style is deviation from a norm*. Of the many definitions of style in modern writings that have adopted this view, Nils Erik Enkvist's is no doubt the most forbidding: 'The style of a text is the aggregate of the contextual probabilities of its linguistic items' [74]. In all these cases, the norm is implied as an important part of the definition. Although Stephen Ullmann regards deviation from a norm as only one of four principles of stylistic description, the other three being choice, poly-valence and evocation, yet deviation seems clearly to be the central one [75]. Choice, in Ullmann's sense, can probably be analyzed to mean deviation: *une robe noire* would be the norm, while *un noir forfait* could then be seen as a deviation from the word-order rule set up by the norm [76]. *Polyvalence* and *evocation*, Ullmann's two remaining principles of stylistic description, are not so much definitions of style as attempts to describe its effect impres-

24

sionistically. Similarly, when Owen Barfield describes archaism in poetic diction as a '...choice of Words, and Grammar', he implies that archaism is a deviation from contemporary usage [77]. In fact, whenever style is regarded as essentially a matter of *choice* between various non-distinctive features of language, it will always be necessary to accept in principle the existence of a norm. The following quotation from Richard M. Ohmann is very revealing in this respect: '...a discussion of style as epistemic choice can operate effectively only over wide areas of prose, where habitual kinds of choice become evident' [78]. Here context, norm and deviation are all introduced as relevant categories for stylistic description. We have already seen that the concept of a linguistic norm underlies the stylistic theories of the Prague school of linguistics, in whose terminology 'foregrounding' is almost synonymous with 'deviation'. Most explicitly the insufficiency of the concept of *choice* has been formulated by Enkvist, and his conclusion again points to the concepts of context, norm and deviation as necessary assumptions for stylistic studies: 'Obviously, to get at style, the investigator must begin with the laborious task of setting up a corpus of reference to find the norm or norms from which a given text differs' [79].

If there is agreement on the necessity of some such concept as the *norm*, this does not mean that there is anything like agreement on the question what the norm is. The basic insight, shared by most writers on the subject, may be quoted in the words of Angus McIntosh: '...the assessment of what is individual in a man's style requires that we should be in possession of some sort of yardstick by which we can assess or measure his use of language. If we say that the later prose of Carlyle is remarkable, this must be in *comparison with something...*' [80].

The something in most theories is supposed to be the context, but here again a number of problems loom large. The idea of a 'norm' against which stylistic features stand out has been implied in European stylistics at least since the days of Bally and plays an important part in Spitzer's writings. To Bally, the norm consisted in the language of abstract statements or in the spontaneous utterances of every-day life, against which stylistically charged language stood out as 'affective'. Spitzer has not even tried to define the norm; the stylistic idiosyncrasies from which he starts his investigations simply 'stand out' from their environment. In Spitzer's writings, a tacit conception of the context as norm seems already implied. It is this notion that modern stylistics has developed further until, in the writings of Michael Riffaterre, the context as norm obtains full theoretical justification.

Modern theories on this matter can for convenience's sake be divided into two main types. There are theories which assume the existence and availability of a linguistic norm, derived from the language as a whole, and

25

obtainable by statistical inventorization of the language. There are also theories which deny the existence of a linguistic norm and assume a contextual norm. A first step towards a solution is taken by Enkvist: '...it seems advisable first to define the norm against which the individuality of a given text is measured, not as the language as a whole, but as that part of language which is significantly related to the passage we are analysing... Now some norms can be defined with perfect rigour... As long as we define the norm so that it yields a meaningful background for the text and feature under analysis, and as long as we limit it with operationally unambiguous procedures, definitions of style as deviations from a norm give us a good first basis for stylistic comparison... The crucial point is that limitations of the norm are based on criteria which can be labelled as contextual' [81].

One of the implications of what Enkvist says is that only co-registerial texts can fruitfully be submitted to stylistic comparison, and therefore that only very limited information can be gleaned from the comparison of texts belonging to different registers. Or, if a single feature is being examined, inter-registerial comparisons can indeed be made, but the resultant insight will be very limited at best. Secondly, it follows from Enkvist's views that only synchronic comparisons can be made if we do not wish to obscure the issue by invoking the complications of historical changes and developments. Diachronic comparisons will therefore always have to restrict themselves to single features, although, of course, the data yielded by a number of such comparisons may provide a basis on which diachronic comparisons of texts can be undertaken. However reliable the norm may be for synchronic comparisons, from a diachronic point of view it will always be unstable. This difficulty is clearly realized by Wimsatt: 'The logical virtues of twentieth-century prose style are scarcely noticeable as such, or are noticeable mainly when absent. They are the norm. They are in principle, however, the same virtues which attract attention as virtuosity in the style of Johnson or in the rhetorical styles of antiquity' [82]. In short: what is the norm today may be a deviation tomorrow. There is no doubt that these objections seriously limit the usefulness of what Enkvist understands by the norm. A related objection to his theory was raised by his reviewer David Crystal: 'It is important, for example, that a theory of style should allow comparison of the language of science and that of religion,and it should be possible to make meaningful statements about major contrasts, such as that between emotive and technical kinds of language, which is still a normal part of many school syllabuses in England. But such general comparative statements require norms larger than that of particular contextual groups, and ultimately a norm based on the language as a whole [83].

Now it is true that Enkvist has specified what he is willing to recognize as context in a systematic way, but in doing so he has complicated his theory to such an extent that it becomes all but unworkable [84]. A much more promising approach to the problem of context is that taken by Michael Riffaterre [85]. To him, linguistic norms - that is, norms derived from a linguistic description of the language as a whole - are irrelevant, because the reader's reaction to stylistic devices will not be based on any such norms, but on his own personal experience with the language, or on a vague and subjective *Sprachgefühl;* there is for each reader only his own personal norm or set of norms, which need to be identical with the linguistic norm. To help himself out of this stalemate, Riffaterre introduces the concept of the context as norm, without implying, as Enkvist does, that stylistic analysis is always done through stylistic comparison with other texts. What Riffaterre is trying to do is to create a possibility for stylistic studies to be meaningful without necessarily being comparative. The term context, then, acquires an essentially different meaning in his theory. It is no longer only an outward set of characteristics with which the text under study is compared; it is primarily an *internal* set of character-istics distinguishing a text from all other texts. He distinguishes between *microcontext* and *macrocontext* first of all [86]. Of a stylistic device that draws attention to itself in a microcontext he gives as an example Corneille's phrase *obscure clarté*. To realize that in this phrase a stylistic device is operating, it is not necessary to have recourse to a linguistic norm, derived from a study of large stretches of text. Such a norm would tell us that the word *obscure* commonly occurs in contexts where the word *clarté* does not occur. However, we would then not know more than the juxtaposition in a microcontext of the two words tells us of its own accord, at first sight as it were.

Riffaterre accepts as stylistic features only such phenomena as can be accounted for in linguistic terms, thus ensuring that what strikes the reader as a stylistic feature is in fact a feature of the text and not merely of the reader's response to the text. To Riffaterre, reader and stylistic analyst are not identi-cal, as they are to Spitzer. The reader's responses are material on which the analyst has to work, rejecting such as are not founded on linguistic features. Thus he distinguishes between style as a function of the text and style as a function of the reader [87], even though the reader comes first and provides the analyst with the materials on which the latter can work.

In a critique of Riffaterre's theory, Samuel R. Levin has pointed out that the idea of the microcontext is untenable, since an actually occurring linguistic element does not constitute such a standard as can be used as a norm [88]. It would, according to Levin, at least require the data furnished by a highly developed structural and statistical semantics to determine which norm is deviated from by the collocation *obscure clarté*. Now, of course Riffaterre's macrocontext leaves open the possibility of reference to such data; if, in the same Corneille text, a number of collocations containing the same or semanti-cally related words could be found, the juxtaposition of *obscure* and *clarté* could be judged as statistically deviating or not [89]. This would, how-

27

ever, lead us straight back into the field of statistical norms derived from the language as a whole. Now, as Levin admits, these are hardly available, least of all in the field of syntax, since we are never interested merely in the *types* of syntactic constructions used in a poem, but always in particular syntactic sequences. Riffaterre's dismissal of linguistic norms as useless is thus shown to be not wholly justified; his own theory smuggles them in again through a backdoor. In a later article, Levin seems, however, to meet Riffaterre half-way again. He distinguishes between internal and external deviation. In the case of internal deviation, statistical norms are not needed, since the work itself provides the norm against which deviations are measured. In the case of external deviations, they could be useful, if they were available, in the lexical and phonological fields; in the syntactic field, Levin still maintains, they are impossible. The objection that must be raised against Levin's distinction of internal and external deviation is that the two do not seem to be clearly separable. Levin quotes archaisms as an example: 'Thus, if archaisms or foreign terms were used sparingly in a poem, they would be internally deviant. If, on the other hand, they saturated a poem, then they might very well serve to establish a norm' [90]. Although the statement makes sense in itself, it still begs the question at what point of frequency a feature is no longer internally deviant and becomes externally so. The decision could only be made on statistical grounds, and so we are back again where we were.

In the last analysis, Riffaterre's theory does not justify the claim that statistical information can be dispensed with in stylistic analysis, especially also because it does not account for repetition as a stylistic device that can be measured only in terms of frequency. The difficulty is not removed by Levin's theory of internal deviation either; in fact it might be said that this theory implies that each literary work carries its own statistics with it. That this is so, is perhaps assumed by certain analyses of literary works that are actually on record, but of which it is extremely doubtful that they have any use at all [91]. Nevertheless, if we are willing to admit that the simple act of reading - or decoding, as many of these writers call it - implies the employment of a great deal of statistical knowledge of which we are not even aware, the theory may be given the semblance of truth. Such a store of unconscious knowledge might be termed 'stylistic competence'. However, in the case of lexical deviations, competence can only be relied on in so far as the semantic rules are incorporated in the syntactic component, in other words, in so far as the lexicon is subject to selectional rules. This is a moot point in the theory of generative grammar [92]. Statistical norms, then, are difficult to get around. Yet it is obviously important to keep in mind René Wellek's warning: 'Statistical frequency necessarily ignores the crucial aesthetic problem, the use of a device in its context' [93].

On the other hand, Crystal's call for a norm 'based on the language as a whole', supported by Levin, does not present a way out of the problem either. First, if deviations are merely judged by their difference from the reader's personal experience with the language, his stylistic judgement will hardly be able to claim any degree of objectivity and truthfulness at all. Second, since, as Levin recognizes, the reader's experience is based on 'everyday language', this view tends to re-open the gap between poetic and non-poetic, or literary and non-literary discourse unduly.

The concept of the norm, applied to context, at present raises as many questions as it answers. An example of the confusion that may arise from the lack of clarity from which these terms suffer, is offered by an article in a linguistic journal. The author based a classroom experiment on an insufficiently clear distinction between linguistic and situational context. The line 'And never lifted up a single stone' was offered to the pupils in two 'contexts'; Wordsworth's poem *Michael* and a building site where a foreman is commenting on a lazy worker. The conclusion could hardly be more than a truism: 'So the conclusion was now drawn that what we call a 'poetic' effect does not necessarily depend on any kind of special or heightened language, the kind normally thought of as 'poetic', but often on 'prosaic' utterances which nevertheless become emotionally highly charged because of their context' [94]. Nobody will deny this, but whereas the context constituted by Wordsworth's poem can be described linguistically, the fictional context of the building site cannot. The distinction between linguistic and situational context that is ignored here parallels the distinction between knowledge of the composition of language and knowledge of our reactions to language. When the teacher offered his pupils the line in the building site context, he was actually asking them *not* to decide whether the line was poetic or not, but whether they could fit the line into the prosaic situation; in other words, he was asking them what the line meant in the particular context. The idea of the context of situation played an important part in the theories of J. R. Firth and has through his influence become an inevitable issue in linguistic science. Its importance to semantics, and historical semantics, is obvious [95]. But since there is necessarily a situational background to any linguistic utterance, linguistic description cannot ignore situational contexts either. Thus, registers can be defined in terms of the situational contexts to which they apply; there may even be a relation between the set of formal features that makes up a register and the organisation of its situational background, as the structuralists maintain. This remains true when literary language is considered: *The Wreck of the Deutschland* differs situationally from *Ode to Autumn,* and therefore an attempt to describe the two poems in registerial terms could reveal something essential about them. On the other hand, A. L. Binns has suggested that in literary language, our knowledge of the imagined situation is derived from the language, whereas in non-literary discourse the language used is partly determined by the context of situation. The word 'partly' takes the sting out of the argument, and blurs the fact that ultimately this view presupposes an essentially different semantics for literary discourse than for non-literary uses of language [96]. This in fact came out in the classroom experiment mentioned above: the teacher was in reality asking questions about the meaning of the Wordsworth line in its different contexts, which was not the same in either case. We may summarize as follows: if we accept the context as norm, we will have to investigate in how far the linguistic context is determined by the situational background or, vice versa, in how far the situational context is 'new' since it is created by the verbal structure of the text. At an extreme point it is possible to envisage literary uses of language that create or invoke entirely new situational contexts, and which can therefore not be described in terms of existing registerial knowledge. The difficulties that new works of literature present to criticism can perhaps be explained with the help of the following proposition: the really new work of literature creates an unheard-of situational context and can only describe it in the language of an unknown register. The 'situation' of *The Waste Land* is so difficult to grasp because it is described in a register that is 'new' and consists of a deliberately startling mixture of elements from different registers that were traditionally kept very clearly apart: the pastoral and the urban, the 'poetic' and the 'prosaic', the ancient and the contemporary, the metrical and the non-metrical, the aristocratic and the vulgar. Eliot does not only confuse registers to arrive at this discontinuous effect; he also mixes idiolects (Shakespeare and the Bible, Spenser and Marvell) and even languages: English, German, French, Italian, Sanskrit and others. The challenge this poem offers consists in its deliberate undermining of our linguistic habits; therefore, linguistic science would seem to be an important tool with which the poem can be successfully approached. It certainly is no less helpful to a reading of *The Waste Land* than mythological information.

Transformational-generative grammar has in recent years offered a promising tool to solve the problem of the norm in at least the field of syntax. The norm would be the whole complex of syntactic patterns that can easily be generated by grammatical rules. The generatability of a structure marks it as being normative. Levin states quite explicitly that poetic deviations are grammatical deviations, although he takes care to make it clear that grammatical deviations are not necessarily poetic [97]. Poetic deviations, according to Levin, are controlled, or even, as Bierwisch claims, exhibit a certain regularity in the way they are used [98]. If poetic deviations occur regularly in spite of their deviant or irregular nature, there must be, one is tempted to conclude, a generative sub-grammar to account for poetic deviations. In fact something like this has been proposed: 'Now, if sequences can in some way be ordered as to the degree of grammaticalness, it may be possible to characterize the language of poetry in terms of the density of these sequences of lower-order grammaticalness' [99].

However attractive the prospects may be that are opened by transformational-generative grammar, which aspires towards an exhaustive description of the grammatical norm and thus claims to offer a reliable tool to decide what is normative and what is deviant, two objections can hardly be overlooked. First of all, the question of the grammatical norm is inextricably linked up with lexical problems. We may quote John Hollander: 'It is very obvious that there is nothing wrong morphologically or syntactically with saying: "That man is pregnant with ideas", for example. There is nothing grammatically wrong with such a sentence in the usual sense; it is just that it cannot be literally true' [100]. Hollander then suggests the terms *literal* and *non-literal* as being crucial for any consideration of literary utterances in a linguistic context; they are more comprehensive than 'grammatical' and 'non-grammatical' and do not isolate the grammatical component of linguistic utterances unduly. Robert J. Scholes objected to Levin's 1963 article on deviation on very similar grounds. According to him, Levin did not clearly enough distinguish between deviation by order on the one hand, and deviation by class membership on the other. Many deviations which Levin marks as grammatical are in fact not so; insisting on the fact that classes in the vocabulary are always open, Scholes defends Dylan Thomas' use of the collocation 'marvel away' as a transitive verb in *Poem in October* as an extension of grammar rather than a deviation from it [101]. Thus, the notion of grammatical normativeness is dependent on the number of rules and refinements of rules that are admitted into the grammar. This again means that a feature that will strike one reader as deviating will appear 'normal' to another reader; both readers bring their own grammar to bear on the text concerned. Here a difficulty arises that may perhaps be described as follows: the grammaticality of a text - apart from its basic generatability - is determined by the reader's or hearer's linguistic creativeness as well as by his competence in the strictly Chomskian sense of the term. This was neatly demonstrated when somebody published a poem in which Chomsky's famous ungrammatical sentence 'furiously sleep ideas green colorless' occurs [102]. What matters is not, of course, whether the poem is a good one, but whether the procedure implied in the composition of the poem is valid. If this is so, the grammaticality of a sentence becomes equivalent to the writer's or speaker's ability to imagine a context for the sentence. Since the context will always be the text in which the sentence is placed, the existence of an extra-textual norm, such as claimed by transformational-generative grammar, becomes questionable.

On the other hand, it might be said that the context provides clues as to what transformations can be applied to account for the ungrammatical character of the sentence. If this is so, the idea of the norm as 'easy generatability' can be salvaged, and the ungrammatical sentence can be referred to the grammatical norm by means of unusual or ad-hoc transformations. This implies a separate grammar for a text containing such an ungrammatical sentence. The implications of this view will be discussed below.

The second objection arises from Bierwisch's claim that poetic deviations from the grammatical norm are regular. It is obvious that in different literary works, different deviations are found, and this makes it difficult to see how a system of regular deviations, or in other words a grammar of deviations can be set up that would be applicable to all literary texts. What regularity is found can only apply to single texts, and if we want to insist on the notion of regularity in deviations we will have to postulate a separate system of rules, in other words a separate grammar, for each literary text and not only for ungrammatical texts. Now theoretically this possibility has been defended by J. P. Thorne [103]. For Thorne, literary texts can be so deviant that any grammar accounting for them would be intolerably complex, or capable of generating a large number of unwanted sentences as well. The way out of the dilemma which he proposes is to regard each text as having a grammar of its own, which ultimately means postulating for each text a separate language. Now there is something very sound in this idea: it allows room for the awareness that each literary work of art to a considerable extent establishes the criteria by which it is to be judged itself. On the other hand, the notion that two English poems are written in different languages will not be easily acceptable to most people. A more serious objection is that Thorne undermines one of the basic assumptions of generative-transformational grammar, namely, the capability of grammar to generate all the 'grammatical' sentences of its language, including also those that occur in otherwise deviating texts. Theoretical though this objection may be, it is nevertheless vital: generative grammar here denies its own tenets. It is true that Thorne speaks of a separate *dialect* for each literary text rather than a separate *language*, emphasizing that the text's grammar should be as nearly isomorphic as possible to that of the language with which the text naturally compares, but he does not seem to realize that, in this line of thought, the privilege of grammaticalness would be restricted to a corpus from which all literary texts would have to be a priori excluded. Moreover, in the case of difficult or strongly deviating poetry there is '...a relationship between the grammar which I propose for the poem and my understanding of it' [104]. If carried to its logical conclusions this would mean that for each poem there would be as many valid grammars as there are different valid responses from readers. Thorne's theory must therefore be rejected: in the end, it makes discussion of literature almost impossible, by assigning each literary work to a language of its own, whose grammar need not even be shared by the next reader.

A related objection to Thorne's proposal to describe the language of literary texts as dialects having grammars of their own has been raised by William O. Hendricks. Thorne's article had been written before 1965, when Noam Chomsky published his *Aspects of the Theory of Syntax,* which enabled Hendricks to recognize many of the deviations that Thorne regards as syntactic as irregularities in the lexical and semantic component. They violate selectional rules rather than strict subcategorizational rules, and therefore do not constitute ungrammaticalness in the *Aspects* sense of the word. Thorne's reply to Hendricks' article does not remove the force of the objection. Grammar, then, would seem to be irrelevant to the analysis of poetry, at least in so far as it is thought that poetic deviations can be interpreted with reference to grammatical rules. M. Riffaterre would seem to agree with Hendricks' view in this respect [105].

It must be realized moreover, that, if the generatability of a structure is applied as a norm, only those deviations can be recognized that result in some degree of ungrammaticalness. Free variations, which do not violate any grammatical rules, cannot be detected in this way. If, therefore, at the present stage of the discussion, it is not clear where the boundary between the grammatical and the semantic component of the grammar is, it can nevertheless be maintained that statistical or other non-grammatical norms will be needed to account for lexical choices. The reader's 'competence' could not replace statistical norms entirely, since in the lexical field the competence of native speakers differs.

In this context, Geoffrey N. Leech's distinction between deviations from surface structure and deviations from deep structure deserves notice. The former have no fundamental effect on the way in which a text is understood; the latter create, as it were, a new dimension to the language in which the text is composed. Leech's terminology here is misleading; he treats deviations of deep structure as cases of 'mistaken selection' whereas in fact they involve violation of strict subcategorizational rules. However, the distinction can be valid for describing the difference between such 'superficial' deviations as abound on every page of *Finnegans Wake,* which leave syntax intact, and the more radical deviations of which Dylan Thomas provides so many examples. Richard Ohmann suggests that deviations from surface structures are purely stylistic and that the content of a literary work resides in the deep structures underlying its sentences. The analysis of a literary work would then have to begin with the discovery of its deep structures. The most far-reaching aspect of Ohmann's view is that 'deep structure' is equated with 'content' and surface structure' with 'form' or 'style', and that the process of reading is equated to the discovery of the deep structures underlying the surface sentences of a text. Similar views are held by J. P. Thorne in a later review-article. Mark Lester, however, to whom most linguistic criticism preceding the transformational-generative school is of little interest simply because in the corpus-based approach taken by structuralism the concept of *choice* could play no role, is very sceptical about the claims of transformational grammar. According to him, the critic is concerned with the lexicon mainly, which is where the writer makes his significant choices. 'The number and range of choices open to a writer in the syntactic rules is minimal when compared with the richness of options in the lexicon' [106]. There can be no doubt, however, that in cases where a literary text contains strong syntactic deviations, the theory of transformational-generative grammar can be of great use in elucidating these deviations and 'restoring' the deep structures or, in other words, the 'regular' context underlying the 'deviating' surface. This would appear to be particularly so in the case of 'nonsense strings' such as are frequently found in the poetry of E. E. Cummings and Dylan Thomas [107].

Hardly less so than the concepts of the norm and the context, the idea of 'deviation' presents a good many problems. First of all, as Sol Saporta points out, deviation must not always be understood as denoting a tendency towards greater irregularity and freedom; it may also mean deviation towards further restrictions than ordinary language imposes [108]. It is characteristic of literary language that it transcends many of the limitations that govern ordinary discourse, but it is no less characteristic for literary language to impose upon itself important restrictions: on the phonetic level, rhyme and metre, on the syntactic level, regularity of structure such as parallelism, on the lexical level, poetic diction. Next, deviations may be internal as well as external, as we have seen. (p.28). Bierwisch has pointed out that it is characteristic of certain literary effects that deviations are made from norms established by the text itself, norms which are in their turn deviations from ordinary language [109]. Then, deviations may be *polemic;* we all know literary works in which strong deviations are enforced from worn-out poetic norms; Eliot and Pound both provide many examples [110]. Again, deviations can be ordered on a scale of what Trevor Hill has called *institutional delicacy* [111]; in other words, register, dialect and idiolect but also jargon, lingo, slang etc., are important considerations that cannot be left out of account in deciding whether a given utterance deviates or not. Lastly, there is the problem of distinguishing between deviations and errors, or, in transformational-generative terms, between ungrammaticalness and poetic ungrammaticalness: 'When is a unique deviation meaningful, and when is it merely a piece of nonsense?' It is a question which concerns literary interpretation in the first place, whether or not it can be answered in terms of linguistic analysis [112].

The 'deviation from a norm' theory, in spite of all the questions it leaves unanswered, has been of great importance to the development of linguistic criticism as the characteristic form stylistic studies take in our days. Important objections can be made against the theory, of which the fact that it suggests a normal-abnormal dichotomy for non-literary and literary language is the most essential. Also, as Fowler remarks, the theory of deviation '...should not replace completely the other approach, the description of a text as a complete and unique unit; nor should it always invite comparison between a particular literary usage and usage in the elusive "normal" speech' [113]. No less relevant is Dell H. Hymes' remark that '...to some "sources", especially poets, style may be not deviation from but achievement of a norm'. When we recognize that a poem observes certain prescriptions of metre or of poetic diction, we might define it according to the extent to which it conforms to these norms as well as according to the extent to which it deviates from the norms derived from uses of language in which these prescriptions do not obtain. Thus poetic language might well be described as the observation of norms instead of as deviation from them, and Ashok R. Kelkar, in an article on the ontology of poetry, comes very close to precisely such a definition: 'A poem is more than a text - it is an aesthetically satisfying text, which observes some or all of the usual language norms discussed earlier and, in addition, some of the stylistic norms in the literary culture' [114]. Finally, we must never forget that '...a mere list of these peculiarities of style cannot explain the critic's response, which depends on a complex interplay of these distinctive features and his own consciousness' [115].

Within the limitations set by these reservations, the deviation-theory can be useful and productive and has already proved to be so in many cases. The question of what exactly constitutes the norm has to be answered each time a stylistic investigation is undertaken, but there is no reason why we should not allow our critical faculties an optimal margin by accepting internal and external context, register, genre, historical period and ultimately the language as a whole as norms, each of them capable of shedding light on the text under study according to its own particular validity. This will make heavy demands on the critic's erudition, intuition and on his experience with the language, and will require a great deal of self-criticism to prevent him from making statements that assume the existence of a theoretical foundation for his approach which is simply not available. If handled responsibly, the approach to literature through the concept of deviation from the norm, is a challenging and stimulating one, even though unshakeable theoretical foundations for the approach have not been laid.

Meanwhile, there can be no doubt that Riffaterre's theory of the context as norm constitutes '...a fertile point of departure for a more conscious reconciliation of linguistics and literary analysis within a general and specific theory of *style* (stylistics)' [116]. The basic assumption beneath Riffaterre's thinking is a very common-sensical one: the style of a text is not a function of the language in which the text is written, or of the genre to which it belongs; it is a function of the text itself. Therefore, both the stylistic norm and the stylistic deviation are functional categories, defining each other every time when a pattern is broken by an unexpected element. The immense advantage of Riffaterre's approach is that it enables the stylistic investigator to proceed without having to arm himself in advance with statistics or with theories concerning what norms he is going to apply to a text. On the other hand, the need to account for his stylistic observations by referring them to their immediate linguistic environment will protect him from making statements that are purely speculative or impressionistic. However, the approach carries certain limitations: its findings cannot be generalized beyond the text that is under scrutiny. It is clear that Riffaterre's procedure could not reveal anything about, say, the style of Augustan poetry unless it could rely on another stylistic procedure to select a representative example. Whether Riffaterre's procedure is in any essential way different from Spitzer's is a debatable point; the difference would seem to lie mainly in the greater accuracy and a built-in mechanism of self-control by means of which Riffaterre's approach tries to safeguard reliability of statement. Nevertheless, the easy applicability of Riffaterre's approach ensures its importance in making the observation of linguistic facts of immediate value for literary studies. If it can be said at all that the second part of this study is based on any stylistic theory in particular, it is based on that of Riffaterre.

There are two conditions which threaten linguistic criticism as a valid and useful if not completely elucidated approach. The first makes it impossible, the second makes claims for it which it cannot justify. Richards' distinction between symbolic and emotive functions of language, if handled in such a way that a dichotomy results in which 'emotive' and 'referential' discourse are opposites, deprives linguistic criticism of even the narrowest ground for its existence. If language has a different function in literary uses of language than in non-literary ones, there is no reason to suppose that linguistic description will reveal anything valuable about literary works. On the other hand, linguistic description or analysis must recognize its inability to compete with literary criticism in a wider and more traditional sense. The claim that linguistic analysis should replace all other forms of criticism has sometimes been made; it is therefore necessary to reject it explicitly. The relation between linguistic criticism and literary criticism can be compared to that between musical analysis and musical criticism. The question whether the first movement of Sibelius' second Symphony has two or three subjects is highly relevant to our appreciation of the piece, but it is not the final question to be asked on the music. Similarly, an insight into the way in which the resources of language are handled in a work of literature is relevant to our appreciation and understanding of the work, but it is not a guarantee that we have grasped its full significance and to our evaluation of the work it is at best subsidiary. This is not to underrate the importance of linguistic analysis, but to place it in its proper perspective. Linguistic analysis has always to an important degree occupied the attention of the great critics; yet they have always gone beyond it. No matter how refined linguistic description will become - and refinement is improvement - it will always stop where literary criticism begins.

It was this second issue that inspired the debate which Roger Fowler and F. W. Bateson conducted in *Essays in Criticism* for almost three years [117]. It was launched by a review of Fowler's *Essays on Style and Language*, in which it was seriously questioned whether linguists were capable of saying anything relevant about literary works from the viewpoint of their particular discipline. Fowler then came to the defence of what he called the 'new movement' of linguistic criticism. Bateson's arguments can be summed up in his own words: '...in literature, language is for the reader a mere preliminary to style...' [118]. A second complaint that ran through the discussion from the beginning was explicitly formulated by E. B. Greenwood, who stated that so far linguisticians (sic) had provided '...pounds of theory, but not even a dram of literary benefit...' [119].

The whole debate was conducted in an atmosphere that unfortunately reawakened the old rivalry between 'language' and 'literature' that traditionally exists in English Departments in Britain and elsewhere. There can be no doubt that this regrettable animosity was resuscitated by Bateson and his adherents rather than by Fowler. In the atmosphere thus generated Fowler did not perhaps always hit on the right arguments, yet the views he propounds are sound enough: 'I do object to the idea of the linguist restricted to providing pre-critical material which the more sensitive critic can use... Linguistic analysis in literary criticism should not function as the first phase of a two-part process, the first mechanical and the second creative and valuable... Linguistic concepts, attitudes and techniques may be useful *within* criticism, it is claimed' [120]. Fowler claims for linguistic analysis a role that is vital to the evaluation that is the ultimate aim of the critical process. Elsewhere Fowler has carefully explained what stages in the critical procedure are represented by linguistic description, stylistic analysis and critical evaluation respectively, and how they are linked and interconnected [121]. Here Fowler has offered the *apologia* for linguistic criticism which the debate with Bateson did not produce. For the stylistic component of criticism Fowler allows the importance of what he calls the 'hunch', the intuitive critical response that the intelligence of the critic recognizes as a useful hypothesis that can serve as a basis for further observations. Exactly the same thing has been said by John Spencer and Michael Gregory [122]; in this respect, linguistic criticism does not essentially differ from Spitzer's stylistic method. Unlike Spitzer, however, Fowler, Spencer and Gregory apply the techniques and attitudes of modern linguistics to evolve the hypothetical impression to a reliable description that may be inspired by but does not rest on a 'hunch'.

Although linguistic criticism is not a discovery procedure which is able to disclose features of literary interest purely by means of a mechanical application of linguistic techniques, these writers nevertheless claim for linguistics a function within criticism. Although there is always subjectivity of response, linguistic criticism can help to remove impressionism of statement. The use of linguistic criticism is mainly in the area of articulation. Fowler does not say that the critical process is complete with a carefully articulated analytical description; he only stresses the necessity of linguistic description and its relevance to criticism in the widest sense. Linguistic criticism must, then, be *selective* and *purposeful,* and it can never be exhaustive. Fowler nicely sums up his position in the following terms: '...to be critics, we must be competent linguists and then become less of linguists' [123]. In the total critical procedure three levels of achievement are distinguished: description, stylistics and criticism, in that order, which is an order of value. If Fowler's opponents had tried to understand what claims linguistic criticism can make and what claims it cannot make, the whole debate might never have taken place. On the other hand, it cannot be denied that Fowler's position is essentially no more advanced than that of Wellek and Warren in their *Theory of Literature* (1949). The chapter 'Style and Stylistics' suggests that linguistics can provide greater methodological rigour to the description of literary texts and thus help criticism to transcend impressionism, but the authors fail to make it clear how the disciplinary affinities between linguistics and literary study can be made into an operational procedure. There is a certain irony in the fact that the theory of linguistic criticism as offered by one of its youngest and most articulate exponents still shows the same inconclusiveness as does the book which, more than any other, helped to create a climate of cooperation and reciprocal influence between linguistics and criticism twenty years ago [124].

Samuel R. Levin and Seymour Chatman have made claims for linguistic criticism that are even more modest than Fowler's. They suggest that the linguistic critic will usually be content to accept the judgements of literary critics, to whom 'superiority of response is accorded, on the basis of their experience, sensitivity, and general critical capacity' [125]. Linguistic criticism in their view can hardly undertake more than finding linguistic correlates for the judgements of the literary critics. To them no more than to Fowler can linguistic criticism be applied as a discovery procedure. The question whether the impact of a poem can be explained entirely in terms of its linguistic composition is to them an open one. The very modesty of the claims they make for linguistic criticism would, however, suggest that, if they were pressed for an answer, it would be negative. Meanwhile, they do not doubt that '...a good deal of significant work can be done in the linguistic analysis of poetry without waiting to see whether and how the question will finally be answered'.

G. N. Leech has tried to state his position on this question in a passage that seems to sum up the consensus of opinion at which the adversaries from the literary and the linguistic camps will eventually meet, and which deserves quoting in full: 'It is artificial to draw a clean line between linguistic and critical exegesis: stylistics is, indeed, the area in which they overlap. Nevertheless, if such a line had to be drawn, I should draw it as follows: the linguist is the man who identifies what features in a poem need interpretation (i.e. what features are foregrounded), and to some extent (e.g. by specifying rules of transference) what opportunities for interpretation are available; the literary critic is the man who weighs up the different possible interpretations. I hasten, however, to make an amendment to this division of labour: it is better to regard linguist and critic not as different people, but as different roles which may be assumed by the same person'[126].

George Steiner has defended the disciplinary role that linguistics may play in criticism: 'Formal logic and modern linguistics cannot do the job of the critic. But the critic, in turn, can ill afford to ignore what they, and linguistics especially, have to offer. I would go further. The current state of criticism is so facile and philosophically naïve, so much of literary criticism, particularly in England and America, is puffed-up book-reviewing or thinly disguised preaching, that a responsible collaboration with linguistics may prove the best hope'. He quotes Eliot's famous dictum that 'something happened to the mind of England' between the time of Donne and that of Browning. If such a statement is to have any meaning, Steiner says, '...it must be accountable to the history of the language' [127].

One of the tasks that linguistic critics will have to set themselves is to decide whether the approach through linguistics should not be restricted to certain aspects of the literary work, in particular the textural aspects. There is some truth in Graham Hough's warning that much that literary students are interested in consists of larger units than linguistic criticism can cope with. These larger structures, such as plot, character and the *ordonnance* of ideas, can be attacked directly, '...short-circuiting the approach through language and style' [128]. With regard to the novel, the problem can be put in terms of a *compositional style* on the one hand and an *architectural style* on the other, the former of which would seem to lend itself to linguistic description more easily and more efficiently than the latter [129].

It is regrettable that the debate on linguistic criticism, its ends, and its relation to literary criticism, has mostly been conducted on a theoretical level, and that concrete instances where linguists can point to specific results that could have been achieved by linguistic criticism only have been rare or non-existent. It is not the task of this chapter, in which a report has been given of the present state of linguistic criticism, to attempt answers to these questions. It is hoped, however, that we will be able to make certain suggestions that will contribute to answering these questions at the end of our study. Those suggestions will be the result not of further theoretical thinking, but will arise from a number of observations to which the concentration on one important problem in literary language - the so-called 'epic preterite' - and its concrete operation in certain literary texts will give rise. Being of a purely empirical nature, the answers we will suggest cannot claim to be definitive or even general. However, it is felt that what is needed now is not in the first place unshakeable theoretical foundations for linguistic criticism on the one hand and for literary criticism on the other, including watertight definitions of either, but practical applications of linguistic knowledge in the discussion of literary texts. To the degree in which such applications are successful, the need for theoretical definitions will be felt to be less pressing.

III Tense in the novel and free indirect style - a linguistic investigation

(1)

From the eighteenth century onwards, novelists have realized that to them more than to any other literary artist, time presented not only a philosophical but also a technical problem, to which the tense system of grammar did not offer a ready-made solution. In modern studies on time in the novel, the following quotation from *Tristram Shandy* invariably crops up: 'A cow broke in (to-morrow morning) to my uncle Toby's fortifications and eat up two rations and a half of dried grass, tearing up the sods with it, which faced his hornwork and covered-way' [1]. The juxtaposition of the time-adverb denoting future and a preterite tense form seems to illustrate an awareness of the difference between time within the novel and time outside the novel - the physical clock-time in which the author lives and the fictional time in which the characters live. Later on in the same passage, Sterne remembers that he had promised the reader to tell something about 'my father lying across his bed, and my uncle Toby in his old fringed chair' within half an hour of fictional time, and, finding that thirty-five minutes of physical time have already passed since the promise was made, jocularly concludes that the story will have to be told in 'five minutes less than no time at all'.

In *The Rise of The Novel*, Ian Watt quotes a passage from *Tom Jones* which shows Fielding struggling with, and defending the same need for the novelist to differentiate between what modern theory calls 'chronological time' and 'fictional time' [2]. It is not difficult to see why this problem should have vexed the eighteenth-century realists in particular, and why they should have tried to give their works the outward appearance of temporal truthfulness by such means as Richardson's carefully detailed time-scheme or Fielding's almanac. The novel was going through the first stages of its development, and had yet to invent its technical conventions, while other genres had inherited theirs from a long tradition. These conventions necessarily entailed suspension of disbelief on the part of a reading public that was being taught by the philosophers and moralists of its age to think realistically and positivistically.

One respect in which a willing suspension of disbelief was requisite was the fact that tenses used in the novel did not have the same temporal implications as tenses used in historical reporting or factual description. To say that 'a cow broke into uncle Toby's fortifications' did not imply that such an event actually took place at a given moment in history, as did a sentence like 'Shakespeare died in 1616'. Sterne's facetious parenthesis 'to-morrow morning' emphasizes the unrealistic function of the preterite in his sentence, thus forcing the reader into suspension of disbelief while at the same time making fun of the reader's as well as the author's ambiguous position as to the temporal orientation in which the novel envelops him. Since non-epistolary novels naturally adopted the preterite as their principal tense of narration, the preterite became the focus where the whole problem of time and tense was most clearly visible and most easily lent itself to serious or light-hearted manipulation. Of course the preterite had traditionally been the narrative tense in epic literature, poetry as well as prose. The novelists of the eighteenth century, however, were acutely conscious that what they were writing were not epics, allegories or moralistic fables. The novel was the literary man's answer to the challenge of realism held out by his age. Naturally enough, writing a story in prose meant exposing oneself to the risk that readers would approach the story with standards derived from non-fictional prose. There were various protections against this misunderstanding. One could incapsulate the danger and make one's novels assume some of the guises of journalistic writing, as Defoe tended to do. One could also, as Fielding did, imitate the epic tradition mockingly. Finally one could always have recourse to the epistolary novel to ensure being taken seriously by a journalistically-minded public. In all these cases, it was imperative to deck out one's story like a piece of realistic writing as much as possible by means of providing a detailed surface adhering closely to social reality. But through all this, the problem of time and tense remained unaffected. In a nutshell, the question was how to reconcile the preterite, traditionally the vehicle of historical narration, with a fictive story that had, when all was said and done, not really happened.

It was not until the twentieth century that the problem was dealt with in a large-scale, comprehensive and systematic manner. Käte Hamburger's *Die Logik der Dichtung* [3] once and for all demonstrated that the preterite in fiction has a function essentially different from its function in non-fiction. Starting from this observation, she arrived at a classification of literary works founded not on the traditional *genres* but on a logical distinction between different kinds of 'Origines'. To her, any literary work constitutes an 'Aussage' (utterance) of an 'I', and she distinguishes three I's: a lyrical I, an historical I and an epic I. She then goes on to classify all literary works under these headings, arriving at a total scheme in which genres are shown to belong together on logical grounds that used to be thought widely separate. Thus all novels, except those narrated by a first-person narrator, as well as dramas and films, are subsumed under the heading fictional, while ballads are logically fictional rather than lyrical. First-person novels do not belong to the class of fiction; however 'feigned' their contents may be, they are not 'fictional'. In true fictions, the fictitious world of the novel constitutes the fictitious *present* of the characters in the novel, the preterite being the vehicle by means of which this present is conveyed. In first-person novels the fictitious world of the novel constitutes the non-fictitious *past* of the narrator; here the preterite conveys *past* and not *present* events [4].

Käte Hamburger's book has been under constant critical fire since the day it appeared [5]. Yet its importance cannot be overvalued. It is her unquestionable merit to have realized that the problem of the preterite in fiction occupies a central position. It is true that she has not succeeded in developing her logical scheme into linguistic description [6]. In fact, the linguistic evidence on which her theory is erected is inadequate. Her view of the first-person novel is a case in point. The need to redefine the novel as a genre became clear to her as a result of certain linguistic peculiarities of the preterite as used in novels. Arguing from these, she arrived at her logical definition of the novel as an utterance of an epic I. Logically, the epic I of third-person novels differs significantly from the narrator-I of first-person novels, as has been explained above. What Käte Hamburger ought to have done at this stage of her argument was to go back to linguistic observation to find out whether the *linguistic* behaviour of the preterite in first-person novels supported her theory by differing from the linguistic behaviour of the preterite in third-person fiction. Logically, nothing is demonstrably wrong with her procedure. However, one feels that something more than a logical approach is called for, namely, a turning back to first-hand observation. In the study of literature, as Spitzer has shown, vicious circles lose their vicious character by becoming philological circles [7]. It is this failure on Käte Hamburger's part to remain in constant touch with the realities of actual literary works and their linguistic features that accounts for the ultimate inadequacy of her genre-theory, for her unacceptable isolation of the first-person novel from the realm of fiction and, connected with the latter point, her insufficient recognition of the role played by free indirect speech [8], resulting in undue simplification of the problem of time and tense. It is these shortcomings that will provide this chapter with its subject matter. However, it is only a matter of giving credit where credit is due to admit that it was Käte Hamburger herself who pointed the way to the problems to be investigated here, just as many of the tools by which our investigation will be carried out have been forged by Käte Hamburger herself.

(2)

In her Preface to *Die Logik der Dichtung* the author states that the problem of the epic preterite is the key to the whole book and the central issue in her philosophy of literary art. The epic preterite is linguistically marked by its ability to be modified by deictic adverbs of time, irrespective of whether these refer to the past, present or future time-spheres [9]. She quotes examples from Alice Berend, Thomas Mann, Bruno Frank, Goethe, Jean Paul and Virginia Woolf. To these many others may be added, not only from German and English but from all Romance languages and from Dutch as well [10]. Adverbs like 'morgen', 'tonight', 'heute' and 'dans une heure', referring to a non-past time-sphere, can modify a preterite tense form; adverbs like 'gestern', referring to a past time-sphere, can modify a pluperfect tense form. To borrow Käte Hamburger's examples, in a novel we could read 'Gestern war Weihnachten gewesen' but not 'Gestern war Weihnachten' [11] while, on the other hand, 'Morgen war Weihnachten' would be possible in a novel only. Thus the author claims to have laid bare a linguistic rule obtaining only in the language of fiction and therefore clearly differentiating the language of fiction from non-fictional discourse [12]:

ADVERBS OF TIME	modifying	PRETERITE	PLUPERFECT
past time reference		—	+
future time reference		+	—

Käte Hamburger does not explicitly discuss the adverb *now* and its equivalents in other modern European languages. She quotes a sentence from Conrad Ferdinand Meyer's novel *Jürg Jenatsch* ('Jetzt erscholl aus der Ferne das Gebell eines Hundes...') [13] in which 'jetzt' modifies a preterite tense form, adding that this does not signal an epic preterite. The sentence therefore is not characteristically one that could occur in a novel only; it is only when later on in the quotation the expression 'schnell bedacht...' occurs, containing one of the verbs she calls 'Verben der Inneren Vorgänge' [14], such as *denken, sinnen, glauben, meinen, fühlen, hoffen,* that we can feel sure that what we are reading is in fact a passage from a novel and not from any other kind of discourse. The dubious status of *now* and its equivalents is in fact undeniable. The word is often semantically too vague to be relied upon as a pointer to a well-defined time-sphere; its meaning frequently shades off into that of a modal adverb or one with a consecutive or causal meaning [15]. Nevertheless, followers as well as critics of Hamburger's thesis agree that *now* in its original temporal sense is one of the deictic adverbs whose occurrence with certain non-present tense-forms is a characteristic feature of the language of fiction. Thus Otto Funke quotes the following sentence from Galsworthy's *Forsyte Saga:* 'She thought of June's father... who had run away with that foreign girl... And when June's mother died, six years ago, Jo had married that woman, and they had two children now...' [16]. There can be no doubt that *now* has its literal temporal meaning here and may therefore be regarded as a deictic adverb. Franz Stanzel endorses Funke's quotation [17]. David Lodge gives *now, yesterday,* and *to-morrow* as examples of deictic adverbs [18]. Roy

44

Pascal mentions *now* as one of the markers of the epic preterite, and Harald Weinrich instances *jetzt* [19].

Now is not only used with the preterite in fiction, but with the pluperfect as well, as the following example illustrates: 'We had now reached the edge of the garden and I turned from him quietly across the lawn' [20]. Therefore our diagram may be enlarged as follows:

ADVERBS OF TIME	modifying	PRETERITE	PLUPERFECT
past time reference		—	+
present time reference		+	+
future time reference		+	—

The essence of Käte Hamburger's theory is that the epic preterite, marked by its capability of being modified by deictic time adverbs referring to the present and future time-spheres, does not itself refer to the past time-sphere or, indeed, to any time-sphere at all. In her own words, the point is that the epic preterite '...seine Vergangenheitsfunktion verliert und dies seine Ursache darin hat, dass die Zeit der epischen Handlung, d.h. aber diese selbst, nicht auf eine reale Ich-Origo, ein "redendes" oder Aussagesubjekt bezogen ist, sondern auf die fiktiven Ich-Origines der Romangestalten' [21]. The function of the preterite in any novel is not to assign the events narrated to any time-sphere at all, but to 'fictionalize' them, to present them as forming an epic fiction instead of a chain of events taking place in a temporal order. This is a basic insight that has influenced all later writers on the theory of the novel without exception. By way of William E. Bull's book [22] it has particularly stimulated Harald Weinrich's major study of the functions of the tenses in narrative and descriptive discourse [23]. It is not an insight arrived at by Käte Hamburger alone; it informs Susanne K. Langer's *Feeling and Form* [24], although the latter's definition of the world of the novel as 'virtual history' or 'virtual past' is of course unacceptable to Käte Hamburger, and it plays an important role in the literary theories of the French structuralists. Thus what Roland Barthes wrote in 1953 about the French Passé Défini may appear now as an imaginative anticipation of what Käte Hamburger was to work out on a theoretical level: 'Its function is no longer that of a tense... Through the preterite the verb implicitly belongs with a verbal chain, it partakes of a set of related and orientated actions, it functions as the algebraic sign of an intention. Allowing as it does an ambiguity between temporality and causality, it calls for a sequence of events, that is, for an intelligible Narrative. This is why it is the ideal instrument for every construction of a world; it is the unreal time of cosmogonies, myths, History and Novels... Behind the preterite there always lurks a demiurge, a God or a reciter... So that finally the preterite is the expression of an order, and consequently of a euphoria' [25]. To

Barthes, the preterite is primarily an instrument by means of which mythological structures are built and marked as such.

(3)

The most important reaction provoked by Käte Hamburger's book is Franz
Stanzel's article 'Episches Praeteritum, Erlebte Rede, Historisches Praesens'
of 1959 [17]. Its main thesis is that a sentence like 'Morgen ging sein Flugzeug'
is not, as Käte Hamburger had claimed, possible in any fictional context, but
only in those which he describes as 'personalen Erzählsituationen': '...wo die
sprachliche Formulierung, die Darstellung vom Standpunkt des Erlebenden,
Betroffenen oder einer am Geschehen aktiv oder als Zuschauer teilnehmenden
Gestalt aus erfolgt...'. He equates such narrative situations with free indirect
speech or thought, concluding that only in free indirect style can adverbs
with future or present time-sphere reference be used to modify preterite tense
forms. He constructs two fictional passages to demonstrate that in directly
narrated contexts, where the author is the 'Aussagesubjekt', temporal adverbs
are employed that have as their point of reference the author's present
moment, such as *damals, am nächsten Tag*. These adverbs have a past time-
sphere reference and are therefore not in conflict with the preterite used
throughout the narration. In free indirect style contexts, on the other hand,
where the 'Aussagesubjekt' is a character within the novel, adverbs can be
used whose point of reference is the present moment of the character, such
as *morgen*. Here the friction between the time-sphere of the adverb and of
the preterite tense of the predicate does exist; in other words, only here can
we speak of an epic preterite in the sense in which Käte Hamburger understood the term. An illustration of Stanzel's thesis is afforded by the following
passage from George Moore's *Esther Waters*, which starts in direct narration,
moves into free indirect style after the sixth sentence, interrupts the interior
monologue with 'She examined it all over', and definitely moves back into
direct narration at the sentence beginning 'Then the desire passed...':

> 'She was in John's room - in the sneak's room. No one was about. She
> would have cut off one of her fingers for the coin. That half-crown
> meant pleasure and a happiness so tender and seductive that she closed
> her eyes for a moment. The half-crown she held between forefinger and
> thumb presented a ready solution of the besetting hardship of her wages.
> She threw out the insidious temptation, but it came quickly upon her
> again. If she didn't take the half-crown she wouldn't be able to go to
> Peckham on Sunday. She could replace the money where she found it
> when she was paid her wages. No one knew it was there; it had evi-
> dently rolled there, and, having tumbled between the carpet and the

wall, had not been discovered. It had probably lain there for months, perhaps it was utterly forgotten. Besides, she need not take it *now*. It would be quite safe if she put it back in its place; on Sunday afternoon she would take it, and if she changed it at once - it was not marked. She examined it all over. No, it was not marked. *Then* the desire passed, and she wondered how she, an honest girl, who had never harboured a dishonest thought in her life before, could desire to steal, and a loathly shame fell upon her'. (Italics mine) [26].

Stanzel's criticism of Hamburger's theory of the epic preterite seems to be compatible with modern linguistic theory. F. R. Palmer, for instance, rejects the traditional statement of tense in terms of present, past and future in favour of a fourfold scheme illustrated by the following sentences:

Present non-future :	I'm reading (at the moment).
Present future :	I'm reading a paper tomorrow.
Past non-future :	I was reading when he arrived.
Past future :	I was reading a paper tomorrow.

The problem can be focused more sharply if we replace the first person pronoun by a third person pronoun. The sentence 'He was reading a paper tomorrow' then stands out from the other three in so far that it cannot be interpreted as referring to an action that is realized in any time-sphere at all, whereas the other three sentences refer to actions realized in the present, future and past time-spheres respectively. The preterite in the fourth sentence may be either a modal preterite (in the case when the sentence is completed by, for instance, 'but he suddenly had to go to America') denoting non-fulfilment of the action, or it may be an epic preterite, signifying that the sentence occurs in a novel or story and represents an utterance of a character in the narrative. Palmer's statement that the four sentences are all grammatical seems meaningless so long as it is not specified in what contexts they are grammatical [27].
  An important fact that may be adduced in order to qualify Stanzel's thesis, and one of which Stanzel himself does not seem to be aware, is that the preterite combines with adverbs having a present or future time-sphere reference not only in free indirect style passages that occur in novels and mark a change of the narrative point of view from the author to one of the characters, a change from a less subjective to a more subjective perspective, but also in other forms of discourse under similar circumstances of heightened subjectivity. The following examples may illustrate this:

'Those marvellous little speeches which sum up, in a few minutes' chatter, all that we need in order to know an Admiral Croft or a Mrs.

Musgrove for ever, that shorthand, hit-or-miss method which contains chapters of analysis and psychology, would have become too crude to hold all that she *now* perceived of the complexity of human nature'.

Virginia Woolf, 'Jane Austen'; *The Common Reader* I, 1925.

'An education at Oxford appealed to a new class of rich and well-to-do men who wished to use it to improve the prospects of their sons. The Colleges were *now* therefore able to charge fees proportionate to the social advantages likely to accrue...'

C. D. Darlington, 'The Uses of Abuses', *Encounter*, January 1967.

'So the conclusion was *now* drawn that what we call a 'poetic' effect does not necessarily depend on any kind of special heightened language, the kind normally thought of as 'poetic', but often on 'prosaic' utterances which nevertheless become emotionally highly charged because of their context'.

P. Edwards, 'Meaning and Context: An Exercise in Practical Stylistics', *English Language Teaching*, XXII, 3; May 1968.

'Having put his religious house in order, Mohammed *now* began to enjoy his power as the undisputed ruler of a large number of tribes'.

Hendrik van Loon, *The Story of Mankind*, 1921, Ch. 28.

The fourth example, taken from a popular book on world history, most clearly offers a narrative context in which it is easy for the reader to identify with Mohammed, i.e. to adopt the point of view of a 'character' within the narrative. Similar uses of *now* as signals of a subjective perspective abound in historical writings: 'Charles *now* had to call parliament again, although it was clear that the commons would *now* destroy the machinery through which the prerogative had been exercised and take vengeance on Laud and Strafford'[28]. Nevertheless it is normal for historical writings to adopt as their principal point of view the author's perspective, as is illustrated by another sentence from van Loon: 'From that time on until the year of his death, Mohammed was fortunate in everything he undertook'. The sentence containing *now* may be said to constitute a deviation from a norm, whose effect in this case is to immerse the reader more deeply in the narrative by inviting his identification with the hero. *Empathy* seems a good term to denote this kind of involvement, which always works through identification with and adopting the perspective of an 'Aussagesubjekt' that is not identical with the narrator, author or speaker of the text concerned. A similar effect of empathy is discernible in the quotation from Virginia Woolf's essay on Jane Austen. It occurs in a passage where Jane Austen is very much imagined as a 'character'; Virginia Woolf is trying to formulate what Jane Austen would have been like if she had been allowed to live - in other words, she is making Jane Austen into a character in a fictive context.

In the second quotation, taken from a letter to the Editor of *Encounter,* the use of *now* can less easily be related to a narrative context - the writer is not telling a story, he is making a point. Yet its obvious effect is to enliven the discourse by inviting the reader's empathy. The passage about the Oxford Colleges may be read as a little story, and the reader can easily adopt the perspective of the 'characters' in that story, i.e. the people who run the colleges, whose 'now' he can make his own once he has become sufficiently engrossed in the story.

The third example, taken from an essay in a linguistic periodical, illustrates how a narrative situation inviting the reader's empathetic involvement can even arise in scholarly discourse.

If the use of *now* with a preterite tense-form is a signal of free indirect style, the four examples discussed above suggest that free indirect style is not restricted to the narrative mode but occurs in other forms of discourse as well. That in fact we have free indirect style here can be made clear from another angle. Harald Weinrich has listed the following linguistic features as signals of free indirect style: demonstrative pronouns, colloquialisms, strings of related words or synonyms, prolepsis [29]. Now a number of these clearly occur in the following passage from Virginia Woolf's essay, immediately preceding our first quotation:

> 'Had she lived a few more years only, all that would have been altered. She would have stayed in London, dined out, lunched out, met famous people, made new friends, read, travelled, and carried back to the quiet country cottage a hoard of observations to feast upon at leisure'.

The implications of what we have found are important. If the epic preterite does not occur in any fictional context but only in such passages as are in free indirect style and have a character within the novel for 'Aussagesubjekt', and if, on the other hand, free indirect style does not only occur in novels but in - theoretically, at least - any form of discourse, the question of the epic preterite is completely open. The problem is in fact no longer one that specifically concerns the language of fiction. The problem of the epic preterite has been replaced by the problem of the preterite in free indirect style. The term 'epic preterite' can no longer be understood as referring to a use of the preterite characteristic of epic literature, but only as denoting the use of the preterite in free indirect style. On the other hand, it is obvious that free indirect style is a characteristically fictional technique, and that even those passages in which it is found outside fiction can more or less easily be shown to possess fictional features.

Meanwhile, the need to redefine free indirect style has become pressing. In a sentence like 'He was reading a paper tomorrow', discussed above, we can say that the sentence cannot be considered to be grammatical as a *realis* statement unless we assume that it is spoken or thought by a fictional character. The same can be said of the sentence 'No, it was not marked' from the George Moore quotation. This use of 'No' is ungrammatical except in direct reporting; hence, a distinctive feature of direct speech is preserved in this sentence which marks it as free indirect style. *No* is in fact a fairly common mark of free indirect style; cf. 'No, he had not been too kind to Tanya' (Iris Murdoch, *The Time of the Angels*, London 1966, p.64) and 'No, never before had he been so ready to take him as he was' (Henry James, *The Ambassadors*, Everyman ed. p.141).

In cases like these, free indirect style may be said to constitute a formal linguistic category. Yet it would be misleading to restrict the term free indirect style to such cases only; many passages in fiction as well as in non-narrative prose represent the point of view of one of the characters within the story, or convey a heightened degree of involvement of the author in his subject-matter, without being marked by unmistakable linguistic evidence. In many cases, such passages show a certain predilection for certain stylistic phenomena that do not in themselves add up to a set of linguistic markers of free indirect style. In other cases, dependence on the context may be the only pointer to free indirect style. If we define free indirect style as a rigid linguistic category, we are therefore likely to oversimplify the important problem of an author's subjective involvement in the object of his writing. Our definition of free indirect style should therefore admit of borderline-cases and gradual transitions. On the other hand, in calling a certain passage free indirect reporting we should base ourselves on linguistic evidence as much as possible, either in the passage itself or in its immediate context. As we shall see, free indirect style is very often marked not by the presence of linguistic features that can be related to a set of rules but by deviations from and contrasts with contextual features. Although it cannot on this ground be called a linguistic category, it certainly is a linguistic phenomenon.

(4)

A confrontation of Käte Hamburger's and Franz Stanzel's positions will be attempted by means of an investigation into the use of tenses in the first chapter of a first-person novel using the preterite as its main narrative tense. A first-person novel has been chosen because it may help to shed light on Käte Hamburger's theory, according to which the preterite in such novels is not an epic preterite but a preterite with a definite past time-sphere connotation, and according to which free indirect style is for that reason impossible in the I-novel [30]. From the confrontation it is hoped that a number of insights will arise that can be further developed in the second half of this chapter.

In the first chapter of Iris Murdoch's *The Italian Girl* (London, Chatto & Windus 1964) the narrator, who is at the same time the main character of the novel [31], revisits his parental home after a long absence when he has received word that his mother has died. This is the basic situation. The novel is concerned with the psychological effects of the visit on the main character. Here an important complication becomes visible: there are two I's. There is the narrator-I, who is at a certain moment - the moment of narration - relating certain events that take place on the time-level on which the story is enacted. This narrator-I exists only in so far as the novel is a written document originating from a personal source. In Wayne Booth's terminology, he is the 'implied author' [32]. There is also the I who plays a role as a character in the novel. The two I's are not identical: the second I is an object of the first I's writing just as the other characters in the book are. The narrator-I exists exclusively on the first level of time: that of the composition of the novel. The second I exists primarily on the second time-level: that of the time when the story unfolds. This is the time-level of the narrative, and the tense form used for this time-level is the preterite. The second I, however, also existed during the time preceding that of the actual narrative, during the years preceding the moment when he revisits the house of his mother or, in other words, during his youth. For this anterior time-level, the pluperfect is the tense normally employed. The first time-level, that on which the narrator-I exists and the actual writing of the memoirs takes place, uses the present and occasionally the perfect tense. Thus we have a perfectly regular and conventional tense sequence that may be represented in the following diagram:

	TIME-SPHERE	TENSE
I	Time of writing (Narrator-I)	present & perfect
II	Time of narrative (Character-I)	preterite
III	Time anterior to narrative (Character-I)	pluperfect
IV	Neutral time-sphere	present

The sequence of tenses implied in this diagram is that of direct narration and non-narrative discourse. Thus, the opening sentence of the chapter is enacted on the second time-level, and uses a past tense, whereas the second sentence moves back into the third time-level - the I's youth - and uses a pluperfect: 'I pressed the door gently. It had always been left open at night in the old days'. It is important to note that the time adverb employed in the second sentence -*in the old days*- has for its point of reference the second time-level, from which it points back into the third. All the pluperfect forms in the chapter (about 40 altogether) can be accounted for in this way; they all of them refer back to 'the old days', i.e. the third time-sphere.

In a few cases, the preterite is used with reference to the third time-sphere. An example is provided by the following passage: 'My mother's name was Lydia, and she had always insisted that we call her by that name. This had displeased my father, but he did not cross her in this or indeed in anything else' (p.17). The second preterite in this quotation *(did not cross)* regularly refers to the anterior past because it occurs in a context dependent on a preceding clause containing a pluperfect; it assumes therefore the perspective of the pluperfect. Similarly, in the sentence 'My father had passed from us almost unnoticed, we believed in his death long before it came' (p.19), the two preterites in the second half of the sentence are 'placed' by the pluperfect in the first. The same explanation holds good for the preterites '...she lost Otto...' (p.18) and '...when she came...' and '...was to look after...' (p.22). The only preterite resisting this explanation is the one in the sentence quoted from p.17: 'My mother's name was Lydia...'. This is indeed a problematic case. For the time being we may suggest that it deliberately places the mother in the second time-sphere instead of the third; in other words, it suggests that in a sense the mother still exists at the moment when the I comes to her cremation. It will appear that this suggestion is borne out by our interpretation of the whole novel.

The third time-sphere, we may conclude, is regularly represented by the pluperfect or by preterites whose proximity to or dependence on pluperfects makes them refer to the anterior past, in other words, makes them virtual pluperfects [33]. Quite as regularly, the first time-sphere is represented by the present and perfect tenses, as the following passages illustrate: 'Otto and I are both very big men...'; 'Although I am not especially a coward I have always been afraid of the dark...' (p.13); '...Otto, who is my senior by two years...' (p.17); 'I can recall...' (two times on p.18); 'Yet my early memories are not of my father...' (p.19); '...whether this was a foible of my mother's I never remember discovering' (p.21). These present tenses either occur in non-temporal predicates and thus constitute neutral presents [34], or they are actual presents referring to actions taking place on the first time-level and directly connected with the writing of the novel itself: the calling up of recollections. In both cases they confirm the regularity of the tense system [35].

The second time-sphere is indicated by the normal narrative preterite: 'I pressed the door gently' (p.11). Although temporal adverbs are comparatively rare in this chapter, it is easy to see that the norm governing their use is that adverbs with a past time reference are used with preterites and have the second time-sphere as their point of reference: 'I reached my own door and opened it wide, and then stopped in my tracks' (p.20); 'Then the form stirred lightly...' (p.20); 'Then I realized that it was only my old nurse, the Italian girl' (p.21); 'I felt his absence then with a quick pathos...' (p.23). Obviously this use of the adverb *then* is in accordance with the regularity of the tense-system employed.

However, a large number of preterites in this chapter is accompanied by the adverb *now*. According to Stanzel, we might expect the passages in which this occurs to be in free indirect style. This is in fact what the text bears out. We may take a very revealing passage on p.12 to illustrate this:

> 'To have come then would have made sense in the light of the last abstract consideration I had for her; after all she was my mother. But to come now that she was dead, to come merely to bury her, to stand in her dead presence with those half-strangers, my brother and my sister-in-law, this was senseless, a mere self-punishment'.

In this passage, *now* contrasts strongly with *then*, both words occurring in the same syntactic setting. The second half of the passage shows a number of characteristics that point to free indirect style: the repetitions, the emotive use of the pronoun *those;* the string of related expressions arranged so as to form a climax. These are all features characteristic of direct speech, or even rhetorical features, which are preserved in free indirect style. On the syntactic level another characteristic of the spoken language stands out: the resumption of the subject, lengthened out by repetitions, by the pronoun *this*. In all these respects, the first half of the quotation offers a striking contrast: there are no repetitions, no emotive words, the syntax is unrhetorical. It is the language of 'abstract consideration' rather than the language of empathetic involvement.

Working back from our analysis of this passage, we may easily recognize some of the same signals of free indirect speech in the following passage on p.11: 'Calling out or throwing stones at windows in such a silence, these were abhorrent things. Yet to wait quietly in the light of the moon, a solitary excluded man, an intruder, this was abhorrent too'. There is the same resumption of the subject by demonstrative pronouns, the same climax of synonymous expressions, the same tone of heightened involvement. By thus observing linguistic details, we discover others until we build up sufficient data to recognize free indirect style and distinguish it from direct narration. An investigation of all the passages where *now* occurs modifying a preterite referring to the second time-sphere soon brings out that in the large majority of cases these passages are signalled by certain verbs or expressions on which they depend or to which they can be related. A few examples may illustrate this: 'I now realized...' (p.13); 'I recalled now...' (p.14); 'The sense of her mortality invaded me now...' (p.16); 'Looking up at the remembered face, I felt a sense of temporal giddiness...' (p.21). From the first chapter the following list of such words can be drawn up:

thought (12,20)
reason (13)
to realize (13)
to recall (14)
perceptible (15)
sense (16)
to seem (17)
to feel (20,21)
to remember (21)

All these verbs and words refer to what Käte Hamburger calls 'innere Vor-gänge' [36]; they denote mental processes implying thought or feeling and it is these thoughts or feelings that are reported in free indirect style [37]. Only in three cases can a passage containing *now* with reference to a preterite not be related to some such verb or expression (pp.12,20 and 21); in fact, as Stephen Ullmann remarks, 'Free indirect speech may stand completely isolated... or there may be some kind of preparation in the context; but in neither case will there be a key verb on which it is syntactically dependent' [38]. It is true that even in those cases where an expression denoting an inner process of thought or feeling does occur there is no syntactic dependence; nevertheless, the relation is very real: there is, more often than not, a linguistic signal in the context preceding the actual passage in free indirect style. Although free indirect style is not always easily recognized on purely formal grounds, it is nevertheless vital for the reader to be able to tell free indirect speech from direct narration. The 'fleeting' or impressionistic character of free indirect style is sometimes considered as its most essential attribute [39], but when it is used in a functional contrast to direct narration, free indirect speech or thought stands or falls by being distinguishable from direct narration. An interesting example of this necessity is provided by a passage from Graham Greene's *Loser Takes All* (London, Heinemann, 1955, p.42): 'I tried to make her return to the Casino and lose a few hundred, but she said she wanted to walk on the terrace and look at the sea. It was an excuse to keep a watch for the *Seagull*. And of course the *Seagull* never came'. The last sentence here must be in free indirect style for the simple reason that it cannot be direct narration: the point is that the *Seagull* does come in the end. The sentence cannot therefore be the 'Aussage' of the narrator-I; it must originate with the character-I. But how is the reader to know? Working from the plot of the novel, he can only interpret the sentence correctly in retrospect, after he has finished the whole book. Yet here again there is perhaps a linguistic signal helping him to read correctly when he comes across the sentence for the first time. The expression 'of course' suggests direct reporting, being more col-loquial than its synonym 'naturally'. The sentence itself does not only report

54

the character's own thoughts, but also his wife's fears, and therefore constitutes an example of free indirect style with a double perspective [40].

The verbs denoting inner processes of thought or feeling and the linguistic features mentioned by Weinrich and Ullmann [29] can be used by writers as signals of the shifting point of view, of heightened empathetic involvement and of free indirect style. Such shifts are not always marked by grammatical or lexical means only; they may also be suggested by other means. A characteristic feature of the first chapter of *The Italian Girl* is a rhythmical alternation of free indirect style passages with passages of direct narration. Most paragraphs begin in direct narration and then move into free indirect thought. The first paragraph already establishes this rhythm; the conclusion is indubitably in free indirect style, being dependent on the verb *to feel* and showing the characteristic repetitions. The same pattern is clearly visible in the second paragraph of p.11, which concludes in direct narration after a strongly emotional passage in free indirect style. Similarly with the second paragraph of p.13, the paragraph beginning at the bottom of p.15 and the whole of the long reminiscent passage in the middle of the chapter. Thus the division into paragraphs may also serve as a help for the reader to distinguish between the various modes of narration.

(5)

In an article called 'Generative Grammars and the Concept of Literary Style' [41] Richard Ohmann, assisted by Morris Halle, explains free indirect style as a 'sequence of transformations'. He uses a passage from Hemingway's story 'Soldier's Home' to illustrate his point:

> 'So his mother prayed for him and then they stood up and Krebs kissed his mother and went out of the house. He had tried so to keep his life from being complicated. Still, none of it had touched him. He had felt sorry for his mother and she had made him lie. He would go to Kansas City and get a job and she would feel all right about it'.

The transformations which Ohmann describes work as follows:

I   *Direct reporting:* He thought: 'She has made me lie'.
    Transformation: change of pronouns and of verb tense:
II *Indirect reporting:* He thought that she had made him lie.
    Deletion of matrix sentence:
III *Free indirect reporting:* She had made him lie.

The tenses of direct speech are shifted according to the rules describing the shifting of tenses in indirect speech, rules described in most conventional grammars [42]. The shifting of pronouns simply means the substitution of third-person pronouns for first-person pronouns. Free indirect style would then seem to differ from indirect speech only in so far that a matrix sentence containing a verb of the *speak, think* or *feel* class has been deleted. As we have seen, however, such a verb, or an expression related to it, is still very often present in the context, although not directly related to the free indirect passage by any syntactic link. This is an important oversight in Ohmann's analysis; the presence of an element for which the grammar cannot account may nevertheless be decisive.

Applied to fiction Ohmann's set of transformations enables us to recognize free indirect style in third-person narratives by a very simple check: third-person pronouns are changed into first-person ones and the deleted clause containing a *speak, think,* or *feel* verb is restored. As an example we may use the sentence from Thackeray quoted by Stephen Ullmann: 'I don't envy Pen's feelings as he thought of what he had done. He had slept, and the tortoise had won the race' [43]. If we strip this of Ohmann's transformations we get: 'I don't envy Pen's feelings as he thought of what he had done. He thought: "I have slept and the tortoise has won the race"'.

Now in the case of a first-person narrative this check is not possible, simply because the narrator and the character whose thoughts or feelings are reported are the same person. Therefore the change of pronouns that is implied in the first transformation is impossible, since the narrator cannot refer to himself by means of a third-person pronoun. This is easily made clear if we attempt Ohmann's transformations in reverse order on a sentence from *The Italian Girl* that is clearly in free indirect style: 'The sense of her mortality invaded me now, and it became inevitable that I should enter her room' (p.16):
Deletion of the matrix sentence restored:

II I felt that the sense of her mortality invaded (was invading) me now and that it became (had become) inevitable that I should enter her room.

Change of pronouns and tense forms restored:

I I felt: 'The sense of her mortality invades me (?) now and it becomes inevitable that I (?) enter her room'.

Clearly in first-person narratives free indirect style results from a different set of transformations than does free indirect style in third-person narratives. This is probably one reason why Käte Hamburger felt that free indirect style does not occur in first-person novels. It is true that one important structural distinction that enables the reader to recognize free indirect style is lost in first-person narrative: the congruence of the pronoun and tense system with that of indirect reported speech or thought. In other words, in third-person narratives the reader need only add a 'silent' *he thought* or *he said* in order to be sure that a certain passage is in free indirect style. In first-person narratives he does not have such a reliable tool to find out whether the 'Aussage-subjekt' of a given passage is the narrator or a character; he can only judge by the presence of a verb or expression denoting an inner process, or by the other linguistic features we have discussed.

How does the first-person narrative make up for this loss? The very fact that narrator and main character are one and the same person makes it imperative that the reader should be able to distinguish between their different points of view. In other words, in I-novels we constantly have to ask ourselves whether what we are reading represents the thoughts or feelings of the narrator-I or of the character-I.

In *The Italian Girl* a different tense system is used for direct narration and free indirect style respectively, and it is this difference only that acts as a structural signal of free indirect style. First of all, in free indirect style the preterite assumes a function that is performed by the present in direct narration: that of the neutral or gnomic tense. That this function of the preterite is characteristic of free indirect style in third-person fiction as well is evident from the same Thackeray passage quoted by Ullmann: 'Oh! it was a coward hand that could strike and rob a creature so tender...'. In the first chapter of *The Italian Girl* an example of this neutral preterite occurs on p.22:

> 'Otto claimed he remembered being wheeled by Maggie in his pram, but this was certainly a false memory: some previous Carlotta, some Vittoria, merged here with her image; they were indeed all, in our minds, so merged and generalised that it seemed as if there had always ever been only one Italian girl'.

That the passage is in free indirect style is suggested by other evidence: the resumption of the object of the first clause by the pronoun *this*, and a number of repetitions of which *always ever* is the most remarkable. The use of the preterite here deviates from the norm which we have found governing those passages that are in direct narration. The action - Otto's claim that he remembers - takes place in the first time-sphere, that of the actual composition of the book, but also in the second and third time-spheres: he has always remembered this. If this were a case of straightforward reporting, the tense employed would normally have been the present tense. We must conclude that the preterite here unambiguously points to free indirect style. Of course the preterite can also have a neutral or gnomic function in indirect reporting: 'He remembered the sun rose in the east'. In such cases, the preterite is explained as a 'preterite of concord' by the grammarians [44], but in our example this explanation can only account for the second of the two preterites since there is no preterite in a headclause with which the verb *claimed* can be said to be in concord.

Another passage where repetitions and a strongly emotive tone suggest free indirect style occurs at the top of p.12:

'It had been foolish, entirely foolish, to come. I ought to have come earlier when she was ill, earlier when she wanted me and wrote in letters which for anger and guilt I could scarcely bear to read, come, come, come'.

Note that the beginning of the passage, containing a pluperfect referring to the third time-sphere, is in direct narration. Very quickly then the passage changes into free indirect style, marked in particular by the striking repetitions. We now find the preterite used for actions in the third time-sphere: 'She was ill...', '...she wanted me...', 'I could scarcely bear to read...'. To explain these preterites as 'virtual pluperfects' as we did with a number of other preterites referring to the third time-sphere would seem far-fetched. It would even be impossible in the following sentence on p.18: 'There was nothing of the artist in her. Yet with this she was a timid woman...'. On the same page two cases occur where the expression 'I can recall...' introduces a passage in which the preterite is consistently used with reference to the anterior past. From all this evidence we can only conclude that in free indirect style Iris Murdoch regularly, though not exclusively, uses the preterite with reference to the anterior past. The regularity constitutes a norm, which in itself is a deviation from the norm governing passages in direct narration. This norm can itself be violated, as happens on p.19, where the phrase 'My early memories are...' introduces a whole string of preterites referring to the anterior past, which is however broken by one pluperfect: 'He had been a sculptor, a painter, an engraver, a stone mason'. Interestingly enough, this deviating pluperfect can be explained as a pluperfect of experience, whose effect is not to assign the action to any time-sphere but to stress its iterative aspect and which, as Zandvoort suggests, does not really differ from the preterite in its purely temporal meaning [45]. Thus the deviation does not imply that the sentence is in direct narration; on the contrary, the deviating pluperfect marks the sentence as particularly emotive in tone, even more so than the surrounding sentences in free indirect style. The point seems to be a vitally important one. We could relate this pluperfect to the abstract and theoretical time-sequence we have established, and then we would have to conclude that the sentence in which it occurs constitutes an utterance of the narrator-I: it would then be an objective piece of information about the father's various professional occupations. If we realize, however, that the pluperfect, occurring as it does in a context governed by preterites, constitutes a deviation from a norm, we can interpret it as an extraordinarily emotional tense form, and we will interpret the sentence rather as expressing the character-I's feelings at the realization that, measured against his father's versatility, he himself is only a very limited talent. The norm, in other words, is always determined by the immediate environment of a feature rather than by abstract or grammatical schemes. Not that we can do without the schemes: we need to recognize the tense-sequence governing free indirect style in order to be able to make the basic distinction between the two I's. In the passage discussed just now, for instance, the pluperfects deviate only from their immediate context, since the paragraph in which they occur opens with a number of pluperfects referring to the third time-sphere, in accordance with the general scheme adopted in this chapter. Measured against this scheme, the pluperfect in 'He had been a sculptor, a painter, an engraver, a stone mason' would have been regular; measured against the preterites in its immediate context it is deviating and marked for emotiveness. The schemes are not in themselves expressive; they are so only to the extent to which they can be deviated from. The pluperfect at the end of the first paragraph of the chapter is another case in point. It occurs clearly in a free indirect style context, marked by emotive repetitions and dependent on the phrase 'I felt a resentment...'. It does not denote a return to objective, direct narration, but through its contrast with its immediate environment is shown to be a modal pluperfect rather than a pluperfect referring to the anterior past; it strongly expresses the I's disappointment that he is not being given a proper reception.

A puzzling and seemingly inconsistent mixing up of preterite and pluperfect tenses occurs on p.17. The second paragraph opens quite regularly in direct narration, using pluperfects for actions in the third time-sphere. The phrase 'In my first memories...' introduces a passage where preterites are used for the anterior past, interrupted by one present tense form referring to the first time-sphere. In the middle of this passage, however, two pluperfects ('had escaped' and 'had run away') occur, while the tone and the general style do not change so that there is no reason to suppose that we are back in direct narration again. Close inspection reveals that these pluperfects do not really refer to the third time-sphere, but to a fourth: they refer to a period of time preceding the time-sphere of the preterites in the passage, which is the third time-sphere proper. Momentarily, for the sake of clarity, the anterior past is divided into a more distant and a more recent anterior past and the distinction is marked by the use of contrastive tense forms for either time-sphere. Corresponding to this shift in temporal perspective there is a shift in narrative perspective; the two pluperfects are dependent on 'it was clear to her' and thus constitute an 'Aussage' of the mother. The contrast introduced here is functional on a different level than the distinction between direct narration and free indirect style. Therefore it does not violate the abstract normative tense-schemes governing the two modes of narration. It does however enlarge their semantic scope: the deviation is again functional within its immediate context. It also suggests that the use of tense forms cannot be explained entirely without recourse to the temporal associations the tenses traditionally carry. To say that tense and time have nothing to do with each other will obviously not do. An almost identical use of the pluperfect contrasting with the preterite in free indirect style, while both refer to the third time-sphere, is afforded by the following sentence from Dickens's *Great Expectations* (New Oxford Ill. Ed. 1953, p.12): 'I had begun by asking questions, and I was going to rob Mrs. Joe'.

The sequence of tenses normatively employed by Iris Murdoch for the free indirect style passages can now be formulated as follows. The preterite is used as a neutral or gnomic tense and it is used with reference to actions taking place in the third time-sphere. The present tense only occurs in interpolations (for instance: '...who is my senior by two years...' p.17) and then it always refers to the first time-sphere. Logically, of course, these interpolations are not in free indirect style themselves, since they are utterances of the narrator-I. The pluperfect is regularly dispensed with and replaced by the preterite; when it does occur, it is deviational, either to mark a distinction between a more distant and a more recent anterior past or to mark modality. We may summarize these findings in the following diagram (cf. p.51):

TIME-SPHERE	TENSE
(I Time of writing (Narrator-I)	Present)
II Time of narrative (Character-I)	Preterite
III Time anterior to narrative (Character-I)	Preterite
IV Neutral time-sphere	Preterite

From these conclusions an important correction of Käte Hamburger's theory of fiction results. The statement that free indirect style cannot occur in the first-person novel because the narrator would cancel himself ('...sich selbst damit aufheben' [46]) and become a function within the narrative, appears to be based on philosophical preconceptions that cannot stand the test of linguistic evidence. The fact that the narrator of first-person fictions can treat himself as a character is not a logical inconsistency, but an important source of tension which the writer can put to dramatic use. Concomitantly, her theory that the epic preterite does not occur in first-person fiction must be discarded. Here Stanzel's criticism points the way. He has demonstrated that the epic preterite occurs in free indirect style only. But as we have seen, free indirect style is by no means restricted to the language of fiction; it can occur in critical writing, historical writing and even in expository discourse. This means that the epic preterite is a linguistic feature not only of epic literature, but - theoretically at least - of any kind of discourse. It is an instrument by means of which empathetic involvement or emotional proximity to an object, a situation or a person can be expressed, and which lends itself to linguistic description to a certain degree. Of course the epic preterite, like free indirect style itself, is a *specific* means of expressing emotiveness; there are others besides it. Although its function in narratives is predominantly important, it cannot form the basis of a theory of literature since it is not an exclusive privilege of literature. The concept of the epic preterite answers to a reality: it denotes a certain type of behaviour of the preterite in certain, fairly well-defined contexts and achieves certain stylistic effects, first of all free indirect style. It is a linguistic phenomenon and not a philosophical concept; it defines certain possibilities inherent in the structure of the language, irrespective of genre, register and dialect. To call free indirect style a stylistic feature, as Ullmann does [47], is misleading; it is not an embellishment, a mere technical variation or an elaboration of a stylistic manner. Its function is more essential than that: it affects directly the relation between the speaker or writer and the object of which he speaks or writes. On the most elementary level, the epic preterite in the sense in which we have defined it as the preterite of free indirect reporting, helps to identify the 'Aussagesubjekt'. In third-person novels it enables us to differentiate between the words and thought of the implied author on the one hand and of a fictional character on the other. In first-person novels it enables us to distinguish between the narrator-I and the character-I. The distinctions we make on this level are absolutely essential to our understanding of the novel; just as essential as, say, our seeing that Edgar in the third act of *King Lear* is not really mad, whereas Lear himself is. On other levels, the epic preterite conveys degrees of subjectivity, telling us about tone, attitude and other expressive subtleties.

An integral linguistic description of the epic preterite has not been attempted here. It is doubtful whether it is possible to set up a completely reliable rule enabling us to tell free indirect speech from direct narration. Various writers have stressed the 'impressionistic character' of free indirect style, implying that it is not clearly marked off from other modes of reporting but can shade off into direct narration or indirect reporting imperceptibly [48]. Ullmann, writing about Flaubert's *Novembre,* another example of a first-person fiction in which free indirect style plays a very important part, says that '...since the narrator is also the chief protagonist in the story, it has to be decided in each case whether he is communicating his present thoughts or those he had at the time of the event' [49]. Yet the decisions need not be made purely inductively; we have seen many cases in which grammatical, lexical and prosodic features identify the origin of thoughts or words.

The linguistic evidence for free indirect style has not been exhaustively described, but it may be claimed that a number of linguistic features have been isolated that enable us to make the basic distinctions. One problem in particular remains. Our investigation may suggest that the use of the epic preterite for actions in the anterior past is characteristic either of Iris Murdoch or of first-person fictions. If this is so, a reasonable explanation would be that in first-person novels the subjective involvement of the narrator in his own past is naturally stronger than the involvement of a narrator in the past of his characters in third-person fictions. Facts are classified according to the temporal scheme in which the pluperfect normally expresses the anterior past. Experiences, on the other hand, are timeless. The non-temporal epic preterite would suggest itself as the appropriate tense form in which to report strongly felt personal experiences. The same explanation would account for the fact that in third-person novels free indirect style sometimes deviates from the pluperfect as the tense used regularly to report actions in the third time-sphere, using preterite tense forms instead. An example is afforded by the passage from *Esther Waters* quoted earlier (p.46), where one preterite is used with reference to the anterior past over against three pluperfects. It is striking that the subject of the preterite is the heroine of the book herself, whereas the pluperfects all have 'it' (i.e. a coin) for their subject. The finding of the coin is presented as an experience and is therefore reported in the non-temporal epic preterite, whereas the actions of which the coin is the subject (rolling on the floor etc.) are not experiences of the heroine and are therefore reported in the less subjective, normative pluperfect.

If this interpretation holds good, it suggests that within the sequence of tenses obtaining for free indirect style and marked off from the sequence obtaining in direct narration, there is room for variation. It also implies that, if separate tense systems exist for first-person free indirect style and for third-person free indirect style, the sequences may overlap, or even contradict each other, as a comparison of the use of the pluperfect in the *Esther Waters* passage with its use in Iris Murdoch's sentence 'He had been a sculptor, a painter, an engraver, a stone mason' (cf. p.58) illustrates. In the first case, the pluperfect would be normative and mark a smaller degree of empathetic subjectivity than the deviating preterite; in the second case, the pluperfect would be deviating and mark a higher degree of empathy.

However logical the language may be in its use of consistent tense schemes, it is obvious that what matters to the reader or critic is not only the awareness of these underlying logical schemes but a sensitive response to microcontextual contrasts. Similarly, the use of tenses is governed by the author's decision to make certain contrasts visible at certain moments rather than by his adhering to a complex set of rigid rules prescribing minutely what tenses can be used in certain contexts and what cannot. Our next concern will be to study the implications of this view with reference to the second major book on the problem of time and tense published in recent years, Harald Weinrich's *Tempus*.

(6)

In 1964 Harald Weinrich published *Tempus: Besprochene und Erzählte Welt* [50], a masterly effort to present a comprehensive view of the time and tense problem in its post-Hamburger stage. There is no doubt that Weinrich was greatly influenced by Käte Hamburger's book and the discussions it provoked, and the debt is not unacknowledged. Weinrich attempts to do what Hamburger had failed to achieve, to treat the problem of the language of literature as a linguistic rather than a logical one: 'Wir brauchen nämlich keine Logik der Dichtung, sondern eine *Linguistik der Literatur*' [51]. His starting point is the Bloomfieldian conception of language as communication and the assumption that the tense-system of every language must have something to do with the linguistic situation of communication, in which language and the world meet ('zusammentreffen'). There are, according to Weinrich, two basic attitudes of the speaker or writer to the world that is the object of his utterance: the 'besprechende' (discussing) and 'erzählende' (narrating) attitude. To each of these different attitudes, a separate tense-system is available. Thus the discussing mode uses a certain set of tenses and the narrative mode uses another. In principle the two sets of tenses cannot be interchangeably used. Weinrich develops this theory mainly with reference to modern French but he claims explicitly that it holds good for all other Romance languages as well, and for German, English, Greek and Latin too. In English, the two tense systems would be as follows (I standing for the discussing and II for the narrating mode):

I	II
he sings	he sang
he has sung	he had sung
he will sing	he would sing
he will have sung	he would have sung
he is singing	he was singing
etc.	*etc.*

All possible combinational forms can be assigned to either I or II, none to both.

Weinrich does not claim complete originality for his theory. He mentions several predecessors, such as Jacques Damourette, Eduard Pichon, Emile Benveniste and William E. Bull, but none of these have developed their views into a coherent theory [52]. How coherent the theory is may appear from some of the linguistic conclusions to which it gives rise, however debatable they may be. Thus, it enables Weinrich to offer a definition of the sentence: a sentence is a linguistic utterance containing at least one tense form but not allowing the occurrence of tense forms from both tense systems [53]. The problem of the compound sentence also appears in a completely fresh light: in Romance languages subclauses are linguistically marked by employing tense forms of group II [54]. Most important, however, is Weinrich's claim to have done away with the category of mood in grammar. What are called modal tense forms are simply 'tense metaphors': the appearance of a II-form in a discussing context constitutes a metaphor since the tense form is used in a foreign context [55]. Tense metaphors in the direction II - I (a group II tense form intruding in a context governed by group I forms) generally introduce a semantic nuance which Weinrich describes as 'eingeschränkte Gültigkeit'. Thus, in the sentence 'I wish I was rich' the metaphorical preterite restricts the reality of what 'to be rich' means. In fact, it expresses that the speaker is not rich. Tense metaphors in the direction I - II introduce a semantic colouring which Weinrich calls 'gespannte Erzählung'; they give the narrative into which they intrude a heightened tension and greater vividness; the historical present is a case in point. The theory enables Weinrich to regard modal tense forms as ordinary tense forms, except that they are used metaphorically. Linguistically they are like 'corpora aliena' intruding into the set of tenses to which they do not belong; semantically they either diminish or enhance the 'reality' of what is said.

Both tense systems have an orientational or 'zero tense': the present in the case of I and the preterite in the case of II. Neither the present nor the preterite contain any information as to time by themselves. The other tenses contain temporal information only relatively, with reference to the zero tense from which they point either backward into the past or forward into the future. Thus *he has sung* refers the action to a time-sphere preceding that of the zero tense. But exact allocation in time is only possible if the zero tense is localized by adverbial modifiers. Similarly, *he sang* does not carry any information as to the time when the action took place; it only contains information about the narrative attitude of the speaker or writer towards the event described. It is here, in his view of the basically non-temporal function of the preterite, that Weinrich differs most strongly from current linguistic ideas. Most modern grammars, however, simply ignore the problem of the epic preterite. By assigning to the preterite a purely narrative function, Weinrich has oversimplified the problem of the preterite in the opposite direction. In fact, according to him, the tenses of group II act as signals that the laws of physical time, obtaining in the discussed world, are suspended in the world of narration. This is indicated by the fact that certain time adverbs (*jetzt, heute, gestern, morgen*) have to be 'translated' into others (*damals, am Vortage, am Tage danach* etc.) when tense forms of group II are used. Only in the case of free indirect speech does this translation not take place; here again, free indirect speech is seen to be firmly rooted in the linguistic system.

Such adverbs, then, do not primarily function as time-indicators, but as 'tense-morphemes'. This becomes especially clear in the case of Camus' *L'Etranger,* written in the tense-system of the discussing mode throughout. Here the adverbs guarantee the continuity the narrative cannot do without. The adverbs are signals of the narrative attitude; they play the role normally fulfilled by the narrative tenses.

Just as all tenses can be arranged in two groups, so can all adverbs of time, corresponding to the discussing and the narrative modes.

I	II
now	then
today	that day
tomorrow	the next day
next week	the next week
etc.	*etc.*

In the case of free indirect speech, when adverbs of class I occur in narrative discourse, we might speak of a 'time adverb metaphor', just as Weinrich speaks of 'tense metaphors'. In other words, adverbs of class I would be normative, and adverbs of class II deviational in non-narrative texts, while adverbs of class I would be deviational in narrations. Apart from isolated cases, such as Camus' *L'Etranger* or Werfel's *Das Lied von Bernadette,* written in the present tense, these rules do in fact obtain. The Camus and Werfel novels might be said to invert the norm deliberately and to be large and elaborate tense metaphors themselves, in Camus' case to create a sense of existentialist absurdity [56] and in Werfel's, to emphazise that he does not want his novel to be read as 'fiction' but as 'reality' [57].

The foregoing is no more than a brief summary of Weinrich's theory. The author's astonishing erudition does not appear from it, nor the brilliance with which he defends his position against cleverly anticipated attacks, or the inventiveness with which many linguistic phenomena are explained by the theory [58]. Yet there are a number of points on which the theory cannot stand detailed investigation. Some of these are so vital that we may well have to reject the whole theory. Even though a definitive evaluation of Weinrich's thesis is not intended here, some of these points cannot be passed by since they relate directly to the subject-matter of this chapter.

First of all, Weinrich reduces the whole concept of the literary genre to typified linguistic situations. Thus the tenses of group II - the tenses used in narrative discourse - predominate in the novel and other kinds of literary narration, while the tenses of group I predominate in the lyric, in drama, in dialogue, in newspaper writing, in literary criticism and in scientific writing [59]. The linguistic situation which he calls narrative is not identical with, but comprises what Aristotle called epic literature. If in narrative pieces of literature tense forms of group I occur, they must be metaphorical. Works such as *L'Etranger* and *Das Lied von Bernadette*, which use group I tenses as their narrative vehicles, fall outside the system and are themselves only metaphorically novels. Now this seems a wilful distortion of facts. The literary genre to which a piece belongs cannot be determined on the ground of its tense system alone. The definition of the novel must be comprehensive enough to include Camus' and Werfel's books. Moreover, as we have seen, it is possible to relate the use of the present tense (a discussing tense) to the tense system used in *The Italian Girl* without assuming metaphorical functions for it; the present tense has a normative function in the tense system employed by Iris Murdoch. Again, the fact that in direct narration Iris Murdoch employs the present as a neutral or, in Weinrich's terms, zero-tense, while in free indirect style she uses the preterite, makes it plain that Weinrich's scheme does not work, unless we assume that such a sentence as 'Otto is my senior by two years' (p.17) contains a tense metaphor heightening the tension of the narrative, or interrupts the narrative and puts us back in the 'besprochene Welt'. Neither of course is true; we have proved that the present tense form in our example is not deviational but adheres to the normative tense-system employed throughout the chapter. We cannot but conclude that Weinrich's distinction between the two tense-systems cannot be offered as a dichotomy.

The fact that the distinction is too rigid explains why Weinrich cannot use it as a peg on which to hang a genre-theory without allowing a wide margin for inconsistencies. An example is afforded by what he writes on historical writing. As we have seen, time adverbs of class I are very common in historical narrative; in other words, free indirect style occurs with great frequency. Now Weinrich makes historical writing into a mixed genre, eloquently defending the irregularity as characteristic of the type: 'Er (sc. the historian) ist einerseits Erzähler des Vergangenen, Geschichtenerzähler wollen wir ruhig sagen. Wer nicht erzählen kann, ist ein schlechter Historiker. Aber der Geschichtsschreiber ist gleichzeitig Wissenschaftler. Er begnügt sich nicht damit, die Vergangenheit zu erzählen, sondern er wil sie auch verstehen, erklären, deuten, lehren oder was immer. Sagen wir es in einem Wort: er wil sie besprechen' [60]. Just as it is obviously untrue that a bad story-teller is necessarily a bad historian, it is hard to believe that the writer of history occupies different positions all the time he is writing; it seems much more natural to explain his changes in style as changes in emotional involvement or empathetic identification with the people he writes about. This already points to a possible substitute for Weinrich's rigid distinction between the two linguistic attitudes of discussing and narrating: the idea of a scale of empathy, which is interpretable in terms of linguistic features, as we have illustrated in the case of free indirect style, where the empathetic identification of 'Aussagesubjekt' and 'Aussageobjekt' is maximal. On this scale both novels and historical narratives could easily be placed: yet, in Weinrich's as well as Hamburger's scheme they typify different kinds of linguistic utterances. It might be claimed that such a scale would be applicable to all modes of discourse, since we have seen that free indirect style occurs theoretically in any kind of utterance. In such a view, the adverb *now* would not be a 'tense-morpheme' but a marker of perspective, just like the definite article in 'the next time' as compared with 'next time'.

If we apply Weinrich's classification of all tenses into two groups to our analysis of the use of tense-forms in the first chapter of *The Italian Girl*, an unexpected parallel appears: passages in direct narration use the present and occasionally the perfect as the tense of zero narration, while passages in free indirect style use the preterite. This suggests that there is a connection between Weinrich's group II tenses and free indirect style. The parallel is not maintained throughout the tense system: as we have seen, direct narration in *The Italian Girl* uses the pluperfect - a group II tense in Weinrich's system - with a distinct though relative temporal meaning, locating its actions in the anterior past. But the parallel also suggests that Weinrich's distinction of the tenses into two sets relating to different kinds of linguistic utterances is false. They can only be related to different degrees of empathy; in other words, they function on a scale of subjectivity, whether of a discussing or of a narrative nature. On the evidence of Iris Murdoch's use of the tenses, it seems appropriate to call Weinrich's narrative tenses 'subjective' and his discussing tenses 'objective', in the sense that in the former there is a greater degree of subjective involvement of the author or speaker in his subject-matter, while in the latter more distance is kept, the subject-matter being treated as an object that lies outside the sphere of the author's personal interests. Of course it is true that in narratives the degree of empathy of the author with his subject-matter will be higher than in other forms of discourse, just as the degree of identification of the reader with the subject-matter will be higher. It is part of the rhetoric of narrative literature that the reader should be stimulated to let himself be engrossed in the story by means of presenting that story as something requiring primarily an emotional response. Nevertheless, we have enough evidence to insist that emotiveness is not the privilege of narrative literature, and that a division of utterances into narrative and discussing ones is over-rigid. Our substitute is a scale of emotiveness on which all linguistic utterances can be placed according to their degree of empathy, which, as we have shown, is to some extent describable in linguistic terms.

Weinrich's tendency to set up over-rigid schemes and to neglect micro-contextual deviations as significant features for the interpretation of the speaker's or writer's attitude towards his object of writing also appears from his treatment of the expanded form in English. One of the differences between the French Passé Défini and Imparfait is, according to him, that within the narrative mode the former tense describes actions taking place in the foreground of the narrative, whereas the Imparfait is used to describe background events. He illustrates this with customary persuasiveness by means of a minute, self-composed fairy-tale: 'Il était une fois une pauvre fillette... - Alors un jeune Prince passa... - le lendemain il l'épousait' [61]. In English, Weinrich claims the function of the background tenses is played by the expanded form, not only in the narrative but in the discussing mode as well. The expanded form does not have a durative or progressive meaning; it merely serves to indicate the background-character of the action described, marking those phases in the narrative that have less relief than others. An example from Hemingway is used to illustrate the point: 'Nick said, "All right". He was looking away so as not to see what his father was doing' [62]. The verb *was looking* does not have a durative aspect, according to Weinrich; it simply indicates that the action of looking away serves here as a background to the action in the foreground. This view of the expanded form is not tenable in view of what modern grammarians tell us about the construction. First of all, in the discussing mode the -ing form is often used to *foreground* an action: 'You're being stupid' has a greater degree of actuality and emphasis than 'You are stupid'. The emotive functions of the expanded form in general do the opposite of pushing an action into the background: 'Who has been tampering with that lock'?; 'Dear me, I'm forgetting my umbrella'! [63]. In narrative contexts this foregrounding effect of the expanded form is no less apparent. Consider the following passage from *The Italian Girl*, pp.20-21:

> 'A woman's voice above me softly spoke my name. I paused now and looked up. A face was looking at me over the bannisters, a face which I dimly, partly recognized. Then I realized that it was only my old nurse, the Italian girl. We had had in the house, ever since we were small children, a series of Italian nursery-maids...'

The passage begins a new paragraph. Characteristically, it opens in the neutral, objective tone of direct narration. With the second sentence, tone and perspective shift; the adverb *now* and the repetition in *dimly, partly* suggest free indirect style. The fourth sentence, beginning with *then*, moves back into direct narration and the passage concludes with a number of pluperfects referring to the third time-sphere. It shows the structure that is characteristically used to construct paragraphs throughout the whole chapter. The third sentence, containing a progressive form, can only be said to give background information in the sense that the action described here is continuative: the woman had been looking at the I already before he looked up at her. The repetitions in this sentence, however, contribute to its dramatic immediacy and thus make it fit the emotionality conveyed by the subjective perspective. Obviously the progressive form does in no way have a 'plot-retarding' or 'backgrounding' effect.

Martin Joos's views of the progressive - or, in his terms, the temporary aspect - strongly resemble Weinrich's and are, in fact, much more cogently argued. First of all, he claims a 'backgrounding' function for the progressive only in narrative contexts, irrespective of whether they use the present or the past tense as their narrative vehicle. Secondly, 'background' actions to him are merely actions that do not advance the narrative; he does not attribute a lower semantic importance to them. However, since Joos's analysis of the functions of the English tenses does not imply any statement about the specific function of the epic preterite - in fact his basic tenet that the past tense always has real past-time reference would seem to rule out the existence of anything like the epic preterite - his theory about the progressive cannot be used as a basis on which to erect a theory of narrative tenses. His analysis is simply irrelevant to the subject of our investigation. The main problem, that of the epic preterite, Joos fails to solve. In fact, the problem is ignored by most modern grammarians who, like Joos, consider the -ed morpheme as having past time meaning (cf. also p.47 and p.64).

We conclude, then, that the expanded form, when it occurs as a deviation in a non-expanded context, may have the same function as a simple past tense form occurring in an expanded context: it emphasizes the action by isolating it, by making it stand out from its context. What is semantically significant is the contrast between expanded and non-expanded tense forms; taken by itself, the expanded form does not signal anything or, rather, may signal anything, foreground as well as background, direct narration as well as free indirect style. That even Joos's and Jespersen's interpretation of the progressive as the aspect used for actions that do not advance the narrative is doubtful, is illustrated by the sentence 'A moment later, like an evil spirit put to flight, I was stumbling away down the stairs' (p.20).

It should be clear that neither Käte Hamburger's nor Harald Weinrich's theories have so far enabled us to set up rigid tense systems that could generally be said to mark different modes of discourse. The epic preterite is not a privilege of the language of epic literature; it is a deviation by means of which a greater degree of empathetic or subjective identification of the writer and the objects of writing is ensured. In other words, it is one of the linguistic means by which the language disciplines the expression of emotiveness. Weinrich's tenses of the discussing and the narrative modes are seen to be based on linguistic preconceptions and pay insufficient attention to the importance of microcontextual deviations as signals of attitude. The language permits the expression of shades of feeling not by adhering to rigid schemes but by allowing deviations from contextual norms and by employing contrasts. Of course

Weinrich's theory of the tense-metaphor proves that he is aware of the significance of the contextual contrast. By constant appeals to the idea of the tense-metaphor his theory could be salvaged to a considerable extent. But the contextual deviation is more immediately relevant than any abstract and general scheme to which each deviation can be related at two or more removes.

An example of Weinrich's over-confidence in schemes and typologies is his statement that no science fiction novel is written in the future tense, a logical consequence of his view that the preterite is the zero tense of all narrative discourse [65]. It may be interesting to investigate the use of tenses in a science fiction novel that is in fact written in the future tense. Not that the fact that a novel is written in the future tense is in itself enough evidence to reject Weinrich's theory; after all, it could always be said that the novel is based on a tense metaphor. We are not so much interested in a refutation of Weinrich's theory, however, as in a number of positive insights the investigation may yield.

(7)

Michael Frayn's *A Very Private Life* (Collins, London 1968) opens as follows: 'Once upon a time there will be a little girl called Uncumber'. The traditional formula of fairy-tale openings leaves no doubt that what is being launched here is a narrative. The zero tense of this narrative is the future tense; it is, however, not entirely free from temporal connotations as are the zero tenses of Weinrich's discussing and narrative modes. For one thing it 'means' that the novel is set in the future, thus acting as a marker of what we know as 'science fiction', a marker dispensed with in most science fiction stories, which use the non-temporal preterite as their zero tense of narration.

The future tense here is the zero tense of a third-person narrative; accordingly, the adverbs of time modifying the future tense have as their point of reference the narrator's present moment: 'Once upon a time...' (p.15), 'then' (pp.5,7), 'at the time' (p.12). The present is used in a way contrasting to the future tense: it is a neutral or iterative tense (pp.6,7,8,12). Here the future tense is employed for what is in the foreground of the action, while the present describes what is habitual to the characters in the narrative; it gives background information which the reader will need in order to understand the story but which does not belong to the story itself.

The preterite is used as a modal preterite (pp.5,12) in a conventional manner; it is also used as a signal of free indirect style. A striking case is the third chapter, which is told in the preterite throughout. On a superficial level, the preterite might here be analysed as referring to the time-sphere preceding that of the narrative proper.The analysis would not be incorrect from the temporal point of view: the chapter tells us about the 'arrival' of Uncumber's artificially hatched baby-brother when Uncumber was three; at the time when the narrative starts, she is five. However, it is not the case that all preterites refer to a past time-sphere from the narrator's point of view; the preterite on p.15 ('Uncumber must have pressed a switch - or moved some kind of lever - she's no idea what it was she *did*') refers to the time-sphere of the narrative itself. The sentence shows some of the marks of free indirect style: the synonymous repetition and the 'inner' verb *she's no idea*. If the third-person pronoun *she* had been used instead of the proper name, we would be in no doubt at all that the sentence was in free indirect style. The same irregularity is observed in the third chapter. The episode opens with an ambiguous sentence: 'It was when she was three' (p.9). The sentence is ambiguous because there is not enough evidence to determine whether it represents the voice of the narrator or the little girl's memory of the occasion. The chapter then assumes the form of a dialogue between the girl and her mother. The whole chapter, however, depends on the verb *to remember*, occurring in a kind of preliminary sentence: 'Uncumber can just remember the arrival of Sulpice' (p.9). There is a strong suggestion that what follows represents the content of the recollection, reported not in conventional free indirect style but in a kind of 'externalized' or 'dramatized' version. The dialogue form is one of the signs of externalization; the retention of the proper name is another. A similar form of externalized free indirect style occurs on p.103, where the thoughts of the heroine assume the form of a story within a story: 'Once upon a time there were real kings and queens in this palace...'. The two cases together demonstrate the unconventional way in which Frayn uses the technique of free indirect reporting. Ohmann's transformational rules cannot account for Frayn's individual style in this respect; for one thing, the shift of pronous very often does not take place. However, free indirect style is clearly recognizable in Frayn's novel; as will appear, it is almost always marked by strong microcontextual deviations. The story within a story just mentioned illustrates this: the use of the preterite here makes it clear that the passage is not an utterance of the narrator, but of the heroine.

Although the preterite is not consistently used with reference to a time-sphere preceding that of the narrative, yet it always carries temporal connotations in this novel except in those cases where it is modal in the conventional sense. In this respect Frayn's non-modal past tenses differ from those of *The Italian Girl*, where the preterite is the main narrative vehicle of the story. In *A Very Private Life* the preterite is always used for actions preceding the *hic et nunc* the narrative has reached at a certain point. The arrival of Uncumber's little brother and the pressing of the switch do not take place in the same time-sphere - the first being part of the narrative's background, the second of the narrative itself - but they can both be related to a moment in time preceding the moment the narrative itself has reached.

However, the book does not employ the future tense as the zero tense of narration throughout. Already very early in the novel we come across present tenses that can only be explained as zero tenses of narration. An example occurs on p.10: '"Do you die when you get old, Mummy?", Uncumber will ask one day. "Sometimes", her mother replies'. Here the adverb *one day* regularly employs the narrator's present moment as point of reference, thus marking the passage as direct narration. At the same time, this adverb makes it clear that the action of *replies* cannot have an iterative aspect. On p.12 the future tense is resumed as the tense of narration, but from now on the zero narrative present becomes more and more frequent until at the beginning of chapter 6 it becomes normative. There are moments when the author deliberately reverts to the zero narrative future ('She's a difficult child, there'll be no doubt'; p.29); there are also moments when he deliberately employs the double meaning which the future tense has now acquired. Thus, on p.65 a chapter opens: 'Again and again Uncumber will try and call Noli'. Does the future tense here function as a narrative future or does it stress the iterative aspect of the action? Similar examples of deliberate ambiguity occur on p.28 ('It's scarcely necessary to say that Sulpice will take *his* shots'), where the future may express volition and habit, and on p.13 ('She will need many more such shots throughout her childhood'), where the future tense has a predictive ring, ominously hinting that Uncumber 'will be a difficult child'. This use of *will* seems to be the twentieth-century equivalent of Wycliff's prophetic shall [66].

The reason why Frayn chose to switch from the future to the present tense for his main narrative vehicle is not hard to find. In a tense-system using the future as its zero tense, the preterite can be used for the projection of events backwards into the past, but for the forward perspective - the projection of events into the future - no tense is available. Thus the choice of the future tense as the zero tense of narration seriously limits the author in his communicational possibilities. In a science fiction novel, as in any novel, there is a present and a past as well as a future; by choosing to tell his story in the future tense Frayn has robbed himself of the possibility to talk of the future within his fictional world. The usual functions of the future tense - i.e. to express futurity, volition and the iterative aspect - are denied to him. The preterite cannot take the place of the zero narrative tense because it has been used with clearly temporal connotations. The only neutral tense open to the author is, then, the present, which so far has not carried temporal associations but only aspectual ones.

Within the new tense system that is gradually substituted for the original one, the present tense becomes the zero tense of narration. It will remain so till the end of the novel. The future tense is free now to be used in its normal functions; henceforth it refers to the future time-sphere (pp.13,25,28,60,98, 115,126,188); it expresses volition (pp.27,31,63) or the iterative aspect (pp.25,

26,42). By a curious reversal of roles the future tense now becomes the vehicle of background information whereas from chapter 6 onwards the present tense consistently relates the events in the immediate foreground of the story. The introductory part of the novel, i.e. the part using the future as the zero tense of narration, now impresses us as constituting a kind of frame or background to the story proper, which stands out against this background as a result of the new function of the present tense. It is obvious that Weinrich's distinction between foreground and background tenses does not stand. Again, these discriminations are not achieved by following a rigid set of rules; they are created by the author's handling of deliberately achieved contrasts. It is also obvious that effects of the same subtlety can be accomplished in narrative prose by using a tense system based on the discussing tenses as by a system derived from the narrative tenses. Yet it would not do to call Weinrich's dichotomy meaningless on these grounds. If we consider Frayn's choice of discussing tenses as a deliberate metaphor, we are made sharply aware of the discussing or didactic intention behind the book, which is clearly offered as a moral fable (not a very profound one, it must be admitted [67]) whose theme is the growing lack of human communication in our technocratic society. On the other hand, most science fiction novels achieve their moralistic and didactic intentions [68] without reverting to the metaphorical use of discussing tenses rather than narrative ones. Weinrich's dichotomy is ultimately based on quantitative evidence only [69]; there does not seem to be any linguistic justification for it.

In order to discover what adjustments the reader of *A Very Private Life* has to make different from those he makes when he reads a past-tense novel, it remains to investigate the use of other tenses. The perfect tense does not present any problems; it is used, in contrast with the zero present, with reference to actions in the non-distant past, mostly in what is known as its resultative function (pp.52,59,101,124,128,130,137-8,152,156,191) and once as a continuative perfect (p.102). In contexts using the future zero tense it does not occur; its logical substitute there is the future perfect.

The preterite is used with a variety of functions in that part of the novel which uses the present as the zero narrative tense. First of all it should be said that on one occasion it is used by mistake, instead of the narrative present: '"I've got the right number?" asked Uncumber' (p.63). This is simply a momentary lapse from the narrative present into the narrative past. Secondly, the preterite is used, though only rarely, to refer to the past time-sphere in direct narration: 'Sulpice has found someone, of course, being Sulpice. He advertised, and had 74 replies, out of whom, after thorough interviewing, he picked a calm, lethargic girl called Nanto-Suleta' (p.46). This quotation shows the difference between the perfect and the preterite as referring to the past time-sphere: the perfect cooperates with the semantic element 'find' to produce a resultative effect, while the preterite denotes the past-ness of the action. A similar use of the preterite occurs in the following sentence: 'A colossal double explosion fills the room, like the one which caught Uncumber off balance in the garden' (p.95). At the same time, the preterite in these cases functions as a marker of background. It not only locates the actions in a more distant past but assigns them to the background of the story. The foreground of the story, i.e. the actual narrative itself, employs tense forms of group I (present and perfect) normatively.

Another function of the preterite is to denote irreality. Regular modal preterites occur throughout the book; they do not have any temporal implications. They frequently occur in conditional clauses (pp.18,24,120) or as modal auxiliaries (pp.88,120,170,186,187). Weinrich's interpretation of the modal preterite as a tense metaphor denoting 'eingeschränkte Gültigkeit' seems particularly apt in a case like the following: 'Sheer disbelief that any day could be as horrible as this one had been - and even if it could, that it could happen to her - overwhelms her' (pp.77-78), where the word *disbelief* suggests the heroine's unwillingness to accept the events that have taken place as reality.

The modal preterite naturally also occurs in free indirect style passages: 'And if Noli can do it, so can she! In these extraordinary circumstances anything is possible. She could go *behind* the holovision network! Round the back of the world!' (p.67). *So* as a signal of free indirect style is almost a hallmark of Frayn's style: 'So Noli's *nek taomoro*. That's what they said about him before, of course' (p.100); 'So this is what she has been protected from for all those years!' (p.119); 'So that's who it was inside - an old woman only a day away from what looks like final death' (p.68). In the sentence 'It looks rather like a toy dog Uncumber had as a child, so perhaps a dog is what it is' (p.101) we observe an irregularity we have already commented on: the retention of the proper name. Of course the retention of the proper name may be a result of the author's attempt to bring home Uncumber's youth and immaturity by making her speak and think as a child.

Free indirect style in this novel ranges from the orthodox variety to an almost imperceptible transition from direct narration to free indirect reporting. A comparison of the two following passages is instructive:

> 'She is so stunned by this unexpected roomful of people that she cannot bring her mind to bear on it at all. Surely her father told her that this was what happened in the olden days, this crowding together to move from place to place? Surely it was all done away with years and years ago' (p.72).

> 'She falls off the roof in her blindness, and when the pain has begun to subside, feels her way back along the conduits to the next house. Once again it refuses to open to her. She tries a fourth house, and a fifth;

and against the wall of the fifth house she finally sinks down, totally exhausted. She huddles up to it to spend the night. At least she *wasn't* driven away here. And she feels slightly less lonely near to other human beings, even if they are on the other side of soundproof walls, and entirely unaware of her existence' (p.152).

In the first passage a great number of linguistic signals of free indirect style can be observed: emotive exclamations, demonstrative pronouns, prolepsis, rhetorical questions, the dependence on expressions denoting an inner process of feeling *(stunned* and the noun *mind)*. In the second passage only the preterite *was* sharply contrasts with its surroundings: the deviation marks a change of perspective from the narrator's point of view to the heroine's; thus the sentence expresses the heroine's feeling of relief at not being driven away from the house as she had been from the other houses. This preterite is a clear example of what Käte Hamburger calls the epic preterite; it does not carry temporal implications since it functions in the immediate foreground of the action, where the present tense is the normative narrative vehicle. At the same time it bears out Stanzel's view that the epic preterite is characteristic of free indirect style. But these statements cannot, in the light of the evidence offered by this novel, be generalized. Investigation will show that this novel employs a tense system in free indirect style passages, in which each tense can carry temporal implications, assigning actions to the time-sphere normally associated with them in direct narration. Thus the present tense refers to the present time-sphere - i.e. the heroine's present time: 'She is tortured by this repetition of "Nek taomoro Noli". Does it mean "Noli isn't here just now?"Or that he's busy? Or asleep? Or does it mean that they don't know him - have never heard of him? But she feels that they do know him. They're trying to tell her *something* about him. That he's somehow gone away, perhaps? People do go away - they do in certain circumstances leave their houses - that's what the emergency stairs are for. Maybe they mean he's sick? Or slightly dead?' (p.65).

The present also functions as a gnomic tense: 'She needs a friend to confide in. But her old friend Rhipsime wouldn't understand thoughts like these at all. And how do you find a friend when you never meet anyone?' (p.41).

The preterite and the perfect can of course refer to the past time-sphere: 'What strange feelings! How terrible that now she has escaped into the real world all she can think about is the unreal one she escaped from!' (p.113). Even the pluperfect is on one occasion used with a regular reference to the anterior past in a reported statement: 'Clearly it must have been the question of whether or not she'd arrived by rocket that they'd been arguing about earlier' (p.107).

It should be obvious, then, that the linguistic signal of free indirect style in this novel cannot be the selection of tenses according to a sequence of tenses differing from that governing direct narration or discussing discourse. Our analysis has already yielded the observation that the epic preterite is not a linguistic signal of fictional language, and that the difference of behaviour between the tenses in direct narration and free indirect style in *The Italian Girl*, apart from the fact that they are not rigorously applied, may be attributable to the circumstance that the book is a first-person novel. In *A Very Private Life* it becomes clear that all tenses can share the same functions in direct narration as in free indirect style.

It follows that linguistic signals are not so much a matter of features selected according to rules as of deviations from norms, marked by clearly visible contrasts with contextual features. The contrasts may exist on any level: they may affect vocabulary, syntax, rhythm and the use of tenses. We have seen many examples where a contrastive use of tenses acts as a signal of free indirect style, whether in its orthodox or in less conventional forms. The contrast is always with a feature in the immediate context, not with a feature in a theoretical or hypothetical scheme. The terms 'norm' and 'deviation' should then, be understood as functional, not as abstract categories. This is in fact a consequence of Riffaterre's view of style as discussed in the previous chapter, which is probably the most fruitful theory of style to have emerged from linguistic criticism, even if it does not answer all the theoretical questions that can be raised. The point is that Riffaterre's notion of the context as norm and of deviation as an unpredictable element occurring in this context, provides a possibility to make the observation of linguistic facts immediately relevant to stylistic analysis without necessitating a definition of the norm as an abstract or ideal unit against which the text under scrutiny is to be measured. The implication of Riffaterre's theory, that any discourse is amenable to stylistic description, justifies the application of linguistic categories to literary language.

The point may be made clearer by means of an analogy which has the additional advantage of showing what place the insights arrived at occupy in the wider area of modern linguistic theories. From Plato's *Cratylus* onwards, and well on into our own century, theories about the expressiveness of sounds and phonemes have been offered by philosophers, linguists and men of literature. In 1921, Edward Sapir suggested that sound-expression arises out of contrasts and similarities between the elements of the phonetic system of a language rather than from inherent expressive qualities of sounds: 'It is even doubtful if the innate sonority of a phonetic system counts for as much, as esthetic determinant, as the relations between the sounds, the total gamut of their similarities and contrasts. As long as the artist has the wherewithal to lay out his sequences and rhythms, it matters little what are the sensuous qualities of the elements of his material' [70]. The example helps us to define the function of the tenses as studied in this chapter as relational rather than inherent, and to emphasize the importance of microcontextual contrasts.

Three more passages may be adduced in order to bring home the point. The sentence 'Obviously it was a wrong number' (p.62), occurring in a passage of direct narration in the present tense, uses the preterite not as a result of any inherent necessity. In the context of the narrative at this point, a present or a perfect tense would be perfectly justifiable. A present tense would simply have carried on the narrative; a perfect tense would have stressed the aspect of continuity; the girl has been getting the wrong connection two times already. The deviation therefore denotes a change of perspective: it tells us that the sentence is not the author's interpretation of the action, but the heroine's emotional reaction to getting a wrong connection twice. If the sentence had contained a present tense, the possibility of our interpreting it as free indirect reporting would not for that reason be ruled out since, as we have seen, it is normal for the present tense to occur in free indirect style with reference to the heroine's present time. But the appearance of a deviating preterite here forces us towards the intended interpretation: it is the only unmistakable signal in the sentence, whereas the adverb 'obviously', denoting a process of thinking and concluding, may or may not be accepted as evidence of free indirect style.

On p.89 an unexpected preterite occurs which serves the same purpose of marking free indirect style: 'Everyone talked at once, advancing explanations to each other. One thing is plain to Uncumber already - she has found 515-214-442-305-217. This whole palace is 515-214-442-305-217! No wonder such a variety of people answered her calls!' The preterite *talked* here deviates from the narrative present, which is for a moment resumed in the second sentence. As always, the grammatical deviation is reinforced with lexical and phonological features: the words *everyone* and *each other* help to stress the emotionality of the passage by 'excluding' Uncumber from the company; colloquial words like *whole* and the expression *no wonder*, denoting an 'inner process', contribute to the same effect. The dash indicates a pause, the exclamation marks function as indicators of intonation. By all these linguistic means, but in the first place by the strong deviation of the preterite *talked*, the whole paragraph is placed inside Uncumber's mind.

In the following passage: 'The whole world suddenly takes on the aspect of a rank heaving mass of maggots, which appears still and solid only if you stand far enough off from it. So this is what she has been protected from for all these years!' (p.119), the unexpected perfect tense at the end is easily accounted for by the orthodox sequence of tenses: it is a regular continuative perfect. Yet by force of its very contrast with the preceding present tenses it helps to steer our reading of the passage: together with the exclamatory *so*, the pronoun *this* and the exclamation mark it signals free indirect style.

Weinrich's statement that the tenses of free indirect reporting are the (background) tenses of the narrative mode [71] has thus been shown to be inadequate. Similarly, his classification of time adverbs into two groups, corresponding with the discussing and the narrative modes, is untenable. Frayn's novel uses the adverb *now* with its literal temporal meaning, referring to the narrative's present moment: 'The sun looked then, in fact, as it looks now from the orbiting satellite cities above the earth. But the scattered waste-products of those cities have now, mercifully, dimmed the glare for those below' (p.39). *Now* here contrasts with *then* and the contrast emphasizes the literal applicability to time of both adverbs. *Then,* as we have seen, is also used as a time adverb in those passages where the future is employed as the zero tense of narration; its temporal implications are then muted. Once the shift to present tense narration has been made, *then* can be used again to refer to the past time-sphere, and so contrast with *now*. But *then* can also be used in free indirect style with reference to the past. On the other hand, *now* is frequently employed in free indirect style passages to mark the shift of perspective from the narrator's point of view to that of the heroine; in other words, as a signal of free indirect style. It marks, not the epic preterite, because the novel is written in the narrative future and present, but what might logically be called the epic present: 'It's ridiculous, she sees that because she knows now what those white figures were' (p.81). Its use in these cases is not, like its use with the epic preterite, a deviation from its use in discussing discourse, since the connotation of present time reference does not clash with the temporal implications of the present tense. Yet it conspicuously occurs with the verb *to see* (in its sense of *understand*) as well as with other verbs denoting inner processes of thought or feeling (pp.81,123,149,187), thus clearly signalling free indirect style. In all these cases its temporal implications are not muted so that it may be said to contrast with an understood *then*. On the last page of the book, there is even a contrast between a free indirect *now* and a *then* of direct narration:

> 'Now Uncumber feels that she really has come to terms with the whole of her past, and settled accounts with it for good and all. Or at any rate, for the next two or three hundred years. Then a *very* strange thing happens to her. In a sudden inexplicable fit of restlessness and dissatisfaction she...
>
> But that's another story'. (p.192).

The conclusion must be that both *then* and *now* can be used in both direct narration and free indirect style and that their semantic function can only be grasped fully if we consider the words as forming a contrasting pair.

If our analysis of the first chapter of *The Italian Girl* has shown that the theories of Käte Hamburger and Harald Weinrich provide an approach to the problem of tense in the novel and to free indirect style in particular, an approach that enables the critic to discover a number of linguistic features without enabling him to set up a rigid rule governing the use of tenses in fictional language, the investigation of *A Very Private Life* has marked the limits of its applicability. In fact, Frayn's novel completely upsets the theory behind the approach. It has been shown to possess its own system of built-in correspondences and contrasts, such as the different functions of the present and future tenses in the first chapters of the book as compared with the rest. These contrasts - especially when they serve to mark free indirect style - largely depend on the conventional temporal implications the tenses have according to traditional grammar. Relatively, at least, tenses do have to do with time, as Weinrich recognizes: 'Nicht die Zeit der Handlung geben die Tempora an, sondern Ordnung und Aspekt der Handlung, diese allerdings in der Zeit' [72]. The indecisiveness of this formulation invites modifications, which our investigation has enabled us to make. The epic preterite is a case in point. Käte Hamburger considers the epic preterite as a tense whose function it is not to locate an action in time or even in Weinrich's 'Ordnung und Aspekt', but to present an action as an epic event in a fictional context. We know, partly from Stanzel, and partly from our own investigations, that the epic preterite really locates an action on a scale of empathy or subjectivity, and depends for its temporal connotation on the surrounding tense-forms. In the case of a past tense narrative, the temporal implications of the preterite are minimal: it may refer to the time-sphere of the narrative, the time-sphere anterior to the narrative or to no time-sphere at all. In the case of a present tense narrative, however, the temporal implications of the epic preterite are more significant: it contrasts with what we have called the epic present. The reason for this difference is obvious: in past tense narrative, the temporal implications of the epic preterite are muted because it cannot be contrasted with the zero tense of the narration, which is preterite as well [73].

The conclusions drawn from our investigation may seem depressingly negative; what else do they amount to besides the undermining of two theories that have provided many of the tools by means of which the investigation was carried out? It seems, however, that a few positive claims can be made. First of all, we have gained a number of insights into free indirect style, which is a richer and more variedly applied linguistic feature than its common definitions suggest. It is not merely a way of reporting; it is a means by which the language disciplines the expression of emotiveness in all modes of discourse. Secondly, it has become clear that the relation between time and tense is more complex than is suggested by such a representative statement as that of William E. Bull, 'No tense form locates an event in time' [74] on the one hand, or the current linguistic definition of the preterite as being marked for past time on the other. Thirdly, our results would indicate that the current view of stylistic signals as deviations from a norm should replace any 'Logik der Dichtung' theories which attempt to press literary language into the strait-jacket of theoretical constructions; in the first analysis the norm is determined by the immediate context. Lastly, we have tried to show that literary works cannot be properly understood if due attention is not paid to the degree of subjective involvement of the author in his created world, and that this involvement is permeable to linguistic description to a fairly high degree of accuracy.

A no less important conclusion that seems to emerge from our findings is that a linguistic criticism will always be a semantic criticism in the last analysis. The material of the literary artist is language, and elements of language necessarily have a semantic function. As we have seen it will not do to consider tense forms as semantically empty as to the temporal location of actions and events. As all language elements, they have a meaning of their own, independent of the individual user. This meaning enables them to enter into significant contrasts with other elements. It is this type of meaning that is studied in grammar; hence, with reference to *A Very Private Life*, knowledge of what grammar says about the functions of the present and future tenses has turned out to be relevant to our understanding of the book. But the literary artist can also use elements of language as tools that he can give a new meaning by means of contrastive arrangements, in which process the normative meaning of language elements may be muted; this happens in the epic preterite. There is, it would seem, a semantics of the language and a semantics of the creative user of the language. Recent theories on the semantics of metaphor provide a parallel: in metaphor, certain semantic features of a lexical item are muted so that others are free to establish links or contrasts [75]. The literary artist is free, then, to handle the language, but his freedom is limited by the inherent semantics of the language. The moment when his deviations can no longer be related to any linguistic norm marks the point at which his art no longer communicates.

IV *The Italian Girl* - an explication

In this chapter it will be attempted to analyse Iris Murdoch's novel *The Italian Girl* [1] on the basis of a linguistic approach the foundations of which have been laid in the previous chapter. The analysis of linguistic features will not be exhaustive. It is merely claimed that certain facts about the use of tenses in the novel provide a clue to the novel's meaning. The observation of these facts can contribute to an analysis and explication of the novel.

A linguistic analysis of any text can be conducted on the phonological, the lexical and the grammatical levels. The preceding chapter has commented on certain grammatical aspects of the language of *The Italian Girl;* these observations will be used as indicators of certain features on the lexical level as well. The phonological level will be left out of consideration, first because in prose-works there is always less organization of phonological material than in poetry, and secondly because it is hoped that the study of a number of grammatical and lexical features will furnish enough data to attempt an analysis of the whole novel. Moreover, the phonological level, at any rate with a non-native speaker, is a matter of individual interpretation to such an extent that too wide a margin of error is left for any arguments based on phonological expressiveness to be convincing. Apart from punctuation, there is too little that can be called upon as objective evidence.

On any level, linguistic analysis ought to be semantic, and analysis ought to lead to explication. Linguistic features will not be observed simply because they occur, enter into patterns or are 'foregrounded', but because they convey something in themselves and because the patterns into which they enter stand in meaningful opposition to other patterns. For that reason an exhaustive inventory of the novel's linguistic features will not be offered here; nothing like a 'grammar' of *The Italian Girl* will be attempted. The selection of those linguistic features that are thought to be meaningful in themselves must be left to the intelligence and discretion of the critic. If the appeal to the critic's or reader's intelligence is rejected as unscientific, linguistic criticism can only become unreadable, purely quantitative and anti-humanistic. The 'critical hunch' has been recognized as a legitimate stage in linguistic stylistics from Leo Spitzer to Roger Fowler.

The choice of *The Italian Girl* as the object of the kind of analysis attempted in this chapter can be justified for two reasons. First, the preceding chapter has used this novel as illustrative material in formulating a number of observations about the use of tenses in fiction and in particular in free indirect style. Thus it is possible to conduct an analysis of *The Italian Girl* based on its use of the tenses in such a way that the argument links up with and profits by what has been said in the preceding chapter and that its working-hypotheses need not be explained all over again. This implies that a linguistic analysis based on the behaviour of the tense-forms can in principle be applied to any novel and in particular to any first-person novel. Thus, the analytic technique proposed here ought to yield very interesting results when applied to, for instance, *Great Expectations,* one of the acknowledged masterpieces of English fiction, in which the question of the narrator's attitude towards the events narrated in his story would seem to be crucial. That *The Italian Girl* should have been chosen for analysis here must be attributed to reasons of economy in the first place, although modesty and a certain fear to rush in on a great and complex masterpiece with tools not yet sharpened in practice and experience, have played a role as well.

There is, however, an entirely different justification for the choice of *The Italian Girl*. As will appear from the analysis offered here, it is an undeniable fact that *The Italian Girl* is an illustration in fictional terms of Iris Murdoch's ideas in the field of moral philosophy, ideas which have been elaborately recorded in a number of articles, book reviews and philosophical essays. The novel propounds a philosophy; it may be felt that it does little else besides. Whatever conclusions one may wish to draw from this regarding the book's literary merits, the advantage to our purpose is that it is possible to analyse the novel from the viewpoint of Iris Murdoch's philosophy as expounded in her essays. This second analysis, based on external evidence, can be applied as an extra-literary check to the first analysis, based on internal linguistic evidence. The first analysis will turn out to be easily verifiable in terms of the second. It is submitted that the verification will prove the correctness of the linguistic analysis.

A linguistic analysis - or rather, an analysis based on linguistic evidence - verified by an analysis based on other sources; this, then, is what the present chapter attempts to do. Beyond this, it has no further pretensions. It is not concerned with a critical evaluation of the book, even though there will be moments in the argument when evaluative conclusions suggest themselves fairly strongly. This, it would seem, cannot and need not be avoided. It would be unnatural to expect from any analysis an absolutely uncommitted attitude as to literary values once the analysis has been completed. However, the analysis itself does not pretend to be evaluative; what it does pretend is to provide the literary critic with material that cannot be ignored in any critical judgement.

There is one feature of *The Italian Girl* which, though it directly concerns its language, transcends the formal linguistic level. The novel contains a number of quotations and allusions to other literary works (the Bible, Shakespeare, Milton, Coleridge, Walter de la Mare) that are obviously relevant to its interpretation. These quotations enrich the novel's meaning significantly and cannot be left out of consideration in trying to define what the novel ultimately means. Quotation and allusion are techniques characteristic of modern literature and modern art in general. In literary works, they could be explained as specific cases of connotation, in which the connoted element is not merely a part of the language's lexicon but, as the case may be, a whole literary work, a moral or philosophical outlook, a cultural tradition, an atmosphere, or even a literary genre or type. Since the quotations and allusions convey connoted meanings, they may be said to form part of the novel's lexicon and deserve at least the attention our analysis will pay to any other elements in the vocabulary of the book.

(1)

As we have seen in the previous chapter, *The Italian Girl* employs a number of devices to mark the different outlooks of the narrator-I and the character-I. The narrator relates in a factual, controlled manner how he revisits his parental home in order to attend his mother's cremation. The tense-system he employs (tense-system I in the previous chapter) is that of straightforward communication, with the present and perfect tenses referring to his own present time-sphere, the preterite to his past time-sphere, which is the time-level on which the story is enacted, and the pluperfect to his anterior past, i.e. the period of his life anterior to his return to the parental home. Particularly in having the present tense for its 'zero tense' or orientational tense (the tense denoting the narrator's here and now) this tense-system recalls Weinrich's tenses of Group I, the tenses of the discussing mode. The fact that the preterite is the novel's main narrative vehicle does not alter this; in the narrator's perspective the preterite is more than a purely narrative tense, but carries temporal associations; it refers to the time of the novel preceding his here and now. In the narrator's perspective, the preterite does therefore not have an 'epic' function.

Such a sentence as 'Although I am not particularly a coward I have always been afraid of the dark...' (p.13) would, in Weinrich's system, be purely discussing and only relatable to the narrative context in which it occurs by means of the concept of 'tense metaphor'. But as we have shown, the present and perfect tenses as used in this sentence are regularly in accord with the tense-system employed throughout the first chapter. The system constitutes a regularity so that the use of these tenses is in no way metaphorical or deviational from the norm adopted by the writer and maintained in the entire context, even if this norm may itself deviate from the norms obtaining in other narrative contexts, in other novels. What matters to us is that the sentence just quoted would occupy a very low place on a scale of empathy; its degree of subjectivity is very low in spite of the fact that it contains a statement of the I about his own character. Of course it would also be wrong to regard this use of the present tense as a historical present common in third-person fictions. As John R. Frey states, the historical present in third-person novels has a function not essentially different from that of the narrative preterite; the differences are merely gradual and can be described in terms of dramatic and subjective effect only. In first-person novels the intruding present tense plays an essentially different role: it identifies the 'Aussage-subjekt'. In our case, the present tense forms unmistakably identify the speaker as the narrator-I [2].

The narrator must not be confused with the author; as we have said before, he is only the 'implied author'. On a purely logical level he is a point of view, a perspective from which the story is presented. As soon as he becomes involved in the goings-on of the story, however, he undergoes a change of identity as a result of his increased commitment: he becomes another I, who functions in the novel as a character just as do the other characters. In fact he becomes the main character in the story: it is with *him* that the novel is really concerned. The difference between the perspective of the second I and that of the first I is reflected in the grammar of his utterances. The second I uses the preterite as his 'zero tense' of narration, i.e. to refer to his present time-sphere, and the time-sphere that was referred to by the pluperfect for the narrator-I is for him evoked by the preterite in its 'epic' function. In Weinrich's terms: he uses the tenses of the narrative mode; to us, his use of the tenses locates his utterances in a high position on a scale of empathy. This change in the tense-systems by means of which the two I's order their experience makes perfect sense in view of their different identities: what is anterior past to the narrator-I at the moment when he reviews the episode in his life with which the novel deals was simply his past while he was involved in the episode itself.

In the tense-system adopted by the character-I, the (epic) preterite is the tense used for both the second and the third time-spheres, i.e. both for the time of his return to the parental house and for the time anterior to that, for his youth in other words. Figuratively, this means that in knocking on the door of his mother's house the principal character knocks on the door of his own childhood, his own past. The visit to the house can thus be seen to be a visit to his own past, to his own soul, and the journey he has undertaken becomes a quest for self-knowledge. Thus the observation of the behaviour of the tense-forms in the novel has already yielded an important clue to the novel's total meaning.

Although this interpretation satisfactorily accounts for Iris Murdoch's grammar of tense, it suggests another complication which necessarily follows from the fact that the novel is a study of the I's psychological and moral development. The 'implied author' is concerned with conveying to his readers that he has become a different human being as a result of the episode related in the book. This means that from a strictly temporal point of view the 'éducation sentimentale' of the I has been completed by the time he starts to write the novel, or at least reached a stage at which it is possible for him to reflect critically on his own development. Yet, the very purpose of the writing, which is to describe the development he undergoes in the form of a narrative consisting of a succession of events ordered in time, makes it necessary to start from a stage in the development *preceding* the formative episode. In other words, the implied author presents us with a fictive version of himself as he was before the episode of the novel takes place. This implies that the implied author is himself present in the novel as a character and that he is more than just a perspective from which the novel is told. The implied author is dealing with two versions of himself: the character-I and the narrator-I, i.e. himself before and himself after the events narrated in the novel. Implied author and narrator-I can be identified in so far as the moral position resulting from the formative episode is shared by them in the first time-sphere, the narrator's here and now. The character-I can be identified with neither; he exists merely on the time-level of the novel itself. Implied author and narrator-I, however, cannot be identified in so far as the implied author is writing about himself, about his own 'éducation sentimentale'.

Given the system of tenses employed throughout the book, it is to be expected that explicit statements about the I's moral outlook and psychological make-up *before* the formative episode must employ the present tense, simply because the time-level on which they are valid is taken by the implied author to be his present time-sphere, an equation inherent in the fictional situation and explicable in terms of the partial identity of implied author and narrator-I. In accordance with our expectation, a number of highly significant present-tense descriptions of the I occur in the novel:

'Although I am not especially a coward I have always been afraid of the dark...' (p.13).

'Drunkenness disgusts me' (p.30).

'I detest scenes and drama' (p.31).

'I have very strong principles on the subject of abortion. It seems to me impossible to gloss over the fact that an abortion is murder, the termination of an innocent life' (p.66).

'I am a man of some temper myself at times...' (p.107).

'I am very literal about promises' (p.114).

To these may be added a few remarks which the I makes in direct speech, and which are also clearly intended to convey the moral outlook of the I before the change of mind that he undergoes as a result of what happens to him in the course of the novel:

'... I don't smoke' (p.36).

'I always prefer standing' (p.38).

'I have unworldly tastes' (p.40; cf. also p.19).

These quotations illustrate that the narrator-I functions in the novel as a character with a well-defined psychological and moral make-up. He is an 'upright' person (p.13), with clear moral principles, ascetic, reliable and self-confident. He is not, however, without certain weaknesses: he is afraid of the dark and liable to fits of temper. His relatives sum him up as '...a bit of a puritan' (p.64). He is also a vegetarian, a quality that fits the general description of his character and also gives rise to a certain amount of symbolism concerning the eating of vegetables and fruit and, in particular, apples. By these means the narrator-I is given a personality and differentiated from the implied author, who is not strictly speaking the 'Aussagesubjekt' of the statements quoted but of the novel considered as a coherent utterance [3].

In one respect, the novel can be considered as the description of a series of experiences that have an unsettling effect on Edmund's carefully arranged and cultivated moral principles and shatter his self-confident puritanism. A basic uncertainty about these principles is there from the beginning:

'In fact I did not drink at all, only I always thought it sounded priggish and aggressive to say so' (p.34).

'I was in fact a vegetarian, though by preference and on instinct rather than on any clear principle' (p.48).

It seems to be significant that these passages, in which certain qualifications concerning Edmund's moral highmindedness are implied of which he seems to be only vaguely aware, should employ the preterite rather than the present tense. They are thus marked off from the present tense passages quoted above in which Edmund relates a number of objective truths about himself in full confidence. The preterite here helps to denote a sense of uncertainty in the narrator-I and also relates these statements to the preterite of narration. The uncertainty conveyed here has something to do with what takes place on the past time-level: the episode told in the novel, resulting in the shedding of certainties and principles. In the tense-system we have discovered in the novel these preterites can be accounted for without recourse to the epic preterite: they refer to the time-sphere of the narrative. Yet once we are aware of the partial identity of the narrator-I with the implied author, we realize that they can be related to the first time-sphere as well. Therefore we have a contrastive use of the present and past tenses with reference to the first time-sphere. We would suggest that with reference to the moral character of the narrator-I the present tense conveys full awareness, self-confidence and objectivity, whereas the preterite suggests uncertainty, semi-awareness and subjectivity.

The term 'full awareness' is open to misunderstanding: it does not denote a moral but simply a psychological state. When the I speaks in the present tense, he is in full possession of a limited vision of himself; when he uses the preterite, he betrays an uncertain realization of the limitedness of his vision. Morally, it is this uncertainty to which he is educated in the course of the novel.

Although the two passages quoted last are not marked for free indirect style by any conventional linguistic signs (there are no verbs denoting an inner process of thought or feeling and there are no repetitions) they nevertheless seem to represent a kind of interior reporting. It is very striking that both passages immediately follow on passages of directly reported speech, in which the 'Aussagesubjekt' can only be the character-I. Thus the passages containing the preterites echo to a certain extent what had been said in the direct speech passages: '"No thanks. I don't drink much". In fact I did not drink at all. . .' (p.34); '"...we are both practically vegetarians..." ...I was in fact a vege-tarian...' (p.48). As a result of these close verbal parallels, the tense forms, occurring in similar contexts, contrast very conspicuously. Owing to this contrast, they acquire symbolic meanings: the present tense, although tech-nically the vehicle of direct reporting by the character-I, is used to denote a state of mind that is associated with the self-confident narrator-I; the preterite, carrying 'epic' connotations as a result of the close juxtaposition to direct reporting which pushes, as it were, the preterite-statements into the perspective of the character-I, is felt to be a free indirect reporting tense-form and to denote a state of mind characterized by uncertainty and the opposite of self-confidence. In both cases, it is the phrase *in fact* which signals the change in the I's state of mind; its meaning could be paraphrased with something like *on second thoughts* and thus the phrase can be said to denote an inner process of thought, becoming virtually a signal of free indirect style.

As Stephen Ullmann has said, free indirect style is particularly suitable for transposing into words what has only been half-formulated in the mind, and for the evocation of semi-conscious or hallucinatory states of mind [4]. A simple example may illustrate the point. Suppose a character in a novel has hurt his wife's feelings. There are three possibilities as to the degree to which he may be aware of what he has done. He may be fully aware of it, he may be un-aware of it, or he may be becoming aware of it. In the first case, the aware-ness may be conveyed by authorial comment *(John knew that he had hurt his wife's feelings)*, or by means of reported speech or thought *(John said: 'I have hurt her feelings')*. In the second case, the unawareness can only be conveyed explicitly by authorial comment *(John never realized that he had hurt his wife's feelings)*. In the third case, however, the developing awareness, the half-realization is aptly conveyed by free indirect style. When we read *John realized that something was wrong. He had hurt his wife's feelings*, we are, as it were, witnesses of the moment the truth begins to dawn on John; we are made aware of something of which John himself is only half aware; we are given a direct glimpse into the workings of John's mind. We see him wrestling with a problem; we are informed about his moral and emotional involvement in something of which he does not have a clear picture himself. We are thus one step in advance of the character, by being admitted into his developing consciousness. Free indirect style is eminently suitable to convey this kind of semi-conscious emotional involvement. It presents a dynamic picture where direct and reported speech are static.

If the development of the I from his initial self-confident highmindedness to a state of mind characterized by uncertainties rather than certainties is the theme of the novel, it is easy to see how Iris Murdoch has employed the technique of free indirect style to reinforce the theme. The first shock to Edmund's self-confidence and faith in his principles comes when he forgets an important appointment with his niece, who is in trouble and expects help from him. However 'literal about promises' he may be, at a moment of crisis he forgets an important promise because his mind is preoccupied with other affairs. The following passage gives his reactions to the experience:

'I had searched for Flora in vain. I had taken the next bus to the railway station, I had telephoned the college, the hostel where she usually stayed, I had even asked for Mr. Hopgood, but no one at the other end seemed to have heard of him. In fact, I had little hope of tracing her: she had run away, she would hide. She had said that she would do what I told her, she had asked me to look after her: and at the crucial moment I had allowed my mind to be too full of other things. It seemed to me that I had undergone some sort of dubious enchantment, I had been, almost as if purposely, captured by magicians. Yet I knew this was but a false excuse. If my heart and mind had been sufficiently full of Flora and her needs I could not possibly have forgotten to look at the time. I knew too that the scene in the summer-house had excited me extremely. I was affected by some old sense of the connection of Otto's life with mine, a sense of our being, though so dissimilar, identical. I but too perfectly understood the attraction to which my brother had succumbed. I felt pity, and yet I also felt myself degraded, tarnished.

It was also now clear that I could not go away. I was a prisoner of the situation. Earlier in the day, wandering in a state of aimless lassitude, I had been sharply tempted to depart. Flora was gone, Isabel was lying down and would see no one, Otto was still immured in the summer-house. I felt awkward, alien, excluded. There was nothing I could do for these people. Yet, ardently as I desired to go, and even as I advised myself to return to my simple world before something worse should happen to me, I knew I could not. It was my duty to stay: that harsh word riveted me to the spot. But it was not only that. I realised with alarm that I *wanted* to stay. I was becoming myself a part of the machine'. (pp.89-90).

The experience involves the I in the problems of his relations: from a high-minded and principled outsider he becomes somebody whose certainties are beginning to crumble and who is beginning to feel part of the whole mess of human relationships above which he thought himself so highly elevated. The whole passage shows a gradual shift from direct narration (cf. the pluperfects at the beginning) to free indirect style. There are suggestions of it as early as the sentence opening with *in fact*, a phrase that occurs also in the two sentences where we have found the preterite to suggest Edmund's basic uncertainty about his moral outlook. Punctuation too helps to reinforce the impression of reported thought; the use of the colon certainly deviates from common practice. With the sentence 'I felt awkward, alien, excluded' we are definitely in free indirect style; the vocabulary here recalls the vocabulary of certain indubitable free indirect style passages in the first chapter (cf. pp. 11,14,20).

The exclusion and detachment, necessary conditions for the maintenance of Edmund's moral outlook, are shattered; the breach of his promise to the girl has made him 'part of the machine'. From now on he is definitely included, committed, involved. The state of inclusion has been bought at the price of one of his most cherished illusions. He can no longer say 'I am very literal about promises'; to become more human, he has had to become less perfect.

The passage just quoted also shows a shift from a tense-system in which the present tense of the narrator-I's detached statements about himself acts as the zero tense of narration, to a tense-system in which the epic preterite of uncertainty and involvement acts as zero tense. Put schematically, the moral development of the I is reflected by a shift from the present to the epic past tense. Immediately upon his arrival at the house, Edmund is welcomed by his brother, his sister-in-law and his niece as a potential saviour, a helper from the outside world who can rescue them from the complex moral entanglements in which they find themselves enmeshed. He seems to have the necessary equipment for such a role. He is single and has no other commitments; he is rational and disciplined. He is a man without a past, and he has a number of principles. But far from recommending him for the role of saviour, these qualities are in fact revealed as shortcomings in the course of the novel. Instead of helping others to find their way out of the moral labyrinth, he himself is lost in it, after having had his principles and certainties taken away. The outsider is to become hopelessly involved; instead of saving, he must be saved. From the arrogant, high-principled narrator-I who voices his opinions in the present tense he develops into the dishevelled, pushed-around, helpless character-I who decides to throw in his lot with his old nurse, but has learnt to speak and think in the preterite of doubt, anguish and pity, which is at the same time the preterite of growing self-knowledge. Thus the use of tense in the novel is an indicator not only of point of view or narrative perspective, but of the main character's position in a moral world [5].

Distinguishing between the various functions of the pronoun I and its various referents is a necessary condition for any proper understanding of the novel. There is the constant need for the reader to ask himself who is the 'Aussage-subjekt' of any given passage. The opening sentence of the book is a case in point: 'I pressed the door gently'. In the first analysis, the I here refers to the implied author or the narrator. It is a purely instrumental pronoun, which can for that reason function as the initiator of the narrative. With the definite article in 'the door', however, the I's involvement in the story is suddenly brought about: he is now talking about a door that is familiar to him. His response to the door - and later on in the opening paragraph to the house - is not that of a narrator; it is that of a character, a human being who has known this door from childhood and cannot help responding to it emotionally. Thus, in the first sentence, both the narrator-I and the character-I are present. The complexity is brought about by the use of the definite article at the very beginning of the story. This is an example of a common and popular technique used by novelists to ensure maximal absorption of the reader in the story that is to be narrated. This use of the definite article has aptly been called 'the familiarizing article' [6]. Its use at the beginning of *The Italian Girl* combines the conventional advantage of spell-binding the reader's attention by what may be called a well-known form of novelistic shock-tactics with the more meaningful effect of creating an ambiguous referent for the pronoun I. Thus the use of the definite article has a retrospective effect on the pronoun that opened the sentence: it suggests that the narrator-I will soon become a character-I, who is himself involved in the events that follow. The I is not simply a narrator who is telling about a door that is pressed; he is also a character who is telling about the door of his parental home; a door which, to him, is charged with a great deal of emotional significance.

We have seen that the two tense-systems employed in the first chapter enable the reader to distinguish between the two I's from the point of view of narrative perspective. We have also seen that already in the opening sentence the distinction is blurred. The result of these two contradictory effects is a form of confusion that is highly characteristic of the novel's technique. In the most general way the confusion may be defined as follows: the story identifies narrator-I and character-I - or, in more conventional terminology, author and main character - while the minimal requirement that any intelligent reading of the novel will entail is that the two be kept carefully apart. The confusion itself points up the necessity to maintain a clear distinction between the two I's, at the same time making such a distinction difficult. This deliberate flirting with obscurity would seem to be an important constituent of the novel's rhetoric. It functions in other ways as well. On the level of the plot a number of questions may be asked on which the reader is kept deliberately in the dark: who is the father of Flora's child, what is David's and Elsa's past history, what does Isabel know of her husband's affairs, what is Maggie's precise status in the household? These and other questions are answered only by last-minute disclosures; before these are reached, the reader may well have lost his way in the labyrinth of hints, suggestions and speculations that the novel offers. It is a dark, obscure novel whose first effect is to confuse the reader rather than enlighten him; yet its ultimate effect is transparent. Deliberate confusion also characterizes a good deal of the symbolism. Yet here again, as we shall see, the total effect is clear.

In a way it might be said that the reader's awareness of the fact that there are two different I's results in a deliberately confusing effect the novel has on the reader's own identity. Identification with the narrator-I is not difficult for the reader. The narrator expresses himself in coherent, confident and therefore convincing terms; the logical and conventional tense-system on which he bases his statements constitutes one way of ensuring the reader's identification with the I. The reader can see what these statements mean, he can see the narrator's point and go along with him. Identification with the character-I is not achieved so smoothly; the illogical tense-system, resulting in free indirect reporting, creates a different bond between reader and I. The reader cannot go along with the character-I's experiences; he is rather drawn along with the character-I in his emotional response to what occurs to him. Thus the novel effects the same uncertainty in the reader as to his moral position in the events narrated as it brings about in the principal character's mind. The two different tense-systems employed in the novel do not only create two different I's; they also create two different readers. Like each of the two I's, each of the two readers is associated with either of the two aspects of the novel, the transparent aspect and the obscure, confusing aspect. Concurrently, to either of the two I's there is a separate reader. The reader who identifies readily with the self-confident, objective narrator-I is, just like the narrator-I himself, educated into the uncertain and committed state of mind characteristic of the character-I. If the novel describes the process of the I's moral education, reading the novel becomes a morally educating experience for the reader; his own identity undergoes a change towards a different moral position, just as does the identity of the I whose story he is reading. This is the ideal effect at which the novel's structure aims; whether the effect is actually achieved at every turn of the narrative, is another matter.

The state of confusion in which both character-I and reader are thrown can be related to an important element in Iris Murdoch's philosophical view of reality, for which she uses the term 'opaque'. For our immediate purpose, it is important to remember that the obscurity, or opacity, of the novel is in the first analysis brought about by the constant shifting between two tense-systems and their corresponding points of view. It is interesting to note that the term that is used in the novel to denote the confusion which Edmund feels on the first night of his visit draws attention to the blurring of temporal distinctions caused by the shifting tense-systems: 'Looking up now at the remembered face, I felt a sort of temporal giddiness...' (p.21).

(2)

As we have seen in the previous chapter, the passage beginning 'Calling out or throwing stones...' (p.11) stands out from its context by a remarkable syntactic feature, the resumption of the subject by means of a demonstrative pronoun. The same function of the demonstrative pronoun is observed in the concluding sentence of the first paragraph on p.12. We have interpreted these passages as being in free indirect style, constituting utterances not of the narrator-I but of the character-I: they reproduce his emotional reactions at the time when they took place rather than the reflections on the events of the narrator-I. This use of demonstrative pronouns in Iris Murdoch's hands almost becomes a hallmark of free indirect style; it occurs towards the end of the lengthy passage quoted above (p.88) and, very effectively, in the last paragraph of the novel: 'The route, yes, that too we would have to discuss'.

Apart from this syntactic feature, the passage on p.11 is made to stand out from its context by a no less remarkable rhythmical characteristic: a broken rhythm, marked by a relatively large number of commas and by repetition of synonymous or related lexical elements. Compared with the opening paragraph on p.11, the rhythm here is jerky and nervous or even slightly panicky. In the sentence opening 'I walked a little...' the rhythm quietens down again and the syntax regains self-control. The moment of panic has passed; the narrator-I, characteristically calm and sober, takes over where the character-I, emotionally involved and therefore disturbed and nervous, broke off. The two different states of mind are related to the two different identities of the I.

The use of *now* with reference to the past time-sphere, used with striking regularity in passages in free indirect style throughout the novel, has a similar consequence for our reading of the book. If the word *now* has preserved any of its original semantic value, its use in these passages cannot be explained unless we assume that the narrator on the first time-level is identifying with the character-I on the second time-level to such an extent that the time-levels merge into one another. Identification here means empathetic or emotional involvement, since on a purely logical level the narrator and the character are already one and the same person in first-person narratives. What happens is that the narrator-I, who set out to tell his story in an objective and detached way, is losing his detachment from what the character-I, who is himself at a former period of his life, is experiencing. What took place is remembered so vividly that it is, so to speak, lifted from the second time-level to the first, from the past to the present, from the *then* to the *now*. The past is recollected so intensely that it becomes the present.

What the reader has to do in reading the novel is constantly to decide whether he is in the past or the present or, in other words, which of the two I's is speaking. As we have seen, the two I's can be related to two different states of mind of the main character: his controlled, principled and self-confident self and his involved, panicking and helpless self. The direction of his moral development is towards the latter state, or rather by way of the latter state towards a maturity characterized by the absence of self-confidence, self-righteousness and a set of untested moral principles.

The main character's visit to his parental home can be described as a return from the present time-sphere to the past time-sphere, the difference between the two being linguistically marked by different tense-systems based on the present tense and the preterite respectively, and therefore showing a resemblance to Weinrich's discussing and narrating modes not envisaged by Weinrich's theory itself. The first time-sphere is at the same time symbolically a moral world, in which the narrator has been able to define himself in terms of a set of convictions and a set of principles by which he ordered his life. It is the world, also, of full consciousness, which claims to be able to account for and regulate his existence adequately by rational means. The second time-sphere comprises a number of experiences directed towards unsettling the certainties of the conscious world; it is the time-sphere of his emotional reactions. The return to the parental home is a symbolic return to his past and to the unconscious or semi-conscious part of his mind. In the tense-system employed to describe the world of the main character's past, the non-temporal epic preterite becomes the timeless preterite of the unconscious, the preterite of free indirect style.

Investigation of the lexicon of the descriptions of the house in the first chapter bears out this interpretation. The following passages are highly relevant:

'... a greater blackness breathed at me from within' (p.11).
'... the thick waiting blackness of the house...' (p.14).
'... the old stuffy foxy darkness of the hall' (p.14).
'It was a weak, dirty, weary sort of dimness' (p.15).
'... the pale, uncertain, yellow light...' (p.15).

'The dim electric light…' (p.16).

'The closed doors breathed a stupefaction of slumber' (p.20).

'… the bleak lighted interior…' (p.21).

From these descriptions two associative fields clearly emerge: the house is *dark* (blackness, darkness, dimness, pale, dim, bleak) and the house is *alive* (breathed, waiting). The house awaits the visitor and envelops him in its darkness rather than receives him. In the traditional symbolism of archetypal psychology, the house, by way of its associations with the feminine aspects of nature, is a symbol of the female unconscious waiting in slumber to be penetrated by the male light of spiritual consciousness, commonly symbolized as light penetrating the dark [7]. The traditional Jungian interpretation of the house-symbol fits the theme of the novel like a glove and provides a good deal of its *apparatus:* the penetration is achieved in the course of the novel when the 'dim electric light' is replaced by the bright light of a stronger bulb which Edmund installs in the kitchen, symbolically the room in the house where the transmutations of the psychic levels take place: '…a very bright light dazzled us. I covered my eyes. Yes, Lydia was dead' (p.142) [8].

Lydia, the mother, is the first of the two female forces inhabiting the house. In her, Edmund's return to his past is clearly seen to be a return to the maternal unconscious, the pre-birth state of immaturity and irresponsibility. To achieve the transmutation to the light of adult manhood, the dark will have to be penetrated by the light of self-knowledge and the mother will have to die. Although the material purpose of Edmund's journey home is to attend his mother's cremation, on a deeper level his mother, and her influence on her children's lives, are still alive at the time when the novel opens. The first indication of this is the symbol of the fern '…which never grew but never died either…' (p.16) seen by Edmund when he arrives at the landing on his way to his mother's room. A second indication is the elaborate description which Iris Murdoch inserts of the mother's hair, which '…seemed vital still… even seemed to move a little…' (p.17) and which is '…live, still burnished…' (p.20). This idea of the mother as a still living force is emphasized very strongly indeed. At the cremation, just before the coffin disappears into the furnace, it is '…as if she were for the last time waiting, that so demanding (a) spirit turned upon the threshold, and we were there in front of her, an embarrassed, pitiful, half-witted crew…' (pp.28-29). Later in the novel Edmund becomes aware that in an important sense his mother has not yet died: 'But I kept seeming to forget that she had died, as if *that* didn't matter, and kept returning in fantasy to the old, undying Lydia that I carried inside me' (p.115)[9].

What forces the undying mother exerted during her life and still exerts after her death appears unambiguously from a survey of the keywords in a number of passages in the first chapter where she is described:

rapacious violence (p.17)
suffocation (p.17)
fiercely (p.17)
grasp (p.17)
control (pp.18,34)
ruthlessness (p.18)
hatred (p.18)
destroyed (p.18)
ruined (p.18)
proud (p.18)
possessive (p.18)
power (pp.18,19)
possession (p.19)
machine (p.19)
strength (p.20)
destroy (p.20)
mutilated (p.20)
devastations (p.32)

Obviously the mother is presented as a destructive force; her pride and her desire to control the lives of her children have caused the moral chaos in which they now live. What is particularly striking is the description of the mother's influence as a destructive machine, an image which returns on pp.19, 52,90,95 and 203. Unlike his brother and sister-in-law, Edmund has escaped from his mother's overbearing influence *(escaped, run away* p.17; *escape* p.18; *escaped* p.19); yet the escape has not really liberated him from his mother's power: 'Of course I had never really escaped from Lydia. Lydia had got inside me, into the depths of my being, there was no abyss and no darkness where she was not' (p.19). To deal with the forces his mother exerts, he has to face them instead of escaping from them; he has to submerge into the dark of his past and to accept the unconscious. He has, in a word, to become a part of the machine before he can be freed from it: 'I realized with alarm that I *wanted* to stay. I was becoming myself a part of the machine' (p.90). If we interpret the mother as a symbol of the debilitating maternal unconscious, the novel makes the point that maturity cannot be attained through denial or escape from the unconscious part of our mind. If we take her to be primarily a symbol of evil, the novel stresses the omnipresence of evil and the need to conquer it not by ignoring it but by knowing it in its full horror. Only then can the darkness of the unconscious be lit, and the phantom-mother be laid.

Obviously both interpretations are valid; they are in fact no more than two possible explications of the mother's symbolic significance. Whatever precisely she stands for, she is a creature of the past. Physically dead when the story opens, she still, by her force and influence determines the events in the novel. Hence, when she is first introduced to us, it is not in the pluperfect of the narrator's anterior past, but in the epic preterite of the character-I's fictional present: 'My mother's name was Lydia...' (p.17). Present as she is deep within him, the I does not think of her in the 'conscious' and objective tense-system based on the present tense, but in the 'unconscious' and 'emotive' epic preterite. In Weinrich's terms, he does not 'discuss' her; he can only 'narrate' her.

Our mother-image is an aspect of our image of the archetypal feminine. In C. G. Jung's words, three essential qualities of the archetypal feminine image are the mother's cherishing and nourishing goodness, her orgiastic emotionality and her darkness, which is the darkness of the underworld. In *Symbole der Wandlung,* Jung has described these contradictory tendencies in the mother-image in terms of the opposite between the 'loving mother' and the 'terrible mother' [10]. If the debilitating and destructive force of maternal femininity is embodied in the 'terrible mother' Lydia [11], the protecting and nourishing aspect of maternal femininity is personified in the 'loving mother' Maria Magistretti, the Italian girl. From very early in the novel onwards, the brother's old nurse is presented as a maternal figure: 'We had had in the house, ever since we were small children, a series of Italian nursery-maids ... so that I have always had, as it were, two mothers, my own mother and the Italian girl' (p.21). Here again there is an unmistakable reference to Jungian symbolism, according to which the nurse is a recognized symbol of motherhood [12]. When Edmund meets the Italian girl again after his long absence, he is strongly aware of the protection and consolation she offers: 'With this came to me some old comforting breath of childhood; warm beds, prompt meals, clean linen: these things the Italian girl had provided' (p.22). The Italian girl does not exist for him as a person in her own right; she is merely an aspect of motherhood which his real mother had failed to effectuate. Silent and almost unobserved she leads her obscure life in the household, more like a shadow of ideal motherhood than like a human being. It is only at the end, when the horrible truth is revealed of the Lesbian relationship between Lydia and Maria (a relationship that we can now see to be a symbolic statement of the fact that the two women represent different aspects of motherhood in the novel's symbolic Jungian scheme), and when it is discovered that Lydia has left her whole fortune to Maria, it is only then that Edmund realizes with a shock that she is a human being: 'I certainly now, and with a fresh sharpness, saw Maggie as a separate and private and unpredictable being. I endowed her, as it were, with those human rights, the right of secrecy, the right of surprise' (pp.164-165). Yet it is not easy for him to discard the comforting conception of Maria as a loving mother-figure even after these revelations have been made: 'Yet at the same time I could not stop assuming that Maggie

- well, that Maggie loved us' (p.165). At the end of the novel, even that assumption is abandoned: 'I saw her now, a girl, a stranger, and yet the most familiar person in the world: my Italian girl, and yet also the first woman, as strange as Eve to the dazed awakening Adam' (p.213). Only then does the possibility of a human relationship with Maggie begin to exist. Edmund is drawn towards her, not so much out of a certainty of love, but out of hope that the newly discovered woman may provide a possibility of life to the new man that he has become himself. It is at this point that the Jungian interpretation of the novel must yield to a philosophical one. Maria as a symbol of ideal motherhood is now seen to turn into Maria as a symbol of Iris Murdoch's philosophical ideas about the particularity of the human individual, a theme which informs not only *The Italian Girl* but her other novels as well, and which will occupy a central position in our analysis of the book. Meanwhile, an important ambiguity becomes visible precisely at this point. If the development of the main character is directed towards a state of psychological and moral independence in which the particularity and separateness of the human individual is respected, a state of mind symbolized by his awareness that the Italian girl has '... acquired, what she never had before, an exterior...' (p.166), nevertheless his relationship with Maria creates a new form of dependence. After having refused his sister-in-law's offer of an apple (p.201), he finally does eat the apple he has received from the Italian girl (pp.207,213). Apart from their sexual connotations, apples symbolize, traditionally as well as in the symbolic scheme chosen for this novel, the totality of a human relationship realized fully on both the physical and the spiritual levels. The fruits which Edmund has made almost his only diet contrast strongly with the vegetables and herbs on which Otto subsists. Yet the fulfilment and totality symbolized by the apple can only be obtained in dependence on an offerer: apples are eaten in communication with another being, or they are merely consumed. The ambiguity implied in the apple-symbol will be seen to be a central part of Iris Murdoch's moral philosophy.

This inherent contradiction is the more apparent since the nature of Edmund's dependence on Maria forms itself one of the main moral issues of the novel. When he arrives at the door in the first chapter and finds it locked, his sense of isolation from the house and its inhabitants makes itself felt to him as a state of exclusion. As we have seen, the exclusion is really caused by his blindness to his own subconscious life; it is in the last analysis a lack of self-knowledge. As always, the importance of this theme is clearly seen in the emphatic vocabulary used by the author:

solitary (p.11)
excluded (pp.11,90,136)
intruder (pp.11,13)

locked out (p.14)
exclusion (p.20)

The clues are not always as obvious as these. A sentence like 'I scratched on the door like a dog' (p.119) conveys the same sense of exclusion without explicit recourse to the lexical field listed above.

The moral development which the main character undergoes is, however, not simply describable in terms of a wish to be included, although that is an important stage of it. As we have said, the involvement in his own subconscious (mirrored by the novel's use of the epic preterite as indicative of the degree of empathetic identification of the narrator-I with the character-I) is a necessary condition for the maturity to which Edmund develops. The word *included* is used in a highly significant sense in an important scene in the novel. Characteristically, it is set in the kitchen, the place where, symbolically, transmutations of a psychological and moral nature are prepared. The main character sits down in the kitchen, where the Italian girl is engaged on the maternal task of washing his brother's underwear: 'I sat down to watch, feeling with a mixture of shyness and familiarity included in the scene, comfortably included in her consciousness...' (p.140). The chapter in which this occurs is entitled *Edmund Runs to Mother*. His sense of inclusion can be comfortable only because he has not yet learnt to know the Italian girl as she is: the worst revelations of the plot have not yet been made. His illusions about Maria Magistretti are still intact; she has not yet acquired an exterior, she is still simply a mother-substitute, preferable to the real mother because she embodies the more comforting aspects of femininity. The inclusion, therefore, is an illusory one, and that is precisely what the word *comfortable* conveys. It is closely related to the terms *consoling* and *consolation* which play such an important part in Iris Murdoch's philosophical writings, as we shall see. They describe all those mechanisms by means of which man shields himself from reality in order to cherish his illusions without disturbance. In his heart, Edmund knows that what he is looking for cannot be found: 'I felt extremely upset, ill-used, lacerated, I wanted comfort: yet how could I ask for it here?' (p.141). Then the scene follows in which he installs a stronger light-bulb in the kitchen, creating for himself a possibility to see Maggie. In the rest of the chapter, he discovers a few things about her 'exterior' which he had never noticed, in spite of their intimate physical contact when he was a child. Thus the possibility of a more mature sense of inclusion is created, which will no longer imply a defensive attitude towards reality.

There are other thematic symbols by means of which Iris Murdoch sets the scene for her hero's moral education [13]. Like the one just investigated, they are all firmly rooted in the surface of the novel's language, and particularly in the lexical elements. Thus we get repeated descriptions of the garden surrounding the house as a jungle. The word *jungle* itself occurs a number of times, once in the phonologically related form *jumble*. An associative field having *jungle* for its key-word clearly pervades the whole novel:

dense (pp.11,35)
rank (p.11)
jungle (pp.11,56,58,176)
overgrown (p.14)
weighed down (p.14)
unkept (p.35)
wild (p.35)
tangle (pp.35,58,61)
implicated (p.35)
riot (p.59)
impassable (p.59)
jumble (p.59)
thick (p.60)
twined (p.61)
knolled (p.61), *etcetera*

The jungle-symbolism constantly applied to descriptions of the garden naturally links up with the symbolic function of the house itself. Forests are familiar to Jungian psychology and anthropology as symbols of the feminine principle or the Great Mother and hence of the unconscious, especially in its hostile and threatening aspects [14]. The garden in *The Italian Girl* is the scene of Edmund's first conversation with Flora, which leads to the first undermining of his conscious self-confidence as a result of his breach of promise, and it is also the scene of his most significant meeting with Maria Magistretti. In both cases the garden (or *The Enchanted Wood,* as one of the chapter-headings calls it) is the background to a powerful manifestation of the unconscious, on the first occasion damaging to the main character's self-confidence, on the second hinting at his prospective union with the Italian girl. The garden-symbolism comes to a climax in the chapter just mentioned. The stagnant water of the pool in the garden binds together the symbols of the house and the jungle-garden in what is according to Jung the most common symbol of the unconscious [15]. The chapter hinges on the fear felt by Edmund - and by the reader - that Flora is going to drown herself in the pool. Her death by water would be easily interpretable as a symbolic gesture of final submission to the evil forces exercised by the unconscious tyranny of Lydia - of her ultimate failure to achieve independence and maturity on the level of moral consciousness. In fact Flora does not commit suicide, but escapes, past the pool, to an unspecified appointment from which she returns healed and fortified, resolved to resume her filial duties.

There can be no doubt that the garden, full of terrors and threats but also offering hints of sylvan delights, functions as a typically Jungian image in the symbolic scheme of Iris Murdoch's novel. Yet, on a more strictly literary level, it also functions as a piece of *genre* scenery, deliberately employing the conventional associations of woods and gardens in adventure stories and romantic tales. Similarly, the house, dark, cavernous, and throbbing with a mysterious life of its own, is a piece of stage-property familiar enough from gothic fiction [16]. These literary conventions are exploited by the author on purpose, just as her plot deliberately uses the tricks of vaudeville comedy: whenever two people are engaged in a scene which ought to remain secret to third parties, somebody may be counted upon to burst into the room [17]. What is in fact striking about the vocabulary applied to the garden is its extreme conventionality. These are exactly the words one would expect to come across in any description of an unkept garden that has been allowed to grow into a jungle. Iris Murdoch's romantic, not to say gothic descriptions can be explained as a reaction against the prevailing modes of realistic writing in modern British fiction [18], but they also serve a purpose of their own. Their points of contact with archetypal imagery make them fit to function as metaphors in a moral fable. They are stereotypes of moral values, not just echoes of literary modes now unfashionable. It would not do to call the usual critical view of Iris Murdoch as a writer of romantic fantasy entirely undeserved, yet such criticism is in danger of wilfully ignoring the novelist's real attempts [19]. The point is that the forms and conventions of romantic fantasy are used by Iris Murdoch to emphasize a distorted view of reality which the novels aim to expose. Thus the gothic house in *The Italian Girl* functions as a symbol of a state of defective awareness and of defective moral insight which must be transcended. Some of the most offensively melodramatic scenes in the novel can be defended on similar grounds. Edmund's sudden embracing of Flora in Ch. 10 is by its very melodrama shown up to be an act of self-pity and self-indulgence. Isabel's baring her breasts to Edmund in Ch. 9 constitutes a romantic gesture evoking precisely the sort of solution to their predicament that the novel denies to be valid: the attempt to seek forgetfulness in self-indulgence. In thus evoking not only literary traditions but also stereotyped moral attitudes and codes of behaviour, the novel defines its own objects of attack. The occasionally cloying lushness of the writing and the extremely gothic quality of the author's poetic imagination should therefore be judged according to the degree to which they fail or succeed to represent the opposites of the values the novel asserts.

It is true, however, that a good deal of the symbolism sprinkled so liberally through Iris Murdoch's novels does not, or only in a trivial manner, contribute to our understanding of what she is trying to convey. If they are heavily loaded with implications of profound significance, these symbolic embellishments often present themselves to the reader as puzzles rather than clarifications and thus contribute to the obscurity achieved by the more irritating aspects of the novel's rhetoric [20]. *The Italian Girl* is certainly not free from these blemishes. Thus there are no less than 21 references to hair - whenever a new character is introduced we get detailed information about his or her coiffure. At every climax in the novel, hair falls loose or even, in one case, is cut off with a pair of scissors. Even if this scene makes sense in the ultimate symbolic scheme of the novel - by losing her hair Maggie acquires an 'exterior' so that Edmund is finally able to become aware of her as an individual human being - one cannot help feeling that the evocativeness of the symbol, which to many critics carries Freudian overtones, has a gratuitous and diffuse effect [21]. Another example of superfluous symbolism in *The Italian Girl* - superfluous, that is, not perhaps in a Freudian sense, but in terms of the novel's real subject-matter - is the habit the characters in the book have of going down on their knees at moments of great emotional stress. It may be that the author intends this prostrated attitude to contrast with Edmund's 'upright' stance as a self-righteous puritan when he visits the house; at the end of the novel, even he has a desire to kneel on the floor (p.211). Yet one does not even wish to pursue this possible clue. If this is what the kneeling down means, one will hardly welcome it as a feature significantly enriching the novel's meaning. Kneeling down is characteristically the attitude Miss Murdoch's characters assume when they are in the thralls of sexual desire (pp.93,108,134,211). The fact that the novel quotes Shakespeare's line 'But to the girdle do the gods inherit' (p.95) [22] suggests that the author may have Lear's purified kneeling to Cordelia in Act IV, scene vii in mind, as a kind of prostration contrasting to that of her own characters. Again, if this is so, some readers may feel that the allusion is a serious insult to literary good manners rather than an enrichment of the novel's significance. If not, one is left with the kneeling down as an instance of the gratuitous trappings from which Miss Murdoch's work is never entirely free [23].

We have used a selected number of linguistic features - the use of the preterite as contrasted with the use of the present tense, the use of free indirect style, certain lexical patterns forming associative fields - as starting-points for our analysis. Without claiming that we have studied all the relevant linguistic features in the text, we may say that a coherent picture of the novel's meaning has emerged. What we have to do next is to study the philosophical implications that have become visible in the course of our analysis so far and to see whether our analysis can stand in the light of the evidence derived from Miss Murdoch's non-fictional writings in which these philosophical implications are dealt with explicitly [24].

In an article entitled 'Against Dryness, A Polemical Sketch' [25], Iris Murdoch has given us her views on the contemporary British novel. According to her, it appears in two characteristic types, one of which she calls 'crystalline', the other 'journalistic' [26]. The crystalline novel is a '...small quasi-allegorical object portraying the human condition'; the journalistic novel is '...a large shapeless quasi-documentary object, the degenerate descendant of the 19th-century novel, telling, with pale conventional characters, some straightforward story enlivened with empirical facts'. She admits to a preference for the crystalline novel, since that is the only form in which novelists deal with the important philosophical and moral questions of our existence anyway. However, the typical crystalline novel is a fruit of romanticism in a later phase. In her opinion, these allegorical fictions aim to *console* the reader by myths or by stories. The consolation which they offer is teleological; elsewhere she calls them theological fictions [27]. These fabrications by means of which the human mind consoles itself, are the result of its innate selfishness and of its unwillingness to face unpleasant realities. 'Our minds are continually alive, fabricating an anxious, usually self-preoccupied, often falsifying *veil* which partially conceals the world' [28]. The depiction of death in literature is a case in point. It is the role of tragedy to show us death without consolation. Only few deaths in literature achieve this: the deaths of Patroclus, of Cordelia, of Petya Rostov in *War and Peace*. What they convey is '...a juxtaposition, almost an identification of pointlessness and value' [29]; in other words, they present the reality of death without consolation. To do this is the proper function of the human imagination; consoling art works by fantasy.

The modern novel is a function of fantasy rather than of the imagination. Fantasy operates either with shapeless daydreams, as in the journalistic story, or with small myths, toys, crystals. Only the imagination deals with reality. In a review of a book by Stuart Hampshire Iris Murdoch has defined the imagination as '...a willed imaginative reaching out towards what is real' [30]. Models for this type of knowledge of which only an imaginative effort is capable are provided by the way in which we really know persons and by the way in which we really appreciate works of art. People are neither 'characters' in the sense of the types of nineteenth-century journalistic fictions, nor abstractions in the sense of allegorical, crystalline fables. People are 'substantial, impenetrable, individual, indefinable and valuable'; they are, in one word, opaque [31]. Works of art, like persons, cannot be known at all unless a 'willed imaginative reaching out' is made. Art offers us delight in the existence of what is excellent; hence art shows us the '...absolute pointlessness of virtue while exhibiting its supreme importance'. This pointlessness is the pointlessness of life itself, and form in art is '...the simulation of the self-contained aimlessness of the universe' [32]. The forms of art reflect the forms of reality; hence the richest appreciation of reality is afforded by the appreciation of art. This is what Iris Murdoch means by her aphorism 'Art is the great clue to morals' [33]. This of course is not an aesthetic philosophy; it does not pose art as the *telos* of life, but it poses the appreciation of art as a model of the highest forms of awareness and knowledge, as a model of a moral attitude [34].

Analogous to her critique of contemporary fiction Iris Murdoch has developed a moral philosophy centred round the problem of the perception of reality. On the one hand, the fantasies of the modern novel, which consoles the reader with teleological or theological fictions, impede the perception of reality such as it really is. On the other hand, 'practical reason', defined as 'the selfish empirical consciousness' [35], is equally unable to account for the opacity of persons and the significant pointlessness of reality. Reality is transcendent in a non-metaphysical and non-religious sense; it is self-contained and continuously baffling [36]. But reality is our basic existential situation, and truth to Iris Murdoch means the perception of reality such as it is, behind the falsifying veil with which our consoling fictions attempt to hide it from our view. Neither the consolations of theological fictions nor those of the metaphysical novel as exemplified by Sartre, Camus and de Beauvoir are truthful in this sense of the word: the patterns which they impose act as impediments to our perception of reality in its self-contained and unpredictable essence [37].

The nature of reality to Iris Murdoch is determined by a quality very close to what determined the nature of reality to Hopkins, *inscape* or *haecceitas*. This appears clearly from a passage in her 1967 Leslie Stephen lecture:

'I am looking out of my window in an anxious and resentful state of mind, oblivious of my surroundings, brooding perhaps on some damage done to my prestige. Then suddenly I observe a hovering kestrel. In a moment everything is altered. The brooding self with its hurt vanity has disappeared. There is nothing now but kestrel. And when I return to thinking of the matter it seems less important. And of course this is something which we may also do deliberately: give attention to nature in order to clear our minds of selfish care' [38].

The transcendence or 'haecceitas' of the reality observed (suggested by the absence of a definite article before the word kestrel on its second occurrence) does not with Iris Murdoch point to a metaphysical or religious interpretation of reality as it does with Hopkins, although her philosophy does not necessarily preclude a religious interpretation either: 'God, if He exists, is good because He delights in the existence of something other than Himself. And that is the condition to be aimed at' [39]. Iris Murdoch's thinking does not attempt to find a justification for reality anywhere else than in reality itself: its *beauty*. The perception of reality begins with the perception of the '...sheer alien pointless independent existence of things' [40], '...the minute and absolutely random detail of the world' [41]; it brings us closer to the world of 'particularity and detail' [42]. The perception of reality is the perception of what is 'out there'; it is the perception of the 'unself'. An occasion for 'unselfing' is the perception of beauty [43]. Hence art is the clue to morals, for goodness and virtue are connected with the attempt to see the unself [44]. 'Virtue is the attempt to pierce the veil of selfish consciousness and join the world as it really is' [45]; 'Virtue... is concerned with really apprehending that other people exist' [46]; love consists in attention to the other person, in the accurate apprehension of the other person's reality [47]. Thus, using the nature of art as a model, we learn about morality, consisting in such qualities as '...justice, accuracy, truthfulness, realism, humility, courage as the ability to sustain clear vision, love as attachment or even passion without sentiment or self' [48].

Literature can help us to discover '...a sense of the density of our lives' [49], of the infinitely complex reality of our dealings with persons. In doing so it fulfils a moral role, enabling us to overcome our selfishness by making us see the unself of other beings and of the world, and thus to become truly free [50]. But it will have to be a literature that refuses to supply the consolations we demand; it will have to be a product of the imagination rather than of fantasy. In this context Iris Murdoch enters a plea for symbolism in the novel. Symbolist literature, whose ideal it is to create works of art that are independent and self-contained *things,* can fulfil a moral function in making us aware of the other. However, the absorption of symbolism by poetry in modern literature has impoverished the art of prose fiction. '"Eloquence" is out of fashion; even "style", except in a very austere sense of this term, is out of fashion'. Prose has become a dry medium, fit for didactic, documentary and expository purposes. In short, modern prose is unimaginative; most modern novels are not 'written' [51]. Iris Murdoch's plea is one for a more richly sensuous prose, imaginative and evocative, using the resources of rhetoric and symbolism; it is a plea for '...the concreteness and the opaque character of poetry' [52]. The novel, being the literary genre most concerned with the existence of particular persons, is clearly a form whose moral function is vitally connected with our conduct, in that it teaches us about 'the other'. But what is needed for the novel is a prose more like Landor's than like Hemingway's.

Although it is not our concern to evaluate *The Italian Girl* against the standards for fiction implied in Iris Murdoch's philosophical system, the fact that the novel can to such a large extent be read as a crystallization of her ideas in fictional form raises a number of issues that should at least be mentioned. First, do the symbols she so lavishly employs enable us to perceive a tran-

scendent reality or do they create a sense of confusion out of which no defin-
able view of reality arises? Do they achieve anything more than, on the one
hand, imposing a pattern of meaning on the story which makes it easily interpretable in terms of the philosophical system, and, on the other, lending the
story an aura of mystery and romance which seeks to confuse the reader
deliberately in order to ensure his absorption in the story? Souvage has
investigated the symbolic structure of *The Bell*, concluding that it was successful because the meaning aimed at could not otherwise be conveyed than by
means of symbols [53]. Obviously the answer to this question will be different
for each novel, but there can be no doubt that the question vitally affects the
validity of Miss Murdoch's indictment against the contemporary English
novel as well as the importance of her own fictional efforts.

The second principal question may be phrased as follows: does Miss Murdoch's idea of the opacity of persons lead to the creation of opaque characters
in her sense of the word, or does it give rise to characters whose behaviour
is merely wayward and unpredictable in accordance with her ideas about the
unpredictable and self-contained pointlessness of reality? [54]. To ask the same
question in other words: in how far do her melodramatic plots reflect her
sense of the density of life? Related to this question is another: are her sensuous style, her romantic or gothic scenery, a real step forward from the dryness
of journalistic or crystalline writing or should they be regarded as an atavistic
return to outmoded literary fashions whose only recommendation is that they
evoke a sense of reality different from the way in which we tend to depict
reality to ourselves in the modern world?

Thirdly, there is the question in how far the success or failure of Miss Murdoch's novels affects the validity of her views on the strictly philosophical
level. In the case of a writer whose novels are so clearly imbued with a system
of moral philosophy, as our analysis will show, to ask this question is not to
commit a breach of discipline, especially not when, as is the case with *The
Italian Girl*, the novel makes sense to the degree in which it is inspired by the
philosophy. Do Miss Murdoch's novels embody a moral attitude that lends
force to the challenge to neopositivism and logical empiricism implied in her
philosophy, or one that is merely an escape from them? The answer to this
question will carry implications not only for her importance as a novelist,
but also for her significance as a philosopher.

(4)

It should be our concern now to find out whether our analysis of *The Italian
Girl*, so far based on linguistic evidence and confirmed by our explication of
the novel's symbolic scheme, makes sense in the light of Iris Murdoch's
system of moral philosophy as sketched in the preceding pages. The answer

to this question will turn out to be affirmative, thus pointing to an unmistakable integrity which the novel possesses, but which should not be offered as evidence contributing to a literary or critical evaluation of the book. We shall only aim to make it clear that the novel constitutes a coherent statement about issues that are central to the whole of Miss Murdoch's fictional output as well as to her philosophical work. The conclusion to be drawn from this fact is that our initial approach to the book, by way of certain linguistic observations concerning the use of the grammatical tenses and the book's vocabulary, has been a valid one and has produced verifiable results [55].

A. S. Byatt's statement that *The Italian Girl* is '...too clear, too patterned, too much of a statement about complexity with too little real complexity of feeling or action' [56] can serve as an indication of the general direction which a critical evaluation of the novel might take. The verdict would certainly seem to find support in the analysis proposed here. Another critical complaint about the novel, '...the violent oscillation between comedy and an altogether deadening seriousness' [57], seems to hint at a quality of the novel's technique we have already pointed to: the deliberate confusion into which the reader is thrown not only concerning the I's moral position in the events narrated, but, concomitantly, also his own, and the resulting uncertainty about what the proper response to the events narrated is. The fact that the story is at times so extravagant that one has difficulty in taking it seriously at all can thus be related to a distinctive trait of the book's rhetoric. Corresponding to the I's uncertainty about the degree of his involvement in the affairs of his relatives, an uncertainty that takes the linguistic form of his wavering between two tense-systems, is the reader's uncertainty whether he should identify with the I. At those moments when the I speaks in the tense-system of self-control and self-confidence based on the present tense, identification is easy enough; in the more lurid scenes, to which the I responds in the tense-system of uncertainty based on the preterite, identification may become very difficult indeed, but is nevertheless imposed by the I-form of the narrative. The resulting strain on the reader's willingness to suspend disbelief may find vent in the form of a complaint about 'violent oscillation between comedy and deadening seriousness'.

The two critical observations quoted above may indicate the way in which the analysis proposed here may contribute to a critical evaluation of the book. To attempt such an evaluation, however, lies outside the scope of the present study. Our immediate concern is to analyse *The Italian Girl* in terms of Iris Murdoch's system of moral philosophy, and to see whether the results of this analysis can be reconciled to what we have learned about the novel from the observation of a number of linguistic features.

The Italian Girl is to an important extent composed in the vocabulary of the author's philosophical writings; some of its key-terms can be related directly to the terminology of the philosophical articles we have quoted in our summary of her philosophical views. A fresh look at these key-terms, with their philosophical implications in mind, will not only provide more clues to an interpretation of the novel; it will also make it clear that the analysis in Jungian terms pursued so far can be directly translated into the terms of Miss Murdoch's philosophy.

The state of mind in which the main character arrives at his mother's house, armed with a set of moral principles expressed in the 'discussing' and objective present tense, and with a puritanical self-righteousness that enables him to make his characteristic assertions of the 'I am...'-type, answers to what in the philosophical writings is called 'the selfish empirical consciousness' [58], a concept which is strongly reminiscent of D. H. Lawrence. The selfish consciousness is a 'veil' [59] that hides the world as it really is from our awareness. What is hidden behind the veil of the selfish empirical consciousness is, on the psychological level, embodied in the irrational unconscious and on the philosophical level in the 'density of life'. Both meanings are explicitly present in the vocabulary of *The Italian Girl*. The 'dense jungle' (pp. 11 and 35) of the garden, symbolizes at the same time the unconscious and the 'density of life', by which we have to understand the transcendent, impenetrable complexity of our existence, which the empirical consciousness fails to understand. Just as the main character has to enter the jungle of his unconscious in order to be delivered from his essentially empirical outlook on life, so he has to be made aware of the density of the life led by his relatives; he has to be immersed in the moral chaos in which they live in order to be freed of his preconceptions as to how people ought to live. The revelation of the opacity of their conduct towards him and towards each other will open his eyes to the transcendent reality they represent in their individual 'other-ness'.

Not that the lives led by the people in the house represent in themselves any value greater than that of Edmund's moral outlook. They are wholly creatures of the unconscious. They daydream, Isabel in her room, carried away by the infatuating music of Sibelius and Wagner which she constantly plays on her gramophone, and Otto in his 'magic brothel', the summer-house in the garden where his mistress lives. These people are 'fairies', 'angels', 'demons' (pp.95,160,173,181) rather than normal human beings. Together these people, and the intricate web of relationships that binds them together, form an image of the psyche itself. They represent the elemental forces of the unconscious, which Edmund has to confront. Iris Murdoch has used the metaphor of the machine for the psyche: 'The psyche is a historically determined individual relentlessly looking after itself. In some ways it resembles a machine; in order to operate it needs sources of energy, and it is predisposed to certain patterns of activity. The area of its vaunted freedom of choice is not usually very great. One of its main pastimes is daydreaming' [60]. The sources of energy on which Isabel and Otto subsist are their sexual relationships with David and Elsa. The automatic and wholly will-less nature of these relationships, from which they can no more escape than from Lydia's posthumous influence, is brought home clearly enough by Miss Murdoch's descriptions of them. At the same time, to Isabel and Otto these relationships are no less necessary as a stage in their moral education than the whole experience related by the novel is to Edmund. 'I am caught in a machine...' Otto confesses to Edmund (p.52), while Edmund, half-way through the novel, realizes 'with alarm' that he has become 'a part of the machine...' (p.90).

Edmund's moral development is a journey from the empirical present, through the unconscious past represented by the jungle of the garden [61], towards a new maturity that has accepted and assimilated the experience of the garden. It is also described as a journey from the North to the South, where he travels with Maggie, on his way to Rome, at the end of the book. The North-South symbolism [62] in the novel, again reminiscent of D. H. Lawrence as well as of E. M. Forster, links up with Plato's parable of the pilgrims in the cave who emerge from the land of shadows into the sun, where reality becomes perceptible to them for the first time. Iris Murdoch has quoted this parable in her Leslie Stephen lecture in order to illustrate her idea of the Good as 'reality perceived as it is' [63]. What is revealed to Edmund in the light of the sun, after the labyrinth of the garden has been traversed and the journey to the South become possible, is truth. Even Otto realizes that there can be no substitute for truth: 'Evil is a sort of machinery. And part of it is that one can't even suffer properly, one enjoys one's suffering. Even the notion of punishment becomes corrupt. There are no penances because all *that* suffering is consolation' (p.52). Just as Otto and Isabel merely console themselves by their penance and thus allow the machine to hold them captive and the evil machinatress Lydia to keep her hold on them, Edmund is also momentarily threatened by the danger of consolation when he allows himself to be 'comfortably included' (p.140) in Maria Magistretti's protective presence. The danger resides in his failure, at that stage of his development, to apprehend the reality of the Italian girl as she really is, and in his desire to sink back instead into the comforting illusion of Maggie as a mother-substitute, a relapse into the unconscious level from which it is painful to emerge. Just as his puritan principles used to console him earlier, his identification with the machine consoles him now. In both states of mind, reality and truth are not accessible. Those in the power of the machine try to lure him into joining their state of self-indulgence in order to achieve for themselves even more consolation, as the scene in which Isabel attempts to seduce Edmund makes clear (pp.108-109).

But Edmund is saved, and by being saved can save the others. Truth and reality are revealed at last. The awareness of reality is described in the novel in terms of the idea of *haecceitas*, just as it is in the philosophical writings. On this level of analysis, Edmund develops from a 'general' person into a 'particular' person, and comes to see reality in particular rather than in general terms. 'You are so good at talking in general terms', Otto tells him (p.99), ironically reflecting on Edmund's habit of stating his untested convictions in sweeping statements of the 'I am...'-type. 'Particularity and detail' [64] as qualities essential of reality function in the novel as the ultimate aim of the development of Edmund's awareness. The first intimation of particularity in the sense of the '...sheer alien pointless independent existence of people and things' [65] comes to Edmund in - characteristically - the kitchen. At this point of the novel (pp.118-119) we get a detailed and minutely realistic description of Maggie engaged in preparing a chicken for dinner. The description is entirely free from symbolic overtones; it is aimed at conveying the particularity of the scene precisely as it is, with Edmund watching. Before this scene, the chapter had opened with a passage in which the narrator evokes the *haecceitas* of a piece of boxwood apparently without being able to relate it either to the plot of the novel or to his own moral development:

'Those who do not work with such material, such thingy, aspects of nature, may not quite imagine or credit the way in which a piece of unformed stuff can seem pregnant, inspiring. I can imagine how a sculptor might feel about a lump of stone, though I have never felt this myself. But pieces of wood can quite send my imagination racing even in the handling of them. There is the lovely difference between boxwood and pear wood, the male and the female of the wood-engraver's world. But there is also the strong individual difference between one piece of boxwood and another. Each one is full of a different picture' (p.113) [66].

As always, the vocabulary of this passage can be related to the terminology of Iris Murdoch's philosophical writings; such words as *individual*, *difference* and *imagination* have already been discussed as denoting important categories in the author's thinking. The word *thingy*, denoting *haecceitas* in a striking manner, recalls Iris Murdoch's use of the word *thing* as a philosophical term no less clearly. Thus she describes the ideal of symbolist art as '...the ideal of the resonant self-contained work of art which makes itself as like as possible to a thing...' [67]. That the ability to apprehend the *thingy* nature of reality is a moral quality, follows from its application to the perception of beauty in art. This is a theme that runs through the novel, whose principal characters are after all artists. It is stated symbolically at the end of Ch. 6, where Edmund finds his brother and his mistress asleep. At this stage of his development (the scene occurs on p.81 of the novel), Edmund is still unable to see his brother and Elsa as individual human beings; they merely represent to him a moral attitude that he finds 'unbearable'. The narrowness of his vision makes it impossible for him to see them as real and particular persons engaged in a real relationship: 'I stared at them until they became a mere pattern of lines, a hieroglyph. I covered them with a rug'. The quality of his vision is symbolically rendered in terms of the art that he has made his profession. As he had said himself: 'The art of the wood-engraver may be deep but it is narrow' (p.27).

Edmund's awareness of the *haecceitas* of things and of people culminates in his awareness of the particular individuality of the Italian girl herself: 'I certainly now, and with a fresh sharpness, saw Maggie as a separate and private and unpredictable being ... Our ancestral nurse was after all just a sort of legend. Maria Magistretti was quite another matter' (pp.164-165). Again the very vocabulary used to convey this sense of reality, which is at the same time a knowledge of truth, reflects the terminology of the philosophical writings: 'privileged separateness' (p.186) echoes *alien* and *independent;* the adjectives *separate, private* and *independent* (p.165) belong to the same associative field and might well be replaced by, for instance, the string *substantial, impenetrable, individual, indefinable* used in 'Against Dryness' [68].

The recognition of Maria Magistretti's individuality marks the point at which maturity, if not reached, does at least become possible for Edmund. His whole development has been directed towards the recognition of the individuality of other people; it has been a process of 'unselfing'. Just as unselfing is associated with the perception of beauty in works of art in the philosophical writings, so the recognition of other people's individuality is presented in terms of the perception of beauty in the novel. Edmund's awareness of David Levkin as a particular human being is phrased in terms that rely heavily on the vocabulary of the philosophical writings: 'I saw him there full of the despair of the very young, the beautiful absoluteness which can drive on towards a lifelong shipwreck' (p.191). There is a close verbal parallel in a philosophical essay: 'What is beautiful must be separate' [69]. If the phrase '...the lovely difference between boxwood and pear wood...' (p.113) can be understood in its full implications by reference to the symbolism of art and artists pervading the novel, David's 'beautiful absoluteness' provides an example of the way in which the novel is in danger of being misread unless the reader brings his knowledge of Iris Murdoch's philosophical system to bear on the book. There is an intention here that is not realized by the novel itself. The rather flaccid sentimentality of the phrase 'beautiful absoluteness', unless taken in the technical sense imported from the philosophical essays, has a 'consoling' effect; it makes Edmund's reaction to David's loneliness feeble and inefficient rather than respectful and resigned. The case is instructive in indicating the extent to which the novel relies on the philosophical system underlying it, while at the same time it makes it clear that the novel's main justification is to illustrate the philosophy.

For, as the novel makes clear, there is nothing consoling about Iris Murdoch's conception of truth: 'Since the catastrophe Otto and David had treated each other with a gentleness, a tenderness almost, which in the midst of such extreme grief on both sides seemed a miracle of attention. There was a respect which resembled love, but no communication' (pp.183-184); 'He was beyond the consolations of guilt. He was beyond even the sober machinery of penitence. He was broken and made simple by a knowledge of mortality' (p.196). Truth leaves these characters unprotected against reality, guarded only by their courage, which is '...the ability to sustain clear vision' [70].

There can be little doubt that *The Italian Girl* can be read as an illustration in fictional terms of Iris Murdoch's moral philosophy. We have cited a case in which to read it as such is in fact the only way in which a passage can be made to mean anything at all. This would suggest that the coherence on various levels of analysis which our investigation has established would be at once the minimal and the maximal definition of the novel's merits. There is also the paradoxical result that a novel which sets out to illustrate the ideas of a philosophical system centred round the unpredictability of reality, should do so by being extremely predictable itself, on the level of plot, symbolism, vocabulary and general structure. The most puzzling question that Miss Murdoch's *oeuvre* raises is: why, given her philosophical ideas, should she have chosen the traditional form of the well-rounded, melodramatic story as the vehicle in which to convey these ideas?

Nevertheless, it is important to stress the overall lucidity and clarity of *The Italian Girl*, especially in view of the common critical notion that her novels are full of obscurity and mystery-mongering [71]. We have admitted the charge of obscurity, insisting, however, that it affects mainly the reader's response towards the story and not the meaning of the story itself, which is so easily verifiable in terms of what we know about Iris Murdoch's philosophy. The book's total effect is transparent, and the terms in which it is to be understood are easily referable to a coherent philosophical view of life. If not every detail has yielded an unmistakable significance, we can at least make out for the novel an integrity of meaning far removed from what the following description of its theme suggests: '...The omnipotence of guilt, sexual in nature, produced as a result of a distortion of the energy of love within a society [72]. Another reviewer realised the importance of the philosophical background behind the novel without being able to relate it to the plot: 'If you think of Iris Murdoch as a philosopher, *The Italian Girl* makes, not sense, but an understandable pattern'. To prove his point he quotes a passage we have already commented upon: 'I stared at them for a while, Adam and Eve, the circle out of which sprang all our woes. I stared at them until they became a mere pattern of lines, a hieroglyph...' (p.81), commenting that this '...doesn't mean anything' [73]. As our analysis has shown, the passage certainly means something, and what it means can be stated with precision in terms of the philosophical background to the novel. It means that Edmund's perception of 'the other' is once again likened to the perception of the individual particularity of the 'thing', the work of art. The scene thus becomes a phase in the process of Edmund's 'unselfing', and contributes to the 'basic simplicity' [74] that characterizes *The Italian Girl* and sets it off from its predecessors *An Unofficial Rose* and *The Unicorn*.

It remains to say a few words about the references and allusions to other works of literature that occur in the novel. In general, they seem to confirm the interpretation submitted here, while at the same time broadening its scope by suggesting further levels on which the interpretation can be validly applied. Apart from the literary allusions, there are a number of musical ones whose effect, though necessarily vague, seems to point in the same general direction. Both the composers referred to, Wagner and Sibelius (pp.34,58,100,131), are typically 'decline of the West' composers, in whose more popular works a self-absorbed romanticism results in diffuseness rather than succinctness of form, in the evocation of atmosphere rather than in clarity of vision. They are composers of the past, of semi-conscious or hallucinatory states of mind. The symbolic use to which they are put can probably best be understood in relation to the symbolic role played by Bach in *The Bell* [75]. Bach's music, in its objectivity and in the clarity of its structure, represents 'clear vision', the perception of the thing 'out there', which amounts, in Iris Murdoch's philosophy, to truth and love. Wagner and Sibelius represent the subjective absorption in the self that precludes truth and love [76]. Thus they form a suitable accompaniment to Isabel's musings in her boudoir.

The literary allusions can be referred to our interpretation of the novel on a much less speculative basis [77]. The quotation from *King Lear*, 'But to the girdle do the gods inherit' (p.95), has already been discussed; it also relates to the symbolism of gods, demons, sprites and fallen angels that plays a minor role throughout the novel. The quotation from Milton on p.97, 'For who would lose, though full of pain, this intellectual being, these thoughts that wander through eternity...' [78], relates to the theme of 'suffering without consolation (p.96) and links Otto and Belial, the fallen angel who in Milton's poem counsels against the 'battle for the recovery of Heaven' because it would result in the undoing of the rebelling angels; it would mean their complete 'unselfing'. From this prospect Belial shrinks, just as Otto shrinks from the prospect of suffering without consolation and illusion, from a form of suffering

112

that would lead to his unselfing. What Otto confesses himself to be incapable of is to pity his mistress, and thus accept her misery, without the consolation of sexual passion. Elsa, who is the most innocent character in the novel, dies a death comparable to that of Cordelia: the sacrificial death of the innocent character makes possible the redemption of those who are not innocent. Only after his mistress has died is it possible for Otto to suffer without consolation. Elsa's death is tragic in the sense in which Iris Murdoch understands the term: it presents death without consolation. Her death makes it possible for the other characters in the book to see themselves as they really are. In Maggie's words: 'But perhaps in the end it simply changed us into ourselves' (p.211).

Thus the Milton quotation throws light on the *Lear* quotation in suggesting that a godlike form of suffering is denied to those who cannot free themselves from bondage to passion: 'To suffer, but purely, without consolation. Yes, to suffer like an animal. That would be godlike' (pp.96-97). Between them the two quotations seem to create an area of meaning which was to be further developed in Iris Murdoch's *The Time of the Angels,* published two years after *The Italian Girl.* There the fallen angels take over after God has died a Nietzschean death, and the novel is concerned with the failure of their endeavours to set up substitutes for the dead God in the form of a purely human, 'pointless' goodness or in the form of absolute will.

The quotations from *Hamlet* and from the Old and New Testaments on p.127 [79], do not relate to the themes and motifs of the novel in any such distinct manner. They would seem to be mainly atmospheric in function, creating a sense of drama and eschatology well adapted to the intense moral questioning to which the characters in the novel subject themselves.

The theme of particularity is what gives the quotation from Coleridge's *Ancient Mariner* its point:

> "'Can you see that cat?" "Yes, of course". "Well, until lately I couldn't have seen it at all. Now it exists, it's there, and while it's there I'm not, I just see it and let it be. Do you remember that bit in *The Ancient Mariner* where he sees the water snakes? "Oh happy living things, no tongue their beauty might declare!" That's what it's like, suddenly to be able to see the world and to love it, to be let out of oneself"' (p.202).

The passage is an exact replica of the passage from the Leslie Stephen lecture quoted before, in which Iris Murdoch illustrates her idea of the necessity to '...give attention to nature in order to clear our minds of selfish care' [80]. The water snakes are symbols of the 'minute and absolutely random detail of the world' [81] which constitutes transcendent reality and the unselfish perception of which is the essence of virtue. The Coleridge quotation is alluded to once more at the moment when Edmund's awareness of the Italian girl as an individual person rather than a mother-substitute finally breaks through: 'I saw her now, a girl, a stranger, and yet the most familiar person in the world... She was there, separately and authoritatively there, like the cat which Isabel had shown me from the window' (p.213). The symbolism of Coleridge's water snakes also explains the mysterious 'dance of the worms' in Ch. 6, a scene in which the nature of reality is still couched in the unconscious magic of the garden, so that perception is only possible on the level of the unconscious. Elsa's *rapport* with the dancing worms is purely instinctive; it marks her as a child of the dark whose wisdom is a necessary condition for maturity but at the same time one that must be transcended: 'The lawn was covered, strewn, with innumerable long glistening worms. They lay one close by the other criss-crossing the green dewy grass with their reddish wet bodies. The lawn was thick with them. They lay extended, long, thin, translucent, their tails in their holes; and as the torch came down, approaching nearer to them, they drew in their length and then whisked back into the earth with the quickness of a snake. I recalled this phenomenon now, which had greatly excited Otto in the days of our youth' (pp.72-73) [82].

The most significant quotation in the novel occurs on the second page: 'Tell them I came and no one answered'. De La Mare's poem 'The Listeners', from which this line is taken, is itself sufficiently eerie to give extra relief to the romantic atmosphere of mystery that pervades the novel. Moreover, the beginning of the novel exactly reproduces the dramatic situation of the poem: in both cases a traveller visits a house in the night; in both cases the scene is moonlit; in both cases nobody answers his knock. De La Mare's house or castle is situated in the middle of a forest, while Iris Murdoch's house is surrounded by the jungle of the garden. Both visitors expected to be received, but find the door locked.

In 'The Listeners', the inhabitants of the house (phantoms, just as the people who inhabit the house of *The Italian Girl* are sprites and demons, while the main inhabitant is dead) bear the blame for whatever goes wrong; the moral responsibility does not lie with the traveller, who 'kept his word'. The novel ironically reverses this aspect of the poem's meaning. After the first crisis in the novel, the first shock to Edmund's confident security about the values he has made his own, he is made to realize that, unlike the traveller of the poem, he has failed to keep his word to his niece. Remembering too late that he promised Flora to discuss her problems with her and help her find a solution during breakfast on the second day of his stay in the house, he rushes to her room and finds her gone, having left a notice on the table: 'I waited and you did not come' (p.88). The line is a precise negative of the poem's 'Tell them I came and no one answered, that I kept my word'. It even contains an echo of the poem's anapaests, and the implication 'you did not keep your word' is clearly understood. In thus reversing the dramatic climax of the poem, the novel places the responsibility of faithfulness and the duty of virtue firmly with the living rather than with the dead and reformulates the poem's vague and elusive morality in precise and concrete terms.

'The Listener' is a poem very popular with explicators and has been subjected to widely divergent interpretations. To one critic it dramatizes '...the moment of challenge and doubt when the isolated soul questions the unanswering universe' [83]; to another it is about Christ, whose offer of communication is rejected by the world of men; something like a verbal equivalent of Holman Hunt's *The Light of the World* [84]. One sometimes cannot help feeling that 'The Listener' is one of those poems deliberately written to confound the critics and to invite interpretation on many levels while firmly resisting definitive decoding. Nevertheless, it has a high degree of particularity at the same time as far as its scenery is concerned; however elusive its ultimate meaning may be, its dramatic situation and its verbal surface are perfectly lucid and unambiguous. In this respect too the poem seems a perfect correlative of Iris Murdoch's novel. Forrest Reid, in his monograph on Walter De La Mare, recognizes in the poem a '...curiosity of observation, (an) interest and joy in the minutest detail of earth's beauty, (a) Pre-Raphaelitism that notes the tiny spotted scarlet beetle on the green blade of grass...' [85]. In other words, De La Mare's poem is characterised by the loving attention to particularity that represents such a high moral value in Iris Murdoch's thinking.

The main theme of the poem is obviously a visit to the past of the traveller himself and here again it links up smoothly with the psychological meaning of the past that lies at the basis of our explication of *The Italian Girl*. The way in which the poem and the novel are related in this respect is brought out by Isabel C. Hungerland's comment on the poem: 'There is, however, a perfectly obvious dramatic structure to the narrative, and one that is suggestive of a wide range of experiences. The story is one of an attempt, motivated by a sense of obligation, to return to a past scene and to persons known in the past; the promise is kept, but only phantoms are there to listen. The theme is, then, a "You can't go home again" theme, with supernatural overtones. It is in this direction that the symbolic aspect of the poem is to be sought. Freudian and Jungian material might be helpful in further exploring the direction of symbols, but it will suffice here to point out that the dramatic structure of the poem is clear, that its line of suggestion is clear, and that there is no need to make an impenetrable mystery of its symbolism, if a broad sense of symbol is kept in mind' [86].

Iris Murdoch's *The Unicorn* has been compared with *Wuthering Heights* [87] and the same resemblance might be claimed for *The Italian Girl*. If the novel belongs to the same class as that 'sport' [88] of English romantic fiction, 'The Listeners' belongs to a related type of English romantic poetry of which

Keats's 'La Belle Dame Sans Merci' is an outstanding example. Thus the fact that she quotes 'The Listeners' even helps to define the genre to which Iris Murdoch's novel belongs. It is a genre that can hardly be called academically respectable in our time, and Iris Murdoch has repeatedly come in for criticism because of the seemingly uncritical way in which she adheres to it. At the same time, the attraction which her Pre-Raphaelitism holds for a large reading public cannot be entirely unconnected with the generally increased interest in the Pre-Raphaelites of the sixties. However this may be, there can be no doubt that the way in which the formal decadence of her novels goes hand in hand with a quest for moral values pursued within the discipline of a coherent though not strikingly original philosophical system, is one of the most puzzling phenomena in contemporary English literature.

V   Conclusion

The debate on linguistic criticism has veered between two extreme positions. At the one end there is Whitehall's prophecy in 1957 that '...eventually the linguist will be the only one capable of analyzing poetry'; at the other, M. A. K. Halliday's statement '...what the linguist does when faced with a literary text is the same as what he does when faced with any text that he is going to describe' [1]. Although both claims seem to imply that linguistic criticism is principally a concrete art rather than an abstract theory, a frequently heard complaint has in fact been that it is mainly concerned with theoretical issues and that it can hardly point to actual cases in which essential things were said about literary works that could not have been said otherwise.

Halliday is aware of this, and in his 1962 article 'Descriptive Linguistics in Literary Studies' proposes to avoid the danger of devoting all his time to the discussion of principles by starting with concrete analyses of some texts, leaving theoretical points to the end of his paper. He offers an analysis of Yeats's poem 'Leda and the Swan' in two respects: the distribution of verbal items in the poem and the use of the definite article. From the former it appears that in this respect the poem resembles a passage from the *New Scientist* concerning the peaceful uses of plutonium. Halliday refrains from drawing any conclusions, stating only that *in this respect* the two texts are alike. From his analysis of the use of the definite article in the poem it appears that, again in this respect, the language of the poem resembles that of tourist guides and exhibition catalogues. Once more Halliday takes care to emphasize that no conclusions can be drawn.

So far, Halliday has remained on the purely descriptive level, the only level on which the applicability of linguistic techniques has not been questioned or attacked. The question arises, however, what the linguistic description has to offer besides purely linguistic information. If it is really true that 'Leda and the Swan' resembles the language of tourist guides and exhibition catalogues - and there are no grounds on which the fact can be denied - one wonders what significance can be lent to the fact outside the sphere of descriptive linguistics. It may be of importance for a linguist who studies the use of the definite article or who is interested in registers, but if a critic were to write that 'Leda and the Swan' was to be read like an extract from an exhibition catalogue we would be surprised; if he were to write that

117

it was to be evaluated accordingly, we would be astonished. It is obvious, then, that the 'literariness' of the poem, the quality for which the critic is interested in the poem, has not been discovered by Halliday's linguistic analysis.

Halliday's refusal to base any conclusions on his descriptions is symptomatic. It betrays an awareness that, as description, linguistic criticism is not criticism at all - in fact, Halliday speaks of linguistic stylistics. From the point of view of nomenclature this term may be preferable, but it does not solve the real problem. Description of linguistic facts does not lead to the discovery of 'literariness' or 'literary quality'; yet there is no reason why literary texts should be discussed at all if not for the sake of their 'literariness'. Accordingly, Halliday's procedure of describing the language of literary texts in the same way as he describes the language of any text can only reveal anything relevant about a literary text if it is assumed that its 'literariness' does not matter.

When linguistic description has been used as a discovery procedure, it has concentrated on the elucidation of phrases like Dylan Thomas's 'a grief ago' and 'to marvel my birthday away' or E. E. Cummings's 'he sang his didn't he danced his did' [2]. However 'literary' or 'poetic' such phrases may be felt to be, and however useful the transformational explanations of such phrases may appear, they have nothing to do with 'criticism' in any sense of the term, but are merely operative as decoding-techniques. The problems presented by such phrases are grammatical; the phrases themselves can only be discussed critically when the grammatical problems have been solved.

The linguistic description of literary texts, we must conclude, is not a useful exercise in its own right beyond the usefulness of describing any text. Literary texts, according to Halliday, can be described in the same way as any text can be described, but the reason why we are interested in a literary text is precisely that it is not like 'any text'. On the other hand, if we want to know whether a text is 'literary' or just like 'any text', linguistic description cannot help us to find the answer, unless we regard 'literariness' as merely characteristic of a certain *type* of text different from other types by linguistic features only. The reduction of literature to a type of text produced by the linguistic system of the language seems to underlie most modern attempts to arrive at a methodology of literary studies [3]. Although greater precision and explicitness of description can undoubtedly be achieved by describing a literary text in terms derived from linguistics, information theory and formal logic, it is not clear that such methods can contribute towards critical evaluation or do justice to the peculiar interest that we take in great literature, an interest that can not be accounted for by any such criteria as perfection or complexity of structure.

There would seem to be, however, a middle ground between linguistic description and the critical evaluation of literary texts, just as there would seem to be a middle ground between the extreme views of Whitehall and Halliday quoted at the beginning of this chapter. As we have demonstrated in our analysis of *The Italian Girl*, the insights afforded by linguistic description can be used on a second level of linguistic criticism: the level of explication. Linguistic features help to explain the 'content' of a work, in particular the relationship between the text itself and the 'Aussagesubjekt', which in the case of Iris Murdoch's novel we have tried to explain in terms of empathetic involvement. Information on this level is more important in shaping our understanding of the literary work than is purely descriptive information from which no conclusions must be drawn. What is elucidated on this level is not simply the linguistic make-up of the text itself, its surface structure, as in the case of 'a grief ago', but the total articulation of the work as an utterance of a subject - a character, persona, or author.

In the case of 'Leda and the Swan' Halliday deliberately refuses to draw any evaluative or even explicatory conclusions from his observations. He does so with an insistence that makes one wonder why the article was written at all - let alone four times reprinted in different forms. However, in a later version of what is to a large extent the same paper, although delivered before a different audience, he reverts to his analysis of the poem, suggesting certain explicatory possibilities implied in his analysis:

> '...the constant use, in a "defining" structure, of non-defining, descriptive modifiers, with deictics demanding reference outside the text... build(s) up a kind of backcloth or tapestry effect, so that the picture is "fixed" and what might otherwise be the narrative of an event becomes an interpretation of it' [4].

The passage contains a vague but remarkable hint at a concrete and detailed explication of the poem, for which Halliday's observations on the use of the definite article could be used as a starting point. That Halliday has not thought it worth while to attempt such an explication may be due to the purism with which he sticks to the descriptive level and as such an instance of the sterility that inevitably results from such a purism. In order to illustrate our notion of a middle ground between description and criticism, where linguistic criticism has something to contribute to literary studies in particular with reference to the relationship between 'Aussagesubjekt' and 'Aussageobjekt', we will briefly sketch the lines along which an explication of 'Leda and the Swan' could be performed.

To begin with, one conclusion must be drawn from Halliday's description, namely that the linguistic facts he notes need to be taken seriously. Let us proceed on the assumption that the language of the poem does in fact resemble the language of tourist guides and exhibition catalogues in one respect. Halliday observes that all the definite articles in the poem except one occur in a non-cataphoric use, i.e. refer to something outside the nominal groups in which they are found. In fact, they refer anaphorically to the title of the poem. Such a high frequency of non-cataphoric deictics is characteristic of the language of exhibition catalogues. Now there is one literary genre that can be considered as the lyric equivalent of a description in an exhibition catalogue: the 'Bildgedicht' [5]. Such poems characteristically use the present tense, as does 'Leda and the Swan'; they also use deictics anaphorically to refer to elements in the painting or sculpture which the poet is contemplating; in linguistic terms, the deictics in a 'Bildgedicht' refer to the situational context.

Käte Hamburger has written revealingly on the function of the present tense in 'Bildgedichte' [6]. In her words, '...das Präsens hält ein augenblicklich Soseiendes fest wie auf einem Bilde, wir könnten sagen, verewigt es...' [7]. In emphasizing the 'objective' and 'eternal' quality of the scene depicted, the 'Bildgedicht' conceals the 'Aussagesubjekt', the I of the poem, the persona or the poet. Nevertheless, the I is always there; the poem can always be related to a subject, an origin, from which it emanates. Now the most striking linguistic fact about 'Leda and the Swan' is one that Halliday does not mention: the sudden change from the present to the past tense in the last sentence of the poem. From the moment the tense changes, the poem is by definition no longer a 'Bildgedicht'; the objective description is suddenly broken off and the hidden 'Aussagesubjekt', the lyrical I, steps into the foreground. Very much as is the case in *The Italian Girl,* the sudden change of tense (in technical terms, the most conspicuous contextual deviation in the poem) denotes a change of perspective. We are no longer given an objective description of a painting or sculpture, but are addressed by the I of the poem, who asks us a direct question, thus betraying his subjective involvement in the scene depicted and described. In terms of sonnet-structure, the moment at which the I, as it were, turns his back to the painting and addresses the reader, marks the *volta* of the poem.

The moment is highlighted by other means. First, the curious typography of the poem already indicates that the *volta* occurs not after the octave, but in the middle of the last line of the first tercet. Secondly, the part of the poem after the *volta* constitutes a single macro-syntactic unit, governed by the preterites *did* and *could*. Thirdly, the only cataphoric use of the definite article which Halliday noted (*the* brute blood of the air) occurs within this unit, so that we may say that the deviating use of the article has the same function as the deviating preterite, i.e. to mark a change of perspective. The change of perspective may be described as one from description to interpretation, as Halliday seems to have surmised in the passage quoted above. However, there would seem to be little doubt that what is also involved is a sudden

120

increase in empathetic involvement: the scene of the rape cannot be objectively described without raising moral and emotional problems.

In making the transition from the descriptive level on which Halliday collected certain linguistic data to the explicatory level on which we have put these data to use, it is hoped that we have come closer to the poem to a significant degree. What we have tried to make clear is, first, that the linguistic description as such remains meaningless if no conclusions are to be drawn from it and, secondly, that the critical discussion of the poem cannot begin until more has been done than is achieved by description only. In the distinct interest that we take in literary works, the relation between 'Aussagesubjekt' and 'Aussageobjekt' plays a vital role, as long as we are not hampered by a conception of literature that pays sole attention to the 'work' to the exclusion of the 'mind' behind the work. In the case of *The Italian Girl* as well as in that of 'Leda and the Swan', our explication, based on linguistic description, has illuminated this central aspect of the two texts by enabling us to make precise statements about point of view and perspective. That in both works the use of the grammatical tenses is an important pointer in this respect may serve as an indication of the kind of linguistic feature that is semantically of maximal relevance.

There is yet the question whether it is through linguistic description only that our explications of the two texts could have been arrived at. In the case of the explication of 'Leda and the Swan' that we have proposed, the answer is clearly negative. Even if the observation of linguistic facts has enabled us to make precise statements about the attitude of the I towards the object of writing, the statements themselves do not reveal anything new. The very fact that the poem is a 'Bildgedicht' is familiar to Yeats-critics from extra-textual sources [8]. Our explication could therefore have been reached by a short cut, by-passing elaborate linguistic descriptions such as offered by Halliday. It remains true, however, that 'Leda and the Swan' is only a real 'Bildgedicht' for as far as the second tercet, and that the change of perspective occurring at that point is marked by linguistic deviations that cannot be referred to external evidence. Thus, the case would seem to suggest that linguistic criticism cannot claim to be a discovery procedure in the sense that it yields insights that cannot be arrived at in any other way, but that it serves as an important detector of internal evidence for explicatory purposes.

In the case of *The Italian Girl*, linguistic description of the behaviour of certain tense-forms was the chief evidence on which we built our explication of the book. Yet here again it is not clear that the explication could not have been arrived at along different lines. In fact we have used the external evidence of Miss Murdoch's non-fictional writings to test our linguistic reading, finding that the results of both analyses paralleled each other even in details, and that satisfactory explications were the results of either approach. Therefore, in this case linguistic description has proved useful as just one way of collecting the data on which an explication can be built. Yet, here again it may be doubted if the 'temporal giddiness' that is so characteristic a feature of that novel could have been formulated with the same degree of precision without recourse to linguistic description. Linguistic criticism cannot help us to discover the literary qualities of a text, but it can enable us to articulate our response to literary qualities.

Our conclusion must be that Whitehall's claim for linguistic criticism is inordinate, while the kind of methodological purism advocated by Halliday tends to reduce the usefulness of linguistic stylistics by blurring the fact that in the study of literary texts linguistic description is never an end in itself but can function as a natural incentive to explication. Beyond explication there is the field of interpretation and evaluation, the goals to which all literary studies must strive. If description, explication and evaluation are the three phases of the critical process, linguistic criticism in what has become the accepted sense belongs properly to the first two. Of course the distinction is artificial; in practice the three phases will be co-existent and not sharply demarcated from each other, just as the linguist will not be sharply distinguished from the critic in the literary man. Linguistic criticism, then, is an ancillary discipline in literary studies. It is not more than that, but it is that. In the philological tradition, it has always been recognized as such. Paradoxically, the stress that modern linguists have laid on description in their eagerness to dissociate themselves from the philological tradition has, in linguistic criticism, led to a procedure that is philological if it is anything at all. It is regrettable that linguistic criticism should have become associated almost exclusively with the application of modern linguistic techniques to the study of modern texts, for it is with older texts, where external evidence is scarce or lacking, that the philological mind is often most keenly stimulated. Meanwhile, if linguistic criticism should come to be seen and appreciated as a revival of the philological instinct, nobody would be the poorer for it.

Notes

Notes to Chapter I

1. Cf. Miriam Allott, *Novelists on the Novel*, London/New York 1959, p.162.
2. Cf. Richard Stang, *The Theory of the Novel in England 1850 - 1870*, London/ New York 1959, esp. pp.2 - 3 and p.46; Kenneth Graham, *English Criticism of the Novel 1865 - 1900*, Oxford 1965, esp. p.97.
3. Vernon Lee, *The Handling of Words*, London 1923, esp. pp.60 ff.
4. *Ibid.* p.72.
5. Ed. R. P. Blackmur, 1934.
6. J. Middleton Murry, *Discoveries*, London 1924, pp.129 ff.
7. Edwin Muir, *The Structure of the Novel*, London 1928, p.149.
8. Anthony Trollope, *Autobiography*, London 1883, Ch. 12.
9. Malcolm Cowley, ed., *Writers at Work; the Paris Review Interviews*, London 1958, p.162.
10. Originally published as an introduction to *Towards Standards of Criticism*, London 1933, a selection of essays from *The Calendar of Modern Letters;* reprinted in *Anna Karenina and Other Essays*, London 1967.
11. *The Calendar of Modern Letters*, repr. London 1966, vol. III, 1926-1927, pp.226-233.
12. F. R. Leavis, *Anna Karenina and Others Essays*, pp.219 ff.
13. Letter to Louise Colet, 24 April 1852; Gustave Flaubert, *Correspondance*, deuxième série, Paris 1910, p.95.
14. Letter to Louise Colet, 1852; *Correspondance*, deuxième série, Paris 1910, p.71.
15. *Scrutiny*, vol. II (1933 - 1934), no. 2.
16. In this respect, as in so many others, the influence of Leavis is evident in the pages of *The Pelican Guide to English Literature*, ed. Boris Ford, London 1954 - 1961. See, for instance, the essay on Meredith by F. N. Lees in vol. 6, pp.324 ff.
17. Kenneth Graham, *op.cit.* pp.39,59, and 120. In Dutch literature, the most clearly naturalist writer is also the most 'poetic' novelist - Louis Couperus.
18. *The Pelican Guide to English Literature*, vol. 6, pp.324 ff.
19. Cf. Irène Simon, *Formes du roman anglais de Dickens à Joyce*, Liège 1949.
20. Introduction to Djuna Barnes, *Nightwood*, New Directions ed., New York 1961, p.XII.
21. Lionel Trilling, *The Liberal Imagination*, Mercury Books, London 1961, p.271.
22. *Ibid.* p.272.
23. J. Tans and others, *Buitenlandse Letterkunde na 1945*, Utrecht/Antwerpen 1964, pp.121 ff.
24. See, for instance, Paul West, *The Modern Novel*, London 1963, pp.41 ff; Rubin Rabinovitz, *The Reaction against Experiment in the English Novel 1950 - 1960*, New York - London 1967, esp. ch. 4.
25. Lionel Trilling, *op.cit.*, p.277.

26. See for this Harold Whitehall's review of Trager-Smith, *An Outline of English Structure*, in *Kenyon Review*, XIII, 1951 pp.710 ff. Cf. also Whitehall's essay 'From Linguistics to Poetry' in Northrop Frye, ed., *Sound and Poetry*, English Institute Essays, Columbia University Press, New York 1957, where Whitehall suggests that eventually the linguist will be the only one capable of analyzing poetry. See also W. G. Hellinga and H. van der Merwe Scholtz, *Kreatiewe analise van taalgebruik*, Amsterdam - Pretoria 1955, passim; Roger Fowler, ed., *Essays on Style and Language*, London 1966, esp. pp.1 ff.; N. E. Enkvist, John Spencer and Michael J. Gregory, *Linguistics and Style*, London 1964, passim; S. Ullmann, *Language and Style*, Oxford 1964, esp. ch. 6; Angus McIntosh and M. A. K. Halliday, *Patterns of Language; Papers in General, Descriptive and Applied Linguistics*, London 1966, esp. p.56; Charles F. Hockett, *A Course in Modern Linguistics*, New York 1958, ch. 63; Robert A. Hall Jr., *Introductory Linguistics*, New York 1964, ch. 69; R. H. Robins, *General Linguistics*, London 1964, pp.368 ff; Karl D. Uitti, *Linguistics and Literary Theory*, Englewood Cliffs, New Jersey 1969, pp.152-153; F. L. Utley, 'Structural Linguistics and the Literary Critic', *Journal of Aesthetics and Art Criticism*, XVIII, 1960, pp.319-328. Cf. also Roger Fowler: 'We can say that modern descriptive linguistics is a natural companion to modern criticism because both are text-centred: both involve analysis, close reading, and both set a premium on accuracy and usefulness of description'. ('Linguistics, Stylistics; Criticism?',*Lingua* XVI, 1966, pp.153-165; esp. pp.157-158). The term 'linguistic criticism' has by now gained general currency. Note that M. A. K. Halliday speaks of linguistic stylistics ('The Linguistic Study of Literary Texts', revised ed. in S. Chatman & S. R. Levin, *Essays on the Language of Literature*, Boston 1967, pp.217-223, esp. p.217).

27. Thomas A. Sebeok, ed., *Style in Language*, Cambridge Mass. 1960. For a review of this book from the point of view of a literary critic see T. A. Birrell, 'Engelse literaire kritiek op zoek naar een methodologie', *Forum der Letteren* 1963, pp.166 ff. For a discussion of the book's influence on the development of linguistic stylistics see Karl D. Uitti, *op.cit.*, pp.201 ff.

28. *Hudson Review*, I, Spring 1948. Reprinted in Robert Scholes, ed., *Approaches to the Novel*, rev. ed., San Francisco 1966; in J. L. Calderwood & H. E. Toliver, eds., *Perspectives on Fiction*, London/New York, 1968; in Schorer's collection of critical essays *The World We Imagine*, London/New York 1969, and in John W. Aldridge, ed., *Essays and Critiques on Modern Fiction*, New York 1952.

29. *Kenyon Review*, XI, Autumn 1949, pp.539 ff. Reprinted in John W. Aldridge, *op.cit.*

30. For Ransom's views on the criticism of fiction and on the function of language in fiction, see 'The Understanding of Fiction', *Kenyon Review*, XII, 1950, pp.197 ff.

31. Martin Turnell, *The Novel in France*, London 1950.

32. Similar arguments are put forward in Ian Watt, *The Rise of the Novel*, London 1957, and Stephen Ullmann, *Style in the French Novel*, Oxford 1964².

33. *Trivium*, IX, 1951.

34. Cf. Helmut Kreuzer & Rul Gunzenhäuser, eds., *Mathematik und Dichtung*, Munich 1967; Jacob Leed, ed., *The Computer and Literary Style*, Kent, Ohio 1966; P. L. Garvin & B. Spolsky, *Computation in Linguistics*, New York 1967; Gordon R. Wood, 'Computer Research, an Adjunct to Literary Studies' in *Papers on Language and Literature*, IV, 1968, pp.459 ff. See also Harold B. Allen, *Linguistics and English Linguistics, a bibl.*, New York 1966, p.9. Two forerunners in this field deserve mention: Vernon Lee (see *The Handling of Words* pp.187 ff.) and George U. Yule, whose *The Statistical Study of Literary Vocabulary* (1944) was reprinted in 1968

(Cambridge Mass.). For a general comment on the use of the computer in stylistic studies see Graham Hough, *Style and Stylistics*, London 1969, pp.53 ff.

35. Harold C. Martin, ed., *Style in Prose Fiction;* English Institute Essays 1958, New York 1959.

36. See the index 'Styles under Scrutiny' in R. W. Baily and D. M. Burton, *English Stylistics: a Bibliography*, Cambridge Mass. 1968; cf. also David Lodge, *Language of Fiction*, London/New York 1966 and Harold B. Allen, *op.cit.*, pp.86 ff. See also G. L. Brook, *The Language of Dickens*, London 1970.

37. Respectively by Roy Pascal in *Modern Language Review*, LX, 1965, pp.12 ff. and by Edgar F. Shannon in *Nineteenth Century Fiction*, X, 1955, pp.141 ff.

38. Jonathan Raban, *The Technique of Modern Fiction*, London 1968, p.15.

39. *T.L.S.*, 22.4.1965. The statement is surprising from a novelist whose own novels bristle with evidence of a strong interest in linguistic *curiosa* on every page.

40. *A Review of English Literature*, VI, April 1965.

Notes to Chapter II

1. See, for instance, such landmarks in descriptive linguistics as George L. Trager and Henry Lee Smith, Jr., *An Outline of English Structure*, Studies in Linguistics, Occasional Papers 3, Washington 1957 (2nd ed.); C. C. Fries, *The Structure of English*, New York 1952; Martin Joos, *The English Verb*, Madison/Milwaukee 1964.
   Most of the older descriptive studies of English, such as the extensive grammars by Poutsma, Jespersen and Kruisinga, are based on literary and non-literary materials at the same time. So is the *Survey of English Usage;* see Randolph Quirk, 'Towards a Description of English Usage', *Transactions of the Philological Society 1960*, Oxford 1961. The *Survey* will, however, discriminate between literary and non-literary usage.

2. Roger Fowler, ed., *Essays on Style and Language*, London 1966, p.10. For a further elaboration of this point by Fowler, see *Essays in Criticism*, XVIII, 1968, pp.170-174. As Garland Canon has pointed out, the main concern of linguistic criticism up to 1960 was the definition of literature by way of formal descriptions of its subclasses. Inevitably, these attempts have all proved abortive. Cf. Garland Canon, 'Linguistics and Literature', *College English*, XXI, 1960, pp.255-260.

3. Susanne K. Langer, *Feeling and Form*, London 1953, p.288; Isabel C. Hungerland, *Poetic Discourse*, University of California Publications in Philosophy, vol. 33, Berkeley/Los Angeles 1958; R. S. Crane, *The Languages of Criticism and the Structure of Poetry*, Toronto 1953, p.100; Cleanth Brooks, 'The Language of Poetry; some Problem Cases', *Archiv für das Studium der neueren Sprachen und Literaturen*, vol. 203, 1967, pp.401-415; Laurence Lerner, *The Truest Poetry*, London 1960, p.221; René Wellek and Austin Warren, *Theory of Literature*, 2nd ed., New York 1955, Ch. 14; Angus McIntosh and M. A. K. Halliday, *Patterns of Language; Papers in General, Descriptive and Applied Linguistics*, London 1966, pp.56 ff; Brian Lee, 'The New Criticism and the Language of Poetry'; A. L. Binns, '"Linguistic Reading": Two Suggestions of the Quality of Literature': G. N. Leech, 'Linguistics and the Figures of Rhetoric', all in Roger Fowler, ed., *op. cit.*; C. J. E. Ball, 'Language for its Own Sake', *Essays in Criticism*, XVI, 1966, pp.220-226, esp. p.224. Cf. also Monroe Beardsley, *Aesthetics*, New York 1958.

4. Angus McIntosh and M. A. K. Halliday, *op. cit.*, pp.64-65; Harold Whitehall and Archibald A. Hill, 'A Report on the Language-Literature Seminar', repr. in Harold B. Allen, ed., *Readings in Applied English Linguistics*, New York 1958, pp.394-398.

5. David Lodge, *Language of Fiction*, London/New York 1966, p.31.

6. Karl D. Uitti, *Linguistics and Literary Theory*, Englewood Cliffs, New Jersey 1969, pp.258-259. This book is indispensable supplementary reading to this chapter, especially since it provides the historical background to linguistic criticism, relating its principal issues to the linguistic views of Plato and Aristotle and to the views of the medieval and renaissance rhetoricians.

7. *Ibid.*, p.258.

8. Laurence Lerner, *op. cit.*, p.129. But see Josephine Miles, 'More Semantics of Poetry', *Kenyon Review* 1940, reprinted in S. Chatman and S. R. Levin, *Essays on the Language of Literature*, Boston 1967, pp.264-268.

9. See,e.g., Roger Fowler, ed., *op. cit.*, p.13; David Lodge, *op. cit., passim;* T. A. Sebeok, ed., *Style in Language*, Cambridge Mass. 1960, p.99.

10. *Encounter*, January 1967, p.88. For information concerning the historical background to the idea of the continuum see K. G. Hamilton, *The Two Harmonies; Poetry and Prose in the Seventeenth Century*, Oxford 1963, which describes the emergence of divergent styles out of a 'continuum' in the 17th century. Related but not identical views are held by Robert Adolph, *The Rise of Modern Prose Style*, Cambridge Mass. 1968, which also discusses other modern views on the subject.

11. William E. Baker, *Syntax in English Poetry 1870 - 1930*, Berkeley/Los Angeles 1967, p.135.

12. T. S. Eliot, 'The Metaphysical Poets', in *Selected Essays*, London 1951[3], p.289.

13. C. K. Ogden and I. A. Richards, *The Meaning of Meaning*, Cambridge 1946[8], *passim* but esp. Ch. VII (the first edition was published in 1923); I. A. Richards, *Science and Poetry*, London 1926.

14. Robert B. Heilmann, 'Poetic and Prosaic: Program Notes on Opposite Numbers', *Pacific Spectator*, V, 1951, pp.454-463.

15. Cleanth Brooks, *The Well-Wrought Urn*, 1947, esp. Chs. 1 and 4. In a later article ('The Language of Poetry; some Problem Cases', *Archiv für das Studium der neueren Sprachen und Literaturen*, vol. 203, 1967, pp.401-415), Brooks seems to have changed his position somewhat. Herbert Read, 'American Bards and British Reviewers', 1962, repr. in *Selected Writings*, London 1963, esp. pp.214 ff. For some comment on Read's views on literary language, see G. S. Fraser, 'The Last English Imagist', *Encounter*, January 1967, pp.86-90.

16. T. A. Sebeok, ed., *op. cit.*, pp.70,403,410 and 417 respectively.

17. Ian Watt, *The Rise of the Novel*, ed. Penguin, London 1963, p.31. Watt's view reflects common eighteenth-century notions; see e.g. Erasmus Darwin, *The Loves of Plants*, 1789, Interlude I, repr. in Scott Elledge, ed., *Eighteenth-Century Critical Essays*, Ithaca N.Y. 1961, vol. 2, pp.1005-1010. Essentially the same view is found in Alexander Bain, *English Composition and Rhetoric*, 2nd enlarged ed., London 1893, Part I, pp.139,144,151,233,263,277. It may be safely assumed that Bain represents the common late nineteenth-century opinions on the matter; see Max I. Baym, 'Science and Poetry', in A. Preminger, ed., *Encyclopedia of Poetry and Poetics*, Princeton, New Jersey, 1965, pp.742-753.

18. See, e.g., G. Storms, 'The Subjectivity of the Style of Beowulf', in *Studies in Old English Literature in Honor of Arthur G. Brodeur*, University of Oregon Books, 1963, and G. Storms, 'Grammatical Expressions of Emotiveness', in *Papers on English Language and Literature*, I, 1965, pp.351-368.

19. Jerome P. Schiller, *I. A. Richards' Theory of Literature*, New Haven and London 1969, p.74.

126

20. See also Karl D. Uitti, *op. cit.*, pp.157 and 240.

21. See R. S. Crane, *op. cit.*, and R. S. Crane and others, *Critics and Criticism Ancient and Modern*, Chicago 1952.

22. Edward Stankiewicz, 'Linguistics and the Study of Poetic Language' in T. A. Sebeok, ed., *op. cit.* See also René Wellek's ironic comment on p.411.

23. Cf. note 17.

24. Richard Stang, *The Theory of the Novel in England 1850 - 1870*, London 1959, pp.187 ff.

25. Marjorie Boulton, *The Anatomy of Prose*, London 1954, pp.95 ff. and 100.

26. Roger Fowler, ed., *op. cit.*, p.144, Iván Fónagy uses the term 'entropic' in 'Communication in Poetry', *Word*, XVII, 1961, esp. p.201. As Levin points out, terms like *foregrounding* and *entropic* do not mean very much more than *striking;* cf. Samuel R. Levin, 'Internal and External Deviation in Poetry', *Word*, XXI, 1965, p.225. For the poetics of the Prague Circle see Paul L. Garvin, transl., *A Prague School Reader on Esthetics, Literary Structure and Style*, Washington 1958 and *Poetics/Poetyka*, Warsaw and The Hague 1961.

27. Tennyson, *Idylls of the King, Vivien*, line 6.

28. See Karl D. Uitti, *op. cit.*, p.144.

29. See Francis Berry, *Poet's Grammar*, London 1958; Donald Davie, *Articulate Energy, An Enquiry into the Syntax of English Poetry*, London 1955; Harry R. Warfel, 'Syntax makes Literature', *College English*, XXI, 1960, pp.251-255; William E. Baker, *Syntax in English Poetry 1870-1930*, Berkeley/Los Angeles 1967; Allan Rodway, 'By Algebra to Augustanism' in Roger Fowler, ed., *op. cit.*, where Rodway uses the term 'animation' in a sense closely related to 'foregrounding'; Nelson W. Francis, 'Syntax and Literary Interpretation', *Monograph Series on Language and Linguistics* no. 13, Washington 1962; Samuel R. Levin, *Linguistic Structures in Poetry*, The Hague 1962; Thomas E. Patton, 'Syntactic Deviance' in *Foundations of Language*, IV, May 1968, pp.138-153. Kenneth L. Pike's article 'Language - Where Science and Poetry Meet' *(College English*, XXVI, 1965, pp.283-292) illustrates to what extremes of technical complication the attempts of modern linguists to apply their theories to literature can go. The article deals with the application of tagmemic theory (in the non-Bloomfieldian sense) to the study of poetry.

30. Roman Jakobson, 'Poetry of Grammar and Grammar of Poetry', *Lingua*, XXI, 1968, pp.597-609.

31. *Ibid.* p.599.

32. 'A Program for the definition of literature', *Texas Studies in English*, XXXVII, 1958, pp.46-52.

33. C. F. Voegelin, 'Casual and Noncasual Utterances within Unified Structure', in T. A. Sebeok, ed., *op. cit.*, pp.57-68.

34. T. A. Sebeok, ed., *op. cit.*, p.351.

35. T. A. Sebeok, ed., *op. cit.*, p.82.

36. U. Weinreich, 'On the Semantic Structure of Language', in *Universals of Language*, ed. J. H. Greenberg, Cambridge Mass., 1963, pp.117-118.

37. pp.26 and 34 respectively.

38. Joseph T. Shipley, ed., *Dictionary of World Literature*, New Revised Edition, Totowa 1966, s.v. 'Poetry and Prose'. That *poetry* may also have a depreciative meaning appears from Hazlitt's essay 'On the Prose-Style of Poets', *The Plain Speaker (Collected Works*, ed. by A. R. Waller and Arnold Glover, vol. VII, London 1903). Hazlitt has been influenced by Coleridge's attacks on poetic prose, and coins an expressive phrase: 'The prose-writer is master of his materials: the

poet is the slave of his style'. (p.9). It is obvious that Hazlitt, no more than Coleridge, does not commit himself to anything like the symbolic-emotive dichotomy; he merely has certain stylistic abuses in mind.

39. An interesting succinct evaluation of the Rimbaud-Mallarmé-Valéry concept of poetic language is, to my mind, Roland Barthes, *Le degré Zéro de l'écritude,* Paris 1953, English translation *Writing Degree Zero,* London 1967, pp.47 ff. For the influence of Valéry in particular, see Laurence Lerner, *op. cit.,* Ch. 6. For a view of these writers as 'rebelling against the system of language', see Giacomo Devoto, *Linguistics and Literary Criticism,* New York 1963, p.122.

40. F. W. Bateson, *English Poetry and the English Language,* Oxford 1934, p.14. It would be worth while investigating in how far this view has limited Bateson's evaluation of English poetry in many respects, e.g. when he states that the 'catholicity of diction', which he regards as a characteristic feature of English poetry after the First World War, was due to a lack of sensitiveness to the connotations of words. It might also help to explain his failure to deal with Yeats and Eliot as late as 1934.

41. *Ibid.* p.86.

42. Thomas Gray, Letter to Richard West, 1742, repr. in E. D. Jones, ed., *English Critical Essays (Sixteenth, Seventeenth and Eighteenth Centuries),* World's Classics, London 1961, pp.265 ff.

43. It is interesting to note that to Gray, prose and poetry in French differed in nothing in his own days. (See the same letter). The break which the French symbolists brought about in literary French must have been vehement indeed. For a modern French study in which the position of the symbolists is still maintained, see Jean Cohen, *Structure du langage poétique,* Paris 1966.

44. Laurence Lerner, *op. cit.,* p.148.

45. Trevor Eaton, *The Semantics of Literature,* The Hague 1966, esp. pp.53,55.

46. Cf. note 14.

47. Philip Rahv, 'Fiction and the Criticism of Fiction', *Kenyon Review,* XVIII, 1956, pp.276-299, esp. p.291.

48. John Crowe Ransom, 'The Understanding of Fiction', *Kenyon Review,* XII, 1950, pp.197-218, esp. p.201.

49. *Ibid.* p.198.

50. For a discussion of this highly theoretical subject see Seymour Chatman, 'On the Theory of Literary Style' (*Linguistics,* XXVII, 1966, 12-25) and 'The Semantics of Style' (in Michael Lane, *Structuralism: A Reader,* London 1970). See also Richard Ohmann, 'Generative Grammars and the Concept of Literary Style', *Word,* XX, 1964, pp.423-440. Wimsatt's concept of style has not always been the same, as Chatman notes; during the Indiana Conference of 1958, however, he clearly inclined towards the Platonic position. Cf. T. A. Sebeok, ed., *op. cit.,* pp.420-421.

51. W. K. Wimsatt, Jr., *The Verbal Icon,* 1954, 'Verbal Style, Logical and Counterlogical'. See also *The Prose Style of Samuel Johnson,* New Haven 1941.

52. T. A. Sebeok, ed., *op. cit.,* p.75.

53. *Ibid.* Note that Levin considers poetic diction as a clear example of external deviation. This would mean that an exhaustive description of a given poetic dialect might reveal structural independence, which would probably be restricted to the lexical component, however. Cf. Samuel R. Levin, 'Internal and External Deviation in Poetry', *Word,* XXI, 1965, pp.225-237.

54. See his letters to Edward Marsh, repr. in A. Beal, ed., *D. H. Lawrence, Selected Literary Criticism,* London 1955, pp.77 ff. See also T. S. Eliot's 1917 essay 'Re-

flections on Vers Libre', repr. in *To Criticize The Critic*, London 1965.

55. T. A. Sebeok, ed., *op. cit.*, p.135. For a short discussion of modern linguistic studies of metre see the article by Levin and Chatman mentioned in note 125.

56. Fred B. Millet, *Reading Fiction*, New York 1950, p.10.

57 Käte Hamburger, *Die Logik der Dichtung*, Stuttgart 1957, p.17. Cf. also p.144: 'Die "Poesie" ihrer Worte, die Stimmung, die sie ausdrücken - die Luft ging durch die Felder, sacht wogten die Aehren, die Wälder rauschten leis, die Nacht war so sternklar -, erwies sich nicht als ausreichendes Kriterium ihrer Unterscheidung von den beiden Prosa-texten'. (The poetry of their words, the atmosphere they evoke - the air stroked the fields, the corn was swaying gently, the woods were murmuring softly, the night was bright with stars - did not prove to be an adequate criterion to distinguish them from the two prose texts.)

58. Käte Hamburger, *op. cit.*, p.168. (The highest and most authentic kind of prose is the lyric.) For a succinct summary of Hamburger's theory see David Lodge, *Language of Fiction*, London/New York 1966, pp.39-40. For a survey of the most important objections that have been raised against Hamburger's ideas, see *Levende Talen*, 1965, pp.137 ff; 1966, pp.130-131 and 733-734; 1967, p.373. See also Volker Klotz ed., *Zur Poetik des Romans*, Darmstadt 1965. Cf. also note 5 to Ch. III.

59. R. W. Emerson, 'The Poet', *Essays First and Second Series*, Everyman's Library, London 1906, p.215; quoted in Owen Barfield, *Poetic Diction*, London 1962[2], p.179. Similar views are held by Giacomo Devoto, who speaks of the 'basic aestheticity of all linguistic creations' *(Linguistics and Literary Criticism*, New York 1963, Ch. IV, esp. p.59); J. B. Greenough and G. L. Kittredge, *(Words and their Ways in English Speech*, New York 1901, esp. Ch. II); V. K. Gokak, *(The Poetic Approach to Language*, Oxford 1952) and George Steiner ('The Language Animal', *Encounter* August 1969, pp.7-24, esp. pp.19-21). On the essentially Platonic nature of this theory of language and on its links with Dante's *De vulgari eloquentia* and Edward Sapir's theory of language, see Karl D. Uitti, *Linguistics and Literary Theory*, Englewood Cliffs, New Jersey 1969, pp.36 ff and p.148.

60. Owen Barfield, *op. cit.*, p.149.

61. J. Middleton Murry, *The Problem of Style*, London 1922, p.125.

62. *Ibid.*, p.71.

63. *Ibid.*, p.67. Cf. also F. L. Lucas, *Style*, London 1955, p. 253.

64. Lucas, *op. cit.*, p.127.

65. Marjorie Boulton, *op. cit.*, p.149; Isabel C. Hungerland, *op. cit.*, esp. Ch. 4. Cf. also G. N. Leech, *A Linguistic Guide to English Poetry*, London 1969, p.147.

66. Winifred Nowottny, *The Language Poets Use*, London 1962, p.122.

67. *Ibid.*, p.123.

68. Roland Barthes, *Writing Degree Zero*, London 1967, p.47.

69. Samuel R. Levin, 'Deviation - Statistical and Determinate - in Poetic Language' *Lingua* XII, 1963, pp.276-290. For a reply to Levin's article see note 101.

70. T. A. Sebeok, ed., *op. cit.*, p.77.

71. Trevor Eaton, *op. cit.*, see e.g. p.40. See also Geoffrey N. Leech, *A Linguistic Guide to English Poetry*, London 1969, p.6. However, as Leech notes on pp.17 ff., certain 'routine licences' that are not exclusively of a metrical nature but still belong to the mechanics of composition, have been preserved in poetry and not in prose - for instance, aphesis and hyperbaton.

72. See, e.g., G. N. Leech, 'Linguistics and the Figures of Rhetoric' in Roger Fowler, ed., *op. cit.*, esp. pp.136 and 141; see also Nils Erik Enkvist, 'On Defining Style', in N. E. Enkvist, John Spencer and Michael J. Gregory, *Linguistics and Style*,

London 1964, p.25. See also R. A. Sayce, 'The Definition of the Term "Style"', in *Proceedings of the Third Congress of the International Comparative Literature Association,* The Hague, 1962, pp.156-166. For a survey of the many different approaches to style that have been taken by modern scholars, see Richard Ohmann, 'Generative Grammars and the Concept of Literary Style', *Word XX,* 1964, pp. 423-440. The new tendency in the definitions of style is summed up by Louis T. Milic: 'The definition of style has come to be made in terms scientific rather than mystical: "a selection of non-distinctive features of language" rather than "style is the ultimate morality of the mind"'. Milic mentions Morris Croll, Leo Spitzer, Erich Auerbach and W. K. Wimsatt Jr. as illustrative of the former trend, while Leonard Bloomfield provided the quotation for the latter. Cf. Jacob Leed, ed., *The Computer and Literary Style,* Kent, Ohio, 1966, pp.80-81.

Stephen Ullmann notes that the definition of style as deviation from a norm is found in Valéry (cf. *Language and Style,* Oxford 1964, p.154). That this idea is not the prerogative of modern scholarship since the days of Bally, is evident from Walter Raleigh, *Style,* London 1897, p.124, and from Samuel R. Levin, who points out: 'The recognition that deviation is a distinguishing mark of poetry is at least as old as Aristotle'. ('Internal and External Deviation in Poetry', *Word XXI,* 1965, p.225).

For similar definitions of style see T. A. Sebeok, ed., *op. cit.,* pp.87,109,293. For a dissenting voice, attacking not only the concept of style as deviation from a norm but some of the more general theoretical assumptions of linguistic criticism, see the extracts from a review by Alphonse G. Juilland, reprinted in S. Chatman & S. R. Levin, *Essays on the Language of Literature,* Boston 1967, pp.374-384.

73. For the background to this phrase, which is a misquotation since Buffon originally wrote 'Les choses sont hors de l'homme, le style est l'homme même' (*Discours sur le style,* 1753), see Enkvist, Spencer and Gregory, *op. cit.,* p.21. Cf. also the phrase 'stylus virum arguit', quoted by Walter Raleigh, *op. cit.,* p.2. Raleigh came across the phrase in Robert Burton's *The Anatomy of Melancholy,* 1621.

74. Enkvist, Spencer and Gregory, *op. cit.,* p.28.

75. S. Ullmann, *Style in the French Novel,* Oxford 1964[2], pp.9-10.

76. *Ibid.,* p.7. Cf. also Ullmann, *Language and Style,* Oxford 1964, p.141.

77. Owen Barfield, *op. cit.,* p.153.

78. Richard M. Ohmann, 'Prolegomena to the Analysis of Prose Style', in Harold C. Martin, ed., *Style in Prose Fiction,* English Institute Essays, New York 1959, p.15. Cf. also Seymour Chatman, 'On the Theory of Literary Style', *Linguistics XXVII,* 1966, pp.13-25, esp. p.21.

79. Enkvist, Spencer and Gregory, *op. cit.,* p.22.

80. Angus McIntosh and M. A. K. Halliday, *op. cit.,* p.47.

81. Enkvist, Spencer and Gregory, *op. cit.,* p.24.

82. W. K. Wimsatt Jr., *op. cit.,* p.205.

83. *Journal of Linguistics,* I, 1965, pp.173-179.

84. Enkvist, Spencer and Gregory, *op. cit.,* pp.30-31.

85. Michael Riffaterre, 'Criteria for Style Analysis', *Word XV,* 1959, pp.154-175. Riffaterre's approach to the study of style bears certain resemblances to that of Leo Spitzer. In the first analysis, stylistic features are detected by observing the reaction of an observant decoder - a careful reader in common parlance. Yet it is interesting to see how Riffaterre tries to avoid Spitzer's dreaded 'circularity of argument': 'In the procedure I propose, the analyst will scrupulously avoid hypotheses on facts thus designated and will wait, before building a structure, until all

signals collected constrain him by their interplay and convergence to an interpretation taking them all into account'. (p.164). For a succinct survey of the most common objections that have been raised against Spitzer's method see Bennison Gray, 'The Lesson of Leo Spitzer', *Modern Language Review*, LXI, 1966, pp.547. 556. For the similarity between the methods of Spitzer and Riffaterre, see also Ullmann, *Language and Style*, pp.127. For an interesting defence of Spitzer against the objections of the 'philological circle', see Giacomo Devoto, *op. cit.*, pp.45 and 149.

86. Michael Riffaterre, 'Stylistic Context', *Word* XVI, 1960, pp.207-218. Both the 1959 and the 1960 articles by Riffaterre have been reprinted in S. Chatman & S. R. Levin, *Essays on the Language of Literature*, Boston 1967.

87. See Karl D. Uitti, *op. cit.*, p.213.

88. Samuel R. Levin, 'Deviation - Statistical and Determinate - in Poetic Language', *Lingua* XII, 1963, pp.276-290.

89. In fact, the example from Pope which Riffaterre quotes in his 1960 article shows the occurrence of such repeated devices. A general weakness of Riffaterre's theory is that it does not account for repetition as a stylistic device. See M. Adriaens, 'Style in W. Golding's *The Inheritors*', *English Studies*, LI, 1970, pp.16-30.

90. Samuel R. Levin, 'Internal and External Deviation in Poetry', *Word* XXI, 1965, pp.225-237, esp. p.230 and 233. Jakobson's *linguistic fictions*, discussed above, are of course externally deviant.

91. See, e.g. T. A. Sebeok, ed. *op. cit.*, pp.109,149,343. For a demonstration that statistical analysis is only meaningful in so far as it is comparative, see Angus McIntosh and M. A. K. Halliday, *op. cit.*, pp.56 ff.

92. See Noam Chomsky, *Aspects of the Theory of Syntax*, Cambridge Mass. 1965, ch. 4.

93. T. A. Sebeok, ed., *op. cit.*, p.417. For a more detailed critique of statistical stylistics, see Richard M. Ohmann, 'Generative Grammars and the Concept of Literary Style', *Word* XX, 1964, p.425.

94. Paul Edwards, 'Meaning and Context: An Exercise in Practical Stylistics', *English Language Teaching*, XXII, 1968, pp.272-277, esp. p.274.

95. On situational context see S. Ullmann, *Semantics*, Oxford 1962, p.50; Enkvist, Spencer and Gregory, *op. cit.*, pp.99 ff; F. W. Bateson in *Essays in Criticism*, vol. XVI, 1966, p.464-465.

96. A. L. Binns, '"Linguistic" Reading: Two Suggestions of the Quality of Literature' in Roger Fowler, ed., *op. cit.*, pp. 118-134, esp. p.122. The same broad distinction is made by Geoffrey N. Leech, who, however, in Ch. 11 of his *A Linguistic Guide to English Poetry*, (London 1969), attempts to present the problem in more concrete terms by studying the linguistic means by which literary texts create their own situational contexts.

97. Samuel R. Levin, 'Deviation in Poetic Language', *Lingua* XII, 1963, pp.276-290. Cf. also Samuel R. Levin, 'Poetry and Grammaticalness', in *Proceedings of the 9th International Congress of Linguistics (1962)*, The Hague 1963.

98. Manfred Bierwisch, 'Poetik und Linguistik' in Helmut Kreuzer and Rul Gunzenhäuser, eds., *Mathematik und Dichtung*, Munich 1967, p.61.

99. Sol Saporta, 'The Application of Linguistics to the Study of Poetic Language' in T. A. Sebeok, ed., *op. cit.*, pp.82-93, esp. p.84.

100. T. A. Sebeok, ed., *op. cit.*, p.403.

101. Robert J. Scholes, 'Some Objections to Levin's "Deviation"', *Lingua* XIII, 1964, pp.189-192. To these objections Levin replied again, *ibid.* pp.193-195.

102. Sister Mary Jonathan, O. P., 'You, Noam Chomsky', *College English* XXVI, 1965, p.395.

103. J. P. Thorne, 'Stylistics and Generative Grammars', *Journal of Linguistics*, I, 1965, pp.49-59.

104. *Ibid.*, p.56.

105. William O. Hendricks, 'Three Models for the Description of Poetry', *Journal of Linguistics*, V, 1969, pp.1-22; J. P. Thorne, 'Poetry, Stylistics and Imaginary Grammars', *ibid.* pp.147-150; M. Riffaterre, 'Describing poetic structures: two approaches to Baudelaire's *Les chats*', *Yale French Studies*, XXXVI-XXXVII, pp.200-242.

106. Geoffrey N. Leech, *A Linguistic Guide to English Poetry*, London 1969, pp.44 ff. and 73; Richard Ohmann, 'Literature as Sentences', *College English*, January 1966, reprinted in S. Chatman & S. R. Levin, *Essays on the Language of Literature*, Boston 1967, pp.231-238; J. P. Thorne, review of William Baker, *Syntax in English Poetry 1870-1930*, in *Review of English Studies*, XX, 1969, pp.241-243; Mark Lester, 'The Relation of Linguistics to Literature', *College English* XXX, 1969, pp.366-375. Marcia R. Lieberman also states that 'poeticness resides in the lexicon'. See 'The New Linguistics and the New Poetics', *College English* XXX, 1969, pp.527-533.

107. See, for instance, the discussions of Cummings's line 'he sang his didn't he danced his did' in Roger Fowler, 'On the interpretation of "nonsense strings"', *Journal of Linguistics* V, 1969, pp.75-83, and in various other articles mentioned in Fowler's footnotes. See also the analyses of passages by Faulkner and Henry James in Richard M. Ohmann, 'Generative Grammars and the Concept of Literary Style', *Word* XX, 1964, pp.423-439; cf. also Ohmann's 'Literature as Sentences', *College English* XXVII, 1966, pp.261-267. (See note 106).

108. T. A. Sebeok, ed., *Op. cit.*, pp.91-92. In Giacomo Devoto's theory, as outlined in *Linguistics and Literary Criticism*, New York 1963, style as realised in actual literary works is essentially a matter of restrictions imposed upon what he calls 'the stylistic antefact'. The theory is heavily committed to de Saussure; apart from *parole* and *langue*, however, he distinguishes a third linguistic plane, *lingua individuale*, or *style*. An author's style is defined by the restrictions on the *lingua individuale* for which it chooses. In spite of the clumsiness of the terminology, Devoto's theory has the advantage of clearly localizing such concepts as *register* and *period style* in the Saussurian scheme. It must be remarked, however, that deviations from the *lingua individuale* need not necessarily be restrictive; they may transgress limits of usage as well as narrow them. In fact, it would perhaps make sense to dispense with the term *deviation* altogether, and talk of *individualization* rather, or *idiolectization*.

109. See Manfred Bierwisch, *op. cit.*, p.61.

110. Helmut Kreuzer and Rul Gunzenhäuser, eds., *op. cit.*, p.279.

111. Trevor Hill, 'Institutional Linguistics', *Orbis* VII, 1958, pp.441-455. See also G. N. Leech, 'Linguistics and the Figures of Rhetoric', in Roger Fowler, ed., *op. cit.*, pp.138-139 and pp.140 ff.

112. Roger Fowler, ed., *op. cit.*, p.152. For an unsatisfactory answer to this question see G. N. Leech, *A Linguistic Guide to English Poetry*, London 1969, pp.59 ff.

113. *Ibid.* p.22.

114. T. A. Sebeok, ed., *op. cit.*, p.109; Ashok R. Kelkar, 'The Being of a Poem', *Foundations of Language*, V, 1969, pp.17-33.

115. William E. Baker, *op. cit.*, p.2.

116. Karl D. Uitti, *op. cit.*, p.213.

117. See *Essays in Criticism*, XVI, 1966, pp.226-228 and 464-465; XVII, 1967, pp.322-347; XVIII, 1968, pp.164-182 and 477-478. See also *T.L.S.* 1970 (23.7, 31.7, 14.8).

118. *Essays in Criticism*, XVIII, 1968, p.181.

119. *Ibid.*, p.478.
120. *Essays in Criticism*, XVII, 1967, p.331.
121. Roger Fowler, 'Linguistics, Stylistics; Criticism?', *Lingua* XVI, 1966, pp.153-165. Reprinted in G. A. Love and M. Payne, eds., *Contemporary Essays on Style*, Glenview, Ill., 1969.
122. Enkvist, Spencer and Gregory, *op. cit.*, p.61.
123. Fowler, 'Linguistics, Stylistics; Criticism?', *Lingua* XVI, 1966, p.159.
124. See Karl D. Uitti, *op. cit.*, pp.185 ff.
125. Samuel R. Levin & Seymour Chatman, 'Linguistics and Poetics', in A. Preminger, ed., *Encyclopedia of Poetry and Poetics*, Princeton, New Jersey 1965, pp.450-457. Similar reservations were made by Chatman at a time when linguistic criticism was still considered a new development; see 'Linguistics and Teaching Introductory Literature' in Harold B. Allen, ed., *Readings in Applied English Linguistics*, New York 1958, pp.407-413.
    It may be worth while quoting William O. Hendricks' attempt to define the relationship between the linguistic and the literary critic in 'Three models for the description of poetry', *Journal of Linguistics*, V, 1969, pp.1-22, esp. p.21. According to Hendricks, the linguist studies the relationships existing in a work of literature, while the literary critic goes on to conceptualize these relationships, giving them verbal interpretative labels. The linguist stops at describing the text formally as a system of pure relationships and oppositions. Geoffrey Leech, in an article entitled '"This bread I break" - Language and Interpretation' *(A Review of English Literature*, VI, 1965, pp.66-75), describes the tasks of the linguistic and of the literary critic as description and interpretation respectively, without making it unambiguously clear what the two terms stand for.
126. G. N. Leech, *A Linguistic Guide to English Poetry*, London 1969, pp.225-226.
127. George Steiner, 'The Language Animal', *Encounter*, August 1969, pp.7-24, esp. pp.19-21.
128. Graham Hough, *Style and Stylistics*, London 1969, p.105.
129. J. Kunst, 'De vertaalbaarheid van de roman', in *Handelingen van het Negenentwintigste Nederlandse Filologencongres*, Groningen 1966, pp.131-133.

Notes to Chapter III

1. *Tristram Shandy*, 1760-1767; Book III, Ch. 38.
2. Ian Watt, *The Rise of the Novel*, London 1957. (Penguin ed. p.26); A. A. Mendilow, *Time and the Novel*, London 1952, p.57.
3. Käte Hamburger, *Die Logik der Dichtung*, Stuttgart 1957. This book collects various articles previously published in periodicals. For a summary of her theory, see Roy Pascal, 'Tense and Novel', *Modern Language Review* LVII, 1962, pp.1-12, and David Lodge, *Language of Fiction*, London/New York 1966, pp.39-40. Käte Hamburger herself acknowledges her indebtedness to various forerunners, esp. Jean Pouillon, *Temps et Roman*, Paris 1946.
4. *Die Logik der Dichtung* p.227; also p.224 *note*.
5. For a bibliography of some of the most important criticism of *Die Logik der Dichtung* see the footnote to Roy Pascal's article; Harald Weinrich, *Tempus*, Stuttgart 1964, p.318 notes 71 and 72, and the articles mentioned in note 58 to Ch. II. In the second edition (Stuttgart 1968) the author has revised some of her views.
6. Cf. Harald Weinrich, *op. cit.*, p.21.
7. See L. Spitzer's essay 'Linguistics and Literary History' in his book of that title,

Princeton 1948. For a defence of the philological circle by a third party see Graham Hough, *Style and Stylistics,* London/New York 1969, pp.59 ff.

8. The term will throughout this chapter be used as an equivalent of 'style indirect libre' and 'erlebte Rede'. It is preferred to the term 'substitutionary speech', proposed in R. W. Zandvoort, *A Handbook of English Grammar,* 9th ed., Groningen 1964, § 772.

9. *Die Logik der Dichtung* p.33.

10. For a French example see Harald Weinrich, *op. cit.* p.18. The following Dutch example resembles Sterne's sentence about the cow that broke into uncle Toby's fortifications in its ironic explication of the time and tense problem: '"Het volgend jaar doe ik het lekker zelf" zei Mevrouw Poppetje toen het haar weer mislukt was op de ladder te komen. En het volgend jaar was nu'. (Mies Bouwhuys, 'Mevrouw Poppetje' in *Kinderverhalen,* Haarlem n.d., p.165.)

11. Except, of course, in dialogue. Since in dialogue the sequence of tenses is always that of non-narrative discourse, passages in dialogue are left out of consideration throughout this chapter. Martin Joos, in *The English Verb,* Madison & Milwaukee 1964, obscures his discussion of the functions of the past and present (or actual, in his terminology) tenses in narratives by not sufficiently distinguishing between narration and direct reporting as it occurs in dialogue (esp. p.125).

12. The method of structural linguistics to study and classify tense forms according to their selection of time adverbs is exemplified by David Crystal, 'Specification and English Tenses', *Journal of Linguistics,* II, 1966, pp.1-34

13. *Die Logik der Dichtung* p.26.

14. *Ibid.* p.40.

15. Some idea of the semantic weakening to which the word *now* is subject may be conveyed by the arrangement of the following sentences, all taken from H. F. Palmer, *A Grammar of English Words,* London 1938, s.v. *now:* Now or never!; We tried one plan and it was no good; now we shall try a second plan; Now what we have to do next is to write to the manager; I see him now and then; You have broken that glass; now I told you not to touch it!; Now then, what do you mean by it?; Now (that) you are a big boy you must behave better. Cf. also the following quotations, all from novels by the Dutch writer Simon Vestdijk: 'Nu hadden de twee agenten geen moeite meer de hun toevertrouwde flatbewoners in de wagen te krijgen' *(De kellner en de Levenden,* 12th ed. Amsterdam 1968, p.13); 'Nu hoefde hij alleen maar iets opzij te kijken, in het glas, om de heer te zien zitten' *(Een moderne Antonius,* 2nd ed. Amsterdam 1966, p.7); 'Jongens en meisjes, joelend en dringend, de leraren met hun geveinsd spottend lachje, traden er nu dus over de drempel...' *(Terug tot Ina Damman,* 4th ed. The Hague n.d. p.7); 'Maar nu ik er in werkelijkheid was, merkte ik, dat er van mijn boek niets deugde' *(Het schandaal der blauwbaarden,* The Hague 1968, p.5); 'Maar nu ik een eigen praktijk had, met mijn naam naast de deur, en een lelijk meisje voor de ochtenduren, voelde ik mij ver boven hem verheven' *(De dokter en het lichte meisje,* 7th ed. Amsterdam 1968, p.60).

16. Otto Funke, 'Zur "erlebte Rede" bei Galsworthy', *Englische Studien* XLIV, 1929, p.454.

17. Franz Stanzel, 'Episches Praeteritum, Erlebte Rede, Historisches Praesens', *Deutsche Vierteljahrsschrift für Literaturwissenschaft und Geistesgeschichte* XXXIII, 1959, pp.1-12 (reprinted in Volker Klotz, ed., *Zur Poetik des Romans,* Darmstadt 1965, pp.319-338).

18. David Lodge, *op. cit.,* p.39.

19. Roy Pascal, *op. cit.*; Harald Weinrich, *op. cit.*, p.57.
20. Iris Murdoch, *The Italian Girl*, London 1964, p.87.
21. *Die Logik der Dichtung* p. 39: '...loses its function to refer to the past, which is caused by the fact that the time of the action, and therefore the action itself, is not related to a real I-origo, a real subject of utterance, but to the fictive I-origines of the characters'.
22. See note 12.
23. See note 5.
24. Susanne K. Langer, *Feeling and Form; A Theory of Art*, London/New York 1953, esp. Ch. 16.
25. Roland Barthes, *Le degré zéro de l'écriture*, Paris 1953. The quotation is from the English translation by Annette Lavers and Colin Smith: *Writing Degree Zero*, London 1967, pp.36-37. On Barthes' criticism and its relation to the Structuralist movement see Martin Turnell, 'The Criticism of Roland Barthes', *(Encounter*, Febr. 1966) and Michael Lane, *Structuralism: A Reader*, London 1970, pp.36-39.
26. George Moore, *Esther Waters*, World's Classics ed. 1964, p.164.
27. F. R. Palmer, *A Linguistic Study of the English Verb*, London 1965, pp.62-63.
28. E. L. Woodward, *History of England*, rev.ed. Penguin 1962, p.99.
29. Harald Weinrich, *op. cit.*, pp.235-237; cf. Stephen Ullmann, *Style in the French Novel*, Oxford 1964 ², p.97.
30. *Die Logik der Dichtung*, esp. p.225 and pp.238-239.
31. This is not always so. Robert Stanton distinguishes between first-person central narrator and first-person peripheral narrator. See *An Introduction to Fiction*, New York 1965, pp.26 ff.
32. Wayne C. Booth, *The Rhetoric of Fiction*, Chicago/London 1961, p.71 and *passim*. Note Spitzer's terms for the two I's: 'erzählendes Ich' and 'erlebendes Ich', discussed by Bertil Romberg in *Studies in the Narrative Technique of the First-Person Novel*, Lund 1962. Wayne C. Booth's 'implied author' derives from 'the speaker made of language alone' proposed by Walker Gibson in an influential article 'Authors, Speakers, Readers, and Mock Readers' in *College English*, XI, February 1950, pp.265-269. See also *Tough, Sweet and Stuffy*, 1966, in which Gibson develops his theory with reference to some stylistic characteristics of modern American prose.
33. Cf. H. Poutsma, *A Grammar of Late Modern English*, Groningen 1928-1929, Part I, 2nd ed., Ch. XVII, § 19, II.
34. R. W. Zandvoort, *op. cit.* § 133.
35. Here again, dialogue has been left out of consideration. It adheres to the same tense sequence.
36. *Die Logik der Dichtung*, p.40.
37. Stephen Ullmann, *Style in the French Novel* p.102.
38. *Ibid.* p.97.
39. Jürgen Peper, *Bewusstseinslagen des Erzählens und erzählte Wirklichkeiten*, Leiden 1966, p.80.
40. The difficulty of identifying a given passage as an 'Aussage' of the narrator or of a character is a conspicuous mark of Henry James's later style. The problem is discussed in Ian Watt's article 'The First Paragraph of *The Ambassadors:* An Explication' in *Essays in Criticism*, X, July 1960, pp.250-274; reprinted in G. A. Love & Michael Payne, eds., *Contemporary Essays on Style*, Glenview, Ill., 1969, pp. 266-283.
41. Richard Ohmann, 'Generative Grammars and the Concept of Literary Style', *Word* XX, 1964, p.435. Reprinted in G. A. Love & M. Payne, eds., *Contemporary Essays*

on Style, Glenview, Ill., 1969, pp.133-148.

42. See R. W. Zandvoort, *op. cit.* § 772 and E. Kruisinga, *A Handbook of Present-Day English*, fifth ed. Groningen 1931-1932, § 2336 ff.

43. Stephen Ullmann, *Language and Style*, Oxford 1964, p.134.

44. E. Kruisinga & P. A. Erades, *An English Grammar*, Vol. I, 8th ed., Groningen 1953-1960, § 185.

45. R. W. Zandvoort, 'On the Perfect of Experience', in *Collected Papers*, Groningen Studies in English V, Groningen/Djakarta 1954, pp.106-121, esp. p.115.

46. *Die Logik der Dichtung* p.225.

47. Stephen Ullmann, *Style in the French Novel* p.95.

48. Jürgen Peper, *op. cit.*, p.80; Stephen Ullmann, *Language and Style* p.135; Harald Weinrich *op. cit.* p.134.

49. Stephen Ullmann, *Style in the French Novel* p.101.

50. W. Kohlhammer Verlag, Stuttgart. The question whether Weinrich's theory does not imply a philosophical distinction between 'performing' and 'informing' language cannot now be discussed. See, in this context, Margaret Macdonald, 'The Language of Fiction', *Proceedings of the Aristotelian Society* 1954, reprinted in J. L. Calderwood & H. E. Toliver, eds., *Perspectives on Fiction*, London/New York 1968, pp. 55-70.

51. Harald Weinrich, *op. cit.* p.21. 'What we need is not a logic, but a linguistics of literature'.

52. A curious parallel to some of Weinrich's points may be found in Ramón Fernandez' essay on Balzac in *Messages*, Paris 1926. The essay is discussed by Edwin Muir in *The Structure of the Novel*, London 1938, pp.119 ff.

53. Harald Weinrich, *op. cit.* p.51.

54. *Ibid.* pp.211 ff.

55. *Ibid.* pp.110,277 ff.

56. Cf. J. P. Sartre's comment: 'Et nous cascadons de phrase en phrase, de néant en néant. C'est pour accentuer la solitude de chaque unité phrastique que M. Camus a choisi de faire son récit au parfait composé'. *Situations I*, Paris 1947, p.117.

57. Harald Weinrich, *op. cit.* pp.78-79.

58. See, for instance, his discussion of the Passé Défini in Ch. X.

59. Harald Weinrich, *op. cit.* p.309; also pp.47-48.

60. *Ibid.* p.84. 'On the one hand, the historian relates the past; he is a story-teller we may say. Anybody who cannot tell stories is a poor historian. But he is at the same time a scholar. He does not content himself with telling about the past; he also wants to understand the past, explain it, interpret it, teach it, and so on. In one word: he wants to discuss it'.

61. *Ibid.* p.159.

62. *Ibid.* p.196.

63. R. W. Zandvoort, *A Handbook of English Grammar*, 9th ed., §§ 93,95.

64. Martin Joos, *The English Verb*, Madison & Milwaukee 1964, esp. p.121 and 126 ff; Paul Roberts, *Modern Grammar*, New York 1968, p.67. Joos's theory of the progressive contains distinct echoes from Jespersen's 'time-frame' (*A Modern English Grammar* IV, vol. III, §§ 12.5-12.6; *The Philosophy of Grammar*, London 1935, pp.277 ff).

65. Harald Weinrich, *op. cit.* pp.19-20.

66. See H. Poutsma, *A Grammar of Late Modern English*, Part II, Groningen 1926, Ch. L, § 34.

67. Some of the critical praise that has been bestowed on the book seems inordinate.

One reviewer, for instance, claimed equality of rank to *Animal Farm;* see *Times Literary Supplement,* 3 October 1968, p.1097.

68. Cf. Kingsley Amis, *New Maps of Hell,* Ballantine Books, New York 1960, p.54: 'Its most important use, I submit, is a means of dramatising social inquiry, as providing a fictional mode in which cultural tendencies can be isolated and judged'.

69. Harald Weinrich, *op. cit.* pp.44 ff.

70. Edward Sapir, *Language,* Harvest Books ed., New York n.d., p.226. Karl D. Uitti recognizes in Sapir's words one of the theses of the Prague school of linguistics *(Linguistics and Literary Theory,* Englewood Cliffs, New Jersey 1969, p.149). Jozef Boets, in a recent exhaustive study of sound expressiveness, arrives at similar conclusions: 'Ik neem wel aan dat de struktuur van de taal hierbij een zeer belangrijke faktor zal zijn... omdat ze aan de zo belangrijke faktoren 'overeenkomst' en 'oppositie' recht kan laten wedervaren, en ons op die wijze een verklaring biedt voor het feit dat de aard van het klankbeleven enigermate van taal tot taal, van dialekt tot dialekt, van gemeenschap tot gemeenschap kan verschillen'. *(Moderne Teorieën in verband met klankexpressie,* Ghent 1965, p.193). (I assume that the structure of the language plays an important role in this respect... because it can do justice to the important factors of 'parallelism' and 'opposition', and thus help to explain the fact that the way in which the expressiveness of sounds is experienced may differ, up to a point, from language to language, from dialect to dialect, from community to community).

71. Harald Weinrich, *op. cit.,* p.235.

72. *Ibid.* p.41. (The tense-forms do not indicate the time of the action, but the arrangement and aspect of the action, although, of course, in time.)

73. Note that Wolfgang Kayser also rejects Käte Hamburger's opinion that the epic preterite carries no temporal implications, and that he recognizes the temporal implications of a tense-form as dependent on its contrast with other tense-forms. ('Wer erzählt den Roman?', in *Die Vortragsreise,* Bern 1958, pp.82-101; repr. in Volker Klotz, *Zur Poetik des Romans,* Darmstadt 1965).

74. William E. Bull, *Time, Tense and the Verb,* Berkeley 1960, p.62.

75. See J. J. Katz & J. A. Fodor: 'The Structure of a Semantic Theory', *Language,* XXXIX, 1963, pp.170-210; Uriel Weinreich. 'Explorations in Semantic Theory' in Sebeok, *Current Trends in Linguistics vol. III,* The Hague 1966; T. A. van Dijk, 'Taaltheorie en literatuurtheorie', *Raster,* III/2, 1969, pp.162-182.

Notes to Chapter IV

1. For a bibliography of Iris Murdoch, see R. L. Widmann, 'An Iris Murdoch Checklist' in *Critique: Studies in Modern Fiction,* X, 1968, pp.17-29, which lists both primary and secondary material. A good deal of bibliographical information concerning the early novels is contained in the footnotes to J. Souvage's article 'The Novels of Iris Murdoch' in *Studia Germanica Gandensia,* IV, 1962, pp.225-252.

2. John R. Frey, 'The Historical Present in Narrative Literature, particularly in Modern German Fiction' in *The Journal of English and Germanic Philology,* XLV, 1946, pp.43-67. This is an important article, with a rich bibliography. The question of the function of the present tense in past-tense first-person fiction as a means to identify the 'Aussagesubjekt' is a vital one. Edgar F. Shannon Jr., in 'The Present Tense in *Jane Eyre*' (*Nineteenth Century Fiction* X, 1955-56, pp.141-145) neglects it completely. That the present tense may also have a mythopoetic function appears from Roy Pascal's 'The Present Tense in *The Pilgrim's Progress*', *Modern*

Language Review, LX, 1965, pp.12-16. On Christopher Isherwood's use of the present tense in *A Single Man* see Jonathan Raban, *The Technique of Modern Fiction*, London 1968, pp.26 ff.

3. A failure to recognize the different function of the implied author as distinguished from the narrator-I is behind Stephen Wall's remark that '...Edmund's shocked Victorian splutter as each new sexual permutation is revealed makes it more difficult for him to carry the weight he has to as the narrator'. *(The Listener,* 10.9.1964, p.401). The Edmund who 'splutters' is, of course, the character-I and not the implied author, as Wall's use of the term narrator suggests.

4. Cf. Stephen Ullmann, *Style in the French Novel*, Oxford 1964, pp.101 and 104.

5. S. W. Dawson, in a review of A. S. Byatt's monograph on Iris Murdoch *(Degrees of Freedom: the novels of Iris Murdoch,* London 1965), shows himself to be completely unaware of the specific dramatic force of the preterite in this novel. He quotes a passage that is clearly in free indirect style in order to illustrate his observation that 'In the later novels, however, we find passages in which we are flatly *told* what characters are thinking and feeling (a telling which has no dramatic life) juxtaposed with touches of "contingency"'. *(Essays in Criticism,* XVI, 1966, p.333). This criticism, ignoring the fact that it is the character-I that does the telling and not the implied author, is a clear example of the kind of blindness that results from failing to realize the basic linguistic facts about literature - in this case, the contrasting functions of the two tense-systems.

6. G. Storms: *The Origin and the Functions of the Definite Article in English*, Amsterdam, 1961, p.13. G. P. Christophersen, *The Articles*, Copenhagen/London 1939, § 32.

7. See J. E. Cirlot, *A Dictionary of Symbols*, London 1962, s.v. *house*. On the archetypal symbolism of dark and light corresponding to the unconscious and the conscious, see C. G. Jung, *Von den Wurzeln des Bewusstseins*, Zürich 1954, Chs. IV and VI.

8. See Cirlot, *op. cit.*, s.v. *house*. Cf. also W. H. Auden's kitchen-poem in *About the House* (London 1966), 'Grub First, Then Ethics (Brecht)', which has for its theme the transformation of food into spirit as a symbol of religious renewal.

9. One wonders whether the curious syntax (surely *I seemed to keep forgetting...* would be more normal) is indicative of free indirect style, since it is probably due to the influence of the spoken language.

10. Zürich 1952; Cf. also *Von den Wurzeln...* Chs. II and III.

11. One may speculate whether the Lydia of the novel is modelled on the Lydia who tells her story to Astolfo in Canto 34 of Ariosto's *Orlando Furioso*, a story that would seem to invite the same Jungian interpretation. This Lydia destroys Alceste, the Thracian knight who loves her, by her cruelty and perverse egotism, and is punished to suffer in Hell. The key-words in which Ariosto depicts her character form an associative field closely resembling that describing the mother-figure in *The Italian Girl: ingrato* (stanza 13), *ingratitudine* (stanza 43), *vinto, prigione* (stanza 25), *vittoria* (stanza 31), *giogo* (stanza 32), *potere* (stanza 30). T. H. Croker, who edited the work with a literal English translation in 1755, translates these key-words respectively *ungrateful, ingratitude, vanquished, prisoner, conquest, yoke, power*. The most popular translation of the work, that by Sir John Harington (1591), re-edited in 1962 (Graham Hough, Centaur Press), which follows the original less closely, has *hard hearts, cruel usage and ungrate, captivated, conquest, yoke* and *power* respectively. Harington uses the word *subjection* (stanza 42) to paraphrase the original *ubbidire* (stanza 40), a licence which can only be called

felicitous in the light of the general tone of the vocabulary. His use of the word *yokefellow* for *consorte* (stanza 37) may or may not be a deliberate attempt to evoke the connotation of subjection so fitting in the context. O.E.D. mentions *yokefellow* as a fairly conventional term for husband or wife from ± 1545 onwards.

12. C. G. Jung, *Von den Wurzeln...*, Chs. II and III.

13. On Iris Murdoch's use of symbolic backgrounds see A. K. Weatherhead, 'Backgrounds with Figures in Iris Murdoch', *Texas Studies in Literature and Language,* X, 1968-69, pp.635-648.

14. See Cirlot, *op. cit.*, s.v. *forest*. On garden and wood symbolism in Iris Murdoch see also James Gindin, *Postwar British Fiction,* Berkeley and Los Angeles/London 1962, pp.183 ff. The Jungian character of most of the symbolism in *The Italian Girl* was recognized by its reviewer Elizabeth Janeway *(The New York Times Book Review,* 13.9.1964, p.5), who goes so far as to call the characters 'anima-figures'.

15. C. G. Jung, *Von den Wurzeln...*, Ch. I.

16. On Iris Murdoch's use of literary and stylistic models see Joseph S. Rippier's chapter on Murdoch in *Some Postwar English Novelists,* Frankfurt/Main 1965. William Hall ('The Third Way; the novels of Iris Murdoch', *Dalhousie Review,* XLVI, 1966-67, p.314) mentions Henry James as the model for *An Unofficial Rose* and D. H. Lawrence as the model for the sixth chapter of *The Sandcastle.* It would seem that the opening chapter of *The Sandcastle* imitates the style of Ivy Compton-Burnett.

17. *The Times Literary Supplement*'s review of the book was aptly entitled 'Enter Someone' (10.9.1964).

18. See 'Against Dryness, a Polemical Sketch' in *Encounter,* Jan. 1961 (henceforth referred to as 'Against Dryness').

19. See, for instance, *The Times Literary Supplement*'s review of *The Unicorn* (6.9.1963) and John Wain's review of *Bruno's Dream* in *The New York Review of Books* (24.4.1969).

20. Cf. G. S. Fraser, *The Modern Writer and his World,* Pelican ed. 1964, p.186.

21. Pp. 15,20,21,25,31-32,43,49,55,59,74,79,88,101,120,125,126,128,134,149,153,169.
P. N. Furbank, in his review of the novel in *Encounter* (November 1964) suggests that in the scene on p.153 the 'oblong knot of hair' reminds Flora of her own abortion. R. Rabinovitz interprets the scene in a no less Freudian sense as a symbolic castration *(Iris Murdoch,* Columbia Essays on Modern Writers, New York/London 1968, p.37). Like *A Severed Head, The Italian Girl* is a favourite with Freudian interpreters; thus, Rabinovitz suggests that the whole book turns round the I's Oedipus complex. The Freudian school is also represented by J. Souvage *op. cit.* and A. S. Byatt *op. cit.* That Iris Murdoch's novels are written with Jung rather than Freud in mind seems to be confirmed by her denial that *A Severed Head* is a satire on psychoanalysis, but rather 'a myth' (cf. 'The Observer Profile' in *The Observer,* 17.6.1962).

22. *King Lear,* IV, iv, 128 (Arden edition).

23. In an interview in *The Times* (13.2.1964) Iris Murdoch has mentioned Shakespeare's 'imaginative scope' as an influence, as well as Henry James, who is 'a pattern man too'.

24. The most elaborate study of Iris Murdoch's philosophical theories, especially as they appear in the novels, is Peter Wolfe's Ph. D. thesis *Philosophical Themes in the Novels of Iris Murdoch* (cf. *Dissertation Abstracts* XXVI, no. 6, December 1965, pp.3357-3358), which was published as *The Disciplined Heart* in 1966 (Columbia, Mo., University of Missouri Press).

25. *Encounter,* January 1961, pp.16-20. Although this is the most frequently quoted of Iris Murdoch's non-fictional writings, her basic ideas are already clearly apparent in her first book, *Sartre, Romantic Rationalist,* Cambridge 1953. For Miss Murdoch's attacks on modern neo-positivistic ways of thinking and her comments on the failure of logical empiricism to come to terms with ethical problems, see her articles 'A House of Theory' *(Partisan Review* XXVI, Winter 1959, pp.17-31) and 'The Idea of Perfection' *(The Yale Review,* LIII, 1963-64, pp.342-380).

26. Graham Martin has applied the distinction between crystalline and journalistic novels to Iris Murdoch's own works, unfortunately confusing the issue by substituting 'novels of character' for the latter type. The crystalline novels are, according to him, *Under the Net, The Flight from the Enchanter, A Severed Head* and *The Unicorn.* ('Iris Murdoch and the Symbolist Novel', *The British Journal of Aesthetics* V, 1965, pp.296-300). To this short list one would certainly feel inclined to add *The Italian Girl.*

27. 'The Sovereignty of Good over Other Concepts', The Leslie Stephen Lecture, 1967, Cambridge 1967, p.3 (henceforth referred to as 'The Sovereignty of Good...'). The same theme is discussed by Frank Kermode in *The Sense of an Ending; studies in the theory of fiction,* New York/London 1967.

28. 'The Sovereignty of Good...' p.10. The allusion to Shelley's sonnet 'Lift not the painted veil...' is revealing for the general platonic trend in Miss Murdoch's thinking.

29. *Ibid.,* p.15.

30. 'The Darkness of Practical Reason', *Encounter,* July 1966, pp.46-50. (Henceforth referred to as 'The Darkness...').

31. 'Against Dryness', p.20. Cf. also Frank Baldanza, 'Iris Murdoch and the Theory of Personality' in *Criticism* VII, 1965, pp.176-189.

32. 'The Sovereignty of Good...' p.13.

33. 'The Darkness...' p.50.

34. The parallels between the liberal-democratic view of the human personality and certain romantic views of art are discussed by Iris Murdoch in an elaborate article 'The Sublime and the Beautiful Revisited' *(The Yale Review,* XLIX, 1959-1960, pp.247-271). It deals in some detail with T. S. Eliot's ideas on personality and on art. It explicitly states that the symbol can be regarded as an analogon of the individual, but not of a real individual (p.260). The subjects dealt with in this article are also covered by William Van O'Connor in 'Iris Murdoch: the Formal and the Contingent', *Critique; Studies in Modern Fiction* III, 1960, pp.34-46.
    It is important to realize that in Iris Murdoch's stories the symbolism of art plays a role entirely opposite to its function in some of the novels and stories of Henry James or in the early novels of E. M. Forster.

35. 'The Sovereignty of Good...' p.22.

36. 'Against Dryness' p.19.

37. See her criticism of the 'metaphysical novel' as practised by the three French writers in 'The Novelist as Metaphysician' and 'The Existentialist Hero' in *The Listener* (16.3.1950 and 23.3.1950 respectively).

38. 'The Sovereignty of Good...' p.11.

39. See the interview with Iris Murdoch in *The Sunday Times* 11.3.1962.

40. 'The Sovereignty of Good...' p.11.

41. *Ibid.* p.13. The word *random* here may contain an echo from Hopkins; see Donald McChesney's comment on the word as used in 'Felix Randal' in *A Hopkins Commentary,* London 1968, p.112.

42. 'The Sovereignty of Good...' p.26.
43. *Ibid.* p.10.
44. Cf. the end of Ch. 14 in *The Bell*, where Dora visits the National Gallery, and also the symbolism of the Tintoretto painting in *An Unofficial Rose*.
45. 'The Sovereignty of Good...' p.23.
46. 'The Sublime and the Beautiful Revisited', *The Yale Review* XLIX, 1959-60, pp. 269-270.
47. 'Virtue is *au fond* the same in the artist as in the good man in that it is a selfless attention to nature: something which is easy to name but very hard to achieve'. ('The Idea of Perfection', *The Yale Review*, LIII, 1963-64, p.377). The term *attention* is Simone Weil's *(ibid.* p.371). For a discussion of the meaning of the idea of love in Iris Murdoch see also R. Rabinovitz, *op. cit.*, p.17.
48. 'The Sovereignty of Good...' p.17. The clearest example of a character who combines the power of clear perception of the artist with the power to love and be compassionate is the portrait-painter Rain Carter in *The Sandcastle*.
49. 'Against Dryness' p.20.
50. Freedom, in Iris Murdoch's philosophy, consists in '...our ability to imagine the being of others...' ('The Sublime and the Good', *Chicago Review* XIII, Autumn 1959, p.42).
51. 'Against Dryness' p.19.
52. 'The Existentialist Hero', *The Listener* 23.3.1950, p.524.
53. J. Souvage, 'Symbol as Narrative Device: An Interpretation of Iris Murdoch's *The Bell*', *English Studies* XLIII, 1962, pp.81-96. A. S. Byatt *(op. cit.*, p.190) disagrees with the interpretation put forward in this article.
54. For an attack of this kind, see S. W. Dawson in *Essays in Criticism* XVI, 1966, pp.330-335. According to Mr. Dawson, the characters are '...manipulated according to a pre-established pattern', while the melodramatic plot shows this pattern in its most abstract form. The answer to this criticism lies in Iris Murdoch's conception of the psyche as a machine, as we shall see. Meanwhile, the danger to lapse into a 'crystalline' type of fiction is a real one to Iris Murdoch, as she confessed in an interview with Frank Kermode: 'One starts off - at least I start off - hoping every time that this is going to happen and that a lot of people who are not me are going to come into existence in some wonderful way. Yet often it turns out in the end that something about the structure of the work itself, the myth as it were of the work, has drawn all these people into a sort of spiral, or into a kind of form which ultimately is the form of one's own mind'. *(Partisan Review* XXX, 1963, pp.62-65). In terms borrowed from her first published novel, in which an awareness of this problem in various forms is a constant theme, there is always the danger that the book may turn out to be '...a travesty and a falsification...' of the reality the book tries to depict. *(Under the Net*, Ch. 4; London 1963 ed. p.70). Frank Kermode has reformulated the difficulty in the following terms: '...Miss Murdoch, as a novelist, finds much difficulty in resisting what she calls "the consolations of form" and in that degree damages the "opacity", as she calls it, of character'. *(The Sense of an Ending*, New York/London 1967, p.130). A. S. Byatt *(op. cit.*, p.190) and Jonathan Raban *(op. cit.*, pp.108-111) have similar criticisms.
55. A general critical problem related to this is whether the novels should be read with the philosophy in mind or not. Frederick J. Hoffman thinks that Iris Murdoch's philosophical writings are '...an extraordinarily intelligent explanation of what she has been doing'. ('Iris Murdoch: The Reality of Persons', *Critique: Studies in Modern Fiction* VII, 1964-65, p.48). On the other hand, Ved Mehta, in

The Fly and the Flybottle (New York 1962, p.54), quotes Miss Murdoch as saying: 'No, I don't think there is any direct connection between my philosophy and my writing. Perhaps they do come together in a general sort of way - in considering, for example, what morality is and what goes into making decisions'. In an interview in *The Times* (13.2.1964) Miss Murdoch has said that it would be fatal if the novels were made a channel for theoretical philosophy. Similar ideas were expressed in interviews in *The Sunday Times* (11.3.1962) and *The Observer* (17.6. 1962).Nevertheless, most critics have assumed that a study of the novels must go hand in hand with a study of the philosophical ideas. J. Souvage's article on the early novels is based on this assumption. The present analysis would seem to prove him right. On the whole we may agree with R. Rabinovitz in this respect: 'The futility of Miss Murdoch's masking of the ideas in her novels, of her denials in interviews that she is a philosophical novelist, should be obvious to the reader who has managed to get through the necessary background material'. (For Souvage's article see note 1; R. Rabinovitz *op. cit.*, p.45).

56. A. S. Byatt, *op. cit.*, p.72.
57. William Hall, '"The Third Way"; The Novels of Iris Murdoch', *Dalhousie Review* XLVI, 1966-67, pp.306-318.
58. 'The Sovereignty of Good...', p.22.
59. *Ibid.*, p.23.
60. *Ibid.*, p.3.
61. The garden as a symbol of the unconscious plays a comparable role in Graham Greene's story 'Under the Garden', in *A Sense of Reality*, London 1963.
62. Pp.35,36,41,79,187. Stephen Wall, in his review of the novel in *The Listener* (10.9. 1964) noted the north-south symbolism, confessing, however, his inability to relate it to the theme of the book.
63. The Sovereignty of Good...', pp.21-22.
64. *Ibid.*, p.26.
65. *Ibid.*, p.11.
66. Cf. P. N. Furbank's discussion of the 'healing motif' in his perceptive review of the novel in *Encounter*, November 1964, pp.88-90.
67. See 'The Sublime and the Beautiful Revisited', *The Yale Review* XLIX, 1959-60, p.263. Similar scenes in which the idea of 'particularity' is evoked by means of minute realistic descriptions are to be found in Ch. 17 of *The Bell*, in which Dora and Toby hoist the bell from the lake, and in Ch. 16 in *The Sandcastle*, in which Donald is rescued from his dangerous position on the tower. On the symbolism achieved by the precision of writing in such scenes see James Hall, 'Blurring the Will: The Growth of Iris Murdoch', *Journal of English Literary History*, XXXII, 1965, pp.256-273.
68. 'Against Dryness', p.20.
69. 'The Sublime and the Beautiful Revisited', *The Yale Review* XLIX, 1959-60, p.259.
70. 'The Sovereignty of Good...', p.17.
71. See e.g. Frederick R. Karl, *A Reader's Guide to the Contemporary English Novel*, New York 1962, pp.260 ff.
72. William Hall, '"The Third Way"; The Novels of Iris Murdoch', *Dalhousie Review* XLVI, 1966-67, p.313. Nor does it make sense to regard Edmund as a kind of '...Parsifal figure hardly distinct from Michael Meade of *The Bell*', as Bernard F. Dick suggests ('The Novels of Iris Murdoch; A Formula for Enchantment', *Bucknell Review* XIV, May 1966, pp.66-68.
73. Christopher Salvesen in *The New Statesman* (11.9.1964, p.365). A similar inability

to place important details of the novel in the context of the book's total meaning is betrayed by Richard Whittington-Egan in his review in *Books and Bookmen* (October 1964, p.20).

74. Kay Dick, review in *The Spectator* (11.9.1964, p.347).
75. See A. S. Byatt, *op. cit.*, pp.77-78 and p.84.
76. In this connection the following statement made by Miss Murdoch in an interview may be relevant: 'I have no intellectual grasp of music and it attacks my emotions directly. Tears will roll down my cheeks at practically any piece of music. It affects me with a sort of desolation. This shows I don't really understand it'. *(The Sunday Times*, 11.3.1962).
77. There are two quotations or allusions which I have not been able to locate: 'Fair flowers and ripe berries' (p.128) and 'An arrow in the side makes poor travelling, only not to run is a worse pain' (p.137). The title of the novel may owe something to *The Italian Maid*, the novel written by Alexander Goodrich in L. P. Hartley's *A Perfect Woman* (1955), which is a surprisingly 'Murdochian' book.
78. *Paradise Lost*, Bk. II, 146-148.
79. *Hamlet* III, ii, 421; I *Kings* 12, 11; *Matthew* 18, 6; *John* 8,7.
80. 'The Sovereignty of Good...', p.11.
81. *Ibid.*, p.13.
82. The passage seems to invite Freudian interpretation in a rather crude and obvious manner. Such an interpretation could only be misleading.
83. C. B. Cox and A. E. Dyson, *Modern Poetry; Studies in Practical Criticism*, London 1963, p.45.
84. J. M. Purcell in *The Explicator*, March 1945.
85. Forrest Reid, *Walter De La Mare; A Critical Study*, London 1929, p.154.
86. Isabel C. Hungerland, *Poetic Discourse*, Berkeley/Los Angeles 1958, p.159.
87. Joseph S. Rippier, *op. cit.*, pp.102-103; cf. also George Whitside, 'The Novels of Iris Murdoch', *Critique: Studies in Modern Fiction*, VII, 1964-65, p.43.
88. F. R. Leavis, *The Great Tradition*, London 1948, p.27.

Notes to Chapter V

1. Harold Whitehall, 'From Linguistics to Poetry', in Northrop Frye, ed., *Sound and Poetry*, English Institute Essays, New York 1957; M. A. K. Halliday, 'Descriptive Linguistics in Literary Studies', 1962; repr. in G. I. Duthie, ed., *English Studies Today, Third Series*, Edinburgh 1964 and in McIntosh & Halliday, *Patterns of Language*, London 1966.
2. See Ch. II, note 107.
3. See, for instance, T. A. van Dijk, 'Metodologie en Literatuurwetenschap', *Levende Talen*, April 1970, 267-286, esp. 280-281.
4. 'The Linguistic Study of Literary Texts', in *Proceedings of the Ninth International Congress of Linguists*, The Hague 1964; rev. version in Chatman & Levin, eds., *Essays on the Language of Literature*, Boston 1967, esp. p.223.
5. The German term is preferred here because it is less ambiguous than its nearest English equivalent, 'emblematic poem'.
6. *Die Logik der Dichtung*, pp.194 ff.
7. '...the present tense serves to fix the essence of something that is momentarily there as on a picture, to eternalize it...'.
8. Cf. Richard Ellmann, *The Identity of Yeats*, 1963[2], esp. the Preface; A. Norman Jeffares, *A Commentary on the Collected Poems of W. B. Yeats*, London 1968, p.296. An important contribution towards the elucidation of 'Leda and the Swan'

was also made by Leo Spitzer in his 1954 essay 'On Yeats's Poem "Leda and the Swan"', reprinted in *Essays on English and American Literature*, Princeton 1962. Spitzer's view that lines 5-6 of the poem are in free indirect style is not substantiated by linguistic evidence, however.

List of works cited

Abbreviations

CE	*College English*
EC	*Essays in Criticism*
ES	*English Studies*
FL	*Foundations of Language*
JL	*Journal of Linguistics*
KR	*Kenyon Review*
MLR	*Modern Language Review*
REL	*A Review of English Literature*
TLS	*The Times Literary Supplement*

A. *LINGUISTIC CRITICISM*

1. *Bibliography*

ALLEN, HAROLD B., *Linguistics and English Linguistics*, New York 1966.
BAILEY, R. W. & BURTON D. M., *English Stylistics: a Bibliography*, Cambridge
    Mass. 1968.
HATZFELD, HELMUT, *Critical Bibliography of the New Stylistics*, Chapel Hill N.C.
    1953.

2. *Books*

ADOLPH, R., *The Rise of Modern Prose Style*, Cambridge Mass. 1968.
ALLEN, HAROLD B., *Readings in Applied English Linguistics*, New York 1958.
BAIN, ALEXANDER, *English Composition and Rhetoric*, 2 vols., London 1893².
BAKER, WILLIAM E., *Syntax in English Poetry 1870-1930*, Berkeley 1967.
BARFIELD, OWEN, *Poetic Diction*, London 1962².
BARRY, JAMES D. & MACDONALD, WILLIAM U., eds., *Language into Literature*,
    Chicago 1965.
BARTHES, ROLAND, *Le degré zéro de l'écriture*, Paris 1953; transl. by ANNETTE
    LAVERS & COLIN SMITH, *Writing Degree Zero*, London 1967.
BATESON, F. W., *English Poetry and the English Language*, Oxford 1934.
BEARDSLEY, MONROE, *Aesthetics*, New York 1958.
BERRY, FRANCIS, *Poet's Grammar*, London 1958.
BOETS, JOZEF, *Moderne Teorieën in verband met klankexpressie*, Ghent 1965.
BOULTON, M., *The Anatomy of Prose*, London 1954.
BROOKE-ROSE, C., *A Grammar of Metaphor*, London 1958.

145

BROOKS, CLEANTH, *The Well-Wrought Urn*, New York 1947.
BULL, WILLIAM E., *Time, Tense and the Verb*, Berkeley 1960.
CHOMSKY, NOAM, *Aspects of the Theory of Syntax*, Cambridge Mass. 1965.
CHATMAN, S. & LEVIN, S. R. eds., *Essays on the Language of Literature*, Boston
COHEN, JEAN, *Structure du langage poétique*, Paris 1966.   [1967
COLERIDGE, S. T., *Biographia Literaria*, London 1817.
CRANE, R. S. & others, *Critics and Criticism Ancient and Modern*, Chicago 1952.
—, *The Languages of Criticism and the Structure of Poetry*, Toronto 1953.
DAVIE, D., *Articulate Energy, An Enquiry into the Syntax of English Poetry*, London
      1955.
DEVOTO, G., *Linguistics and Literary Criticism*, New York 1963.
DUTHIE, G. I., ed., *English Studies Today, Third Series*, Edinburgh 1964.
EATON, TREVOR, *The Semantics of Literature*, The Hague 1966.
ELLEDGE, SCOTT, ed., *Eighteenth-Century Critical Essays*, Ithaca N.Y. 1961.
ENKVIST, N. E., SPENCER, J. & GREGORY M. J., *Linguistics and Style*, London
      1964.
FOWLER, ROGER ed., *Essays on Style and Language*, London 1966.
FRIES, C. C., *The Structure of English*, New York 1952.
FRYE, NORTHROP ed., *Sound and Poetry*, English Institute Essays, New York 1957.
GARVIN, PAUL L. ed., *A Prague School Reader on Esthetics, Literary Structure and
      Style*, Washington 1958.
— &SPOLSKY, B. eds., *Computation in Linguistics*, New York 1967.
GREENBERG, J. H. ed., *Universals of Language*, Cambridge Mass. 1963.
GREENOUGH, J. B. & KITTREDGE, G. L., *Words and their Ways in English Speech*,
      New York 1901.
GOKAK, V. K., *The Poetic Approach to Language*, Oxford 1952.
HALL, ROBERT A. Jr., *Introductory Linguistics*, New York 1964.
HAMILTON, K. G., *The Two Harmonies: Poetry and Prose in the Seventeenth
      Century*, Oxford 1963.
HELLINGA, W. G. & VAN DER MERWE SCHOLTZ, H., *Kreatiewe analise van
      taalgebruik*, Amsterdam/Pretoria 1955.
HOCKETT, C. F., *A Course in Modern Linguistics*, New York 1958.
HOUGH, GRAHAM, *Style and Stylistics*, London 1969.
HUNGERLAND, ISABEL C., *Poetic Discourse*, Univ. of California Publications in
      Philosophy, vol. 33, Berkeley/Los Angeles 1958.
JESPERSEN, O., *A Modern English Grammar on Historical Principles*, 7 vols., Heidel-
      berg 1909-1949.
—, *The Philosophy of Grammar*, London 1935.
JOOS, MARTIN, *The English Verb*, Madison/Milwaukee 1964.
KREUZER, H. & GUNZENHÄUSER, R. eds., *Mathematik und Dichtung*, Munich
      1967².
KRUISINGA, E. & ERADES, P. A., *An English Grammar*, vol. I, 8th ed., Groningen
      1953-1960.
LANE, MICHAEL ed., *Structuralism: A Reader*, London 1970.
LEE, VERNON, *The Handling of Words*, London 1923.
LEECH, G. N., *A Linguistic Guide to English Poetry*, London 1969.
LEED, J. ed., *The Computer and Literary Style*, Kent, Ohio 1966.
LERNER, LAURENCE, *The Truest Poetry*, London 1960.
LEVIN, SAMUEL R., *Linguistic Structures in Poetry*, The Hague 1962.
LOVE, G. A. & PAYNE, M. eds., *Contemporary Essays on Style*, Glenview, Ill. 1969.

LUCAS, F. L., *Style*, London 1955.
MARTIN, HAROLD C. ed., *Style in Prose Fiction;* English Institute Essays 1958, New York 1959.
McINTOSH, A. & HALLIDAY, M. A. K. eds., *Patterns of Language: Papers in General, Descriptive and Applied Linguistics*, London 1966.
MIDDLETON MURRY, J., *The Problem of Style*, London 1922.
NORMAN JEFFARES, A. ed., *New Attitudes to Style*, a special issue of *REL*, VI, April 1965.
NOWOTTNY, W., *The Language Poets Use*, London 1962.
OGDEN, C. K. & RICHARDS, I. A., *The Meaning of Meaning*, Cambridge 1923.
PALMER, F. R., *A Linguistic Study of the English Verb*, London 1965.
PALMER, H. F., *A Grammar of English Words*, London 1938.
POUTSMA, H., *A Grammar of Late Modern English*, Groningen 1926-29.
PREMINGER, A. and others, eds., *Encyclopedia of Poetry and Poetics*, Princeton 1965.
RALEIGH, W., *Style*, London 1897.
RICHARDS, I. A., *Science and Poetry*, London 1926.
ROBERTS, P., *Modern Grammar*, New York 1968.
ROBINS, R. H., *General Linguistics: An Introductory Survey*, London 1964.
SAPIR, EDWARD, *Language*, New York 1921.
SEBEOK, T. A., ed., *Style in Language*, Cambridge Mass. 1960.
—, *Current Trends in Linguistics*, vol. III, The Hague 1966.
SCHILLER, J. P., *I. A. Richards' Theory of Literature*, New Haven/London 1969.
SHIPLEY, J. T. ed., *Dictionary of World Literature*, rev. ed. Totowa 1966.
SPITZER, LEO, *Linguistics and Literary History*, Princeton 1948.
—, *Essays on English and American Literature*, Princeton 1962.
STORMS, G., *The Origin and the Functions of the Definite Article in English*, Amsterdam 1961 (Inaugural Address).
TRAGER, G. L. & SMITH, H. L., *An Outline of English Structure*, Studies in Linguistics, Occasional Papers 3, Washington 1957[2].
UITTI, KARL D., *Linguistics and Literary Theory*, Englewood Cliffs N.J. 1969.
ULLMANN, S., *Semantics*, Oxford 1962.
—, *Language and Style*, Oxford 1964.
—, *Style in the French Novel*, Oxford 1964[2].
WELLEK, R. & WARREN, A., *Theory of Literature*, New York 1955[2].
WIMSATT, W. K. Jr., *The Prose Style of Samuel Johnson*, New Haven 1941.
—, *The Verbal Icon*, New York 1954.
YULE, G. U., *The Statistical Study of Literary Vocabulary*, Cambridge Mass. 1944.
ZANDVOORT, R. W., *Collected Papers*, Groningen Studies in English V, Groningen 1954.
—, *A Handbook of English Grammar*, 9th ed. Groningen 1964.

3. Articles

AARTS, JAN, 'A Note on the Interpretation of "he danced his did"', to be published in *JL*, VII (1971).
ADRIAENS, M., 'Style in William Golding's *The Inheritors*', *ES*, LI (1970), 16-30.
BALL, C. J., 'Language for its Own Sake', *EC*, XVI (1966), 220-226.
BARTHES, ROLAND, 'Historical Discourse' in LANE, *Structuralism*.
BICKERTON, D., 'Prolegomena to a Linguistic Theory of Metaphor', *FL*, V (1969), 34-52.

147

BIERWISCH, M., 'Poetik und Linguistik' in KREUZER/GUNZENHÄUSER, *Mathematik und Dichtung*.

BINNS, A. L., 'Linguistic Reading: Two Suggestions of the Quality of Literature' in FOWLER, *Essays on Style and Language*.

BIRRELL, T. A., 'Engelse literaire kritiek op zoek naar een methodologie', *Forum der Letteren*, IV (1963), 166-176.

BROOKS, CLEANTH, 'The Language of Poetry; some Problem Cases', *Archiv für das Studium der neueren Sprachen und Literaturen*, vol. 203 (1967), 401-415.

BUTTERS, R. R., 'On the interpretation of "deviant utterances"', *JL*, VI (1970), 105-110.

CARSON, GARLAND, 'Linguistics and Literature', *CE*, XXI (1960), 255-260.

CHARLESTON, B. M., 'A Reconsideration of the Problem of Time, Tense and Aspect in Modern English', *ES*, XXXVI (1955), 263-278.

CHATMAN, SEYMOUR, 'On the Theory of Literary Style', *Linguistics*, XXVII (1966), 12-25.

—, 'The Semantics of Style' in LANE, *Structuralism*.

—, 'Linguistics and Teaching Introductory Literature' in ALLEN, *Readings* ...

CRYSTAL, DAVID, 'Specification and English Tenses', *JL*, II (1966), 1-34.

DIJK, T. A. VAN, 'Taaltheorie en literatuurtheorie', *Raster* III/2, 1969, 162-182.

—, 'Metodologie en Literatuurwetenschap', *Levende Talen*, April 1970, 267-286.

EDWARDS, PAUL, 'Meaning and Context: an Exercise in Practical Stylistics', *English Language Teaching*, XXII (1968), 272-277.

ELIOT, T. S., 'Reflections on Vers Libre' (1917), repr. in *To Criticize the Critic*, London 1965.

—, 'The Metaphysical Poets' (1921), repr. in *Selected Essays*, London 1951[3].

ENKVIST, N. E., 'On Defining Style' in ENKVIST/SPENCER/GREGORY, *Linguistics and Style*.

FÓNAGY, I., 'Communication in Poetry', *Word*, XVII (1961), 194-218.

FOWLER, R. & BATESON, F. W., 'Language and Literature', a debate; *EC*, XVI (1966), 226-228 and 464-465; XVII (1967), 322-347; XVIII (1968), 164-182 and 477-478.

FOWLER, R., 'Linguistics, Stylistics; Criticism?', *Lingua*, XVI (1966), 153-165.

—, 'On the Interpretation of nonsense strings', *JL*, V (1969), 75-83.

FRANCIS, N. W., 'Syntax and Literary Interpretation', Monograph Series on Language and Literature no. 13, Washington 1962.

FRASER, G. S., 'The Last English Imagist', *Encounter*, Jan. 1967.

GRAY, B., 'The Lesson of Leo Spitzer', *MLR*, LXI (1966), 547-556.

HALLIDAY, M. A. K., 'The Linguistic Study of Literary Texts' in *Proceedings of the Ninth International Congress of Linguistics*, The Hague 1964; rev. version in CHATMAN/LEVIN, *Essays on the Language of Literature*.

—, 'Descriptive Linguistics in Literary Studies' in DUTHIE, *English Studies Today*, Third Series and in McINTOSH/HALLIDAY, *Patterns of Language*.

HEILMAN, ROBERT B., 'Poetic and Prosaic: Program Notes on Opposite Numbers', *Pacific Spectator*, V (1951), 454-463.

HENDRICKS, WILLIAM O., 'Three Models for the Description of Poetry', *JL*, V (1969), 1-22.

HILL, A. A., 'A Program for the Definition of Literature', *Texas Studies in English*, XXXVII (1958), 46-52.

HILL, TREVOR, 'Institutional Linguistics', *Orbis*, VII (1958), 441-455.

JAKOBSON, R., 'Poetry of Grammar and Grammar of Poetry', *Lingua*, XXI (1968), 597-609.

KATZ, J. J. & FODOR, J. A., 'The Structure of a Semantic Theory', *Language*, XXXIX, (1963), 170-210.

KELKAR, A. R., 'The Being of a Poem', *FL*, V (1969), 17-33.

LEE, BRIAN, 'The New Criticism and the Language of Poetry' in FOWLER, *Essays on Style and Language*.

LEECH, G. N., 'Linguistics and the Figures of Rhetoric' in FOWLER, *Essays on Style and Language*.

—, '"This bread I break" - Language and Interpretation' *REL*, VI (1965), 66-75.

LESTER MARK, 'The Relation of Linguistics to Literature', *CE*, XXX (1969), 366-375.

LEVIN, SAMUEL R., 'Poetry and Grammaticalness' in *Proceedings of the Ninth International Congress of Linguists*, The Hague 1964.

—, 'Deviation - Statistical and Determinate - in Poetic Language', *Lingua*, XII (1963), 276-290.

—, 'Internal and External Deviation in Poetry', *Word*, XXI (1965), 225-237.

— & CHATMAN, S., 'Linguistics and Poetics', in PREMINGER, *Encyclopedia of Poetry and Poetics*.

LIEBERMAN, M. L., 'The New Linguistics and the New Poetics', *CE*, XXX (1969), 527-533.

MILES, JOSEPHINE, 'More Semantics of Poetry', *KR* 1940, repr. in CHATMAN/ LEVIN, *Essays on the Language of Literature*.

OHMANN, RICHARD, 'Prolegomena to the Analysis of Prose Style' in MARTIN, *Style in Prose Fiction*.

—, 'Generative Grammars and the Concept of Literary Style', *Word*, XX (1964), 423-440; repr. in LOVE/PAYNE, *Contemporary Essays on Style*.

—, 'Literature as Sentences', *CE*, XXVII (1966), repr. in CHATMAN/LEVIN, *Essays on the Language of Literature*.

PATTON, T. E., 'Syntactic Deviance', *FL*, IV (1968), 138-153.

PIKE, KENNETH L., 'Language - where Science and Poetry Meet', *CE*, XXVI (1965), 283-292.

QUIRK, RANDOLPH, 'Towards a Description of English Usage', *Transactions of the Philological Society 1960*, Oxford 1961.

READ, HERBERT, 'American Bards and British Reviewers' (1962), repr. in *Selected Writings: Poetry and Criticism*, London 1963.

RIFFATERRE, M., 'Criteria for Style Analysis', *Word*, XV (1959), 154-175; repr. in CHATMAN/LEVIN, *Essays on the Language of Literature*.

—, 'Stylistic Context', *Word*, XVI (1960), 207-218; repr. in CHATMAN/LEVIN, *Essays on the Language of Literature*.

—, 'Describing Poetic Structures: two approaches to Baudelaire's "Les Chats"', *Yale French Studies*, XXXVI-XXXVII, 200-242.

RODWAY, ALLEN, 'By Algebra to Augustanism' in FOWLER, *Essays on Style and Language*.

SAPORTA, SOL, 'The Application of Linguistics to the Study of Poetic Language', in SEBEOK, *Style in Language*.

SAYCE, R. A., 'Literature and Language', *EC*, VII (1959), 119-134.

—, 'The Definition of the Term "Style"', in *Proceedings of the Third Congress of the International Comparative Literature Association*, The Hague 1962.

SCHOLES, ROBERT J., 'Some Objections to Levin's "Deviation"', *Lingua*, XIII (1964), 189-192.

149

STANKIEWICZ, E., 'Linguistics and the Study of Poetic Language', in SEBEOK, *Style in Language.*

STEINER, GEORGE, 'The Language Animal', *Encounter*, August 1969.

STORMS, G., 'The Subjectivity of the Style of *Beowulf*', in *Studies in Old English Literature in Honor of Arthur G. Brodeur*, Univ. of Oregon Books, 1963.

—, 'Grammatical Expressions of Emotiveness', *Papers on English Language and Literature*, I (1965), 351-368.

THORNE, J. P., 'Stylistics and Generative Grammars', *JL*, I (1965), 49-59.

—, 'Poetry, Stylistics and Imaginary Grammars', *JL*, V (1969), 147-150.

—, review of BAKER, *Syntax in English Poetry 1870-1930, Review of English Studies*, XX (1969), 241-243.

TURNELL, M., 'The Criticism of Roland Barthes', *Encounter*, Febr. 1966.

UTLEY, F. L., 'Structural Linguistics and the Literary Critic', *Journal of Aesthetics and Art Criticism*, XVIII (1960), 319-328.

VENDLER, HELEN H., review of FOWLER, *Essays on Style and Language*, EC, XVI (1966), 457-465 (with a postscript by BATESON).

VOEGELIN, C. F., 'Casual and Noncasual Utterances within Unified Structure' in SEBEOK, *Style in Language.*

WARFEL, H. R., 'Syntax Makes Literature', *CE*, XXI (1960), 251-255.

WEINREICH, U., 'On the Semantic Structure of Language' in GREENBERG, *Universals of Language.*

—, 'Explorations in Semantic Theory', in SEBEOK, *Current Trends in Linguistics III.*

WHITEHALL, H. & HILL, A. A., 'A Report on the Language-Literature Seminar' in ALLEN, *Readings in Applied English Linguistics.*

WHITEHALL, H., review of TRAGER-SMITH, *An Outline of English Structure, KR*, XIII (1951), 710 ff.

—, 'From Linguistics to Poetry' in FRYE, *Sound and Poetry.*

WOOD, G. R., 'Computer Research, an Adjunct to Literary Studies', *Papers on Language and Literature*, IV (1968), 459 ff.

B. *THE NOVEL*

1. *Bibliography*

SOUVAGE, J., *An Introduction to the Study of the Novel*, Ghent 1965.
(Part II, 'A Systematic Bibliography for the Study of the Novel', 103-242).

2. *Books*

ALDRIDGE, JOHN W. ed., *Essays and Critiques on Modern Fiction*, New York 1952.

ALLOTT, MIRIAM, *Novelists on the Novel*, London/New York 1959.

AMIS, KINGSLEY, *New Maps of Hell*, London/New York 1960

BOOTH, WAYNE C., *The Rhetoric of Fiction*, Chicago 1961.

BROOK, G. L., *The Language of Dickens*, London 1970.

CALDERWOOD, J. L. and TOLIVER, H. E. eds., *Perspectives on Fiction*, London/ New York 1968.

COWLEY, MALCOLM, ed., *Writers at Work; the Paris Reviews Interviews I*, London 1958.

FLAUBERT, GUSTAVE, *Correspondance, deuxième série*, Paris 1910.

FORSTER, E. M., *Aspects of the Novel*, London 1927.
GIBSON, WALKER, *Tough, Sweet and Stuffy*, New York 1966.
GRAHAM, KENNETH, *English Criticism of the Novel 1865-1900*, Oxford 1965.
HAMBURGER, KÄTE, *Die Logik der Dichtung*, Stuttgart 1957; 1968².
KAYSER, WOLFGANG, *Die Vortragsreise. Studien zur Literatur*, Bern 1958.
KERMODE, FRANK, *The Sense of an Ending; Studies in the Theory of Fiction*, London/New York 1967.
KLOTZ, VOLKER ed., *Zur Poetik des Romans*, Darmstadt 1965.
LANGER, SUSANNE K., *Feeling and Form; A Theory of Art*, London 1953.
LEAVIS, F. R., *The Great Tradition*, London 1948.
—, *'Anna Karenina' and Other Essays*, London 1967.
LEE, VERNON, *The Handling of Words*, London 1923.
LIDDELL, R., *A Treatise on the Novel*, London 1947.
—, *Some Principles of Fiction*, London 1953.
LODGE, DAVID, *Language of Fiction*, London/New York 1966.
LUBBOCK, PERCY, *The Craft of Fiction*, London 1921.
MARTIN, HAROLD C. ed., *Style in Prose Fiction*, English Institute Essays 1958, New York 1959.
MENDILOW, A. A., *Time and the Novel*, London 1952.
MIDDLETON MURRY, J., *Discoveries*, London 1924.
MILLETT, FRED B., *Reading Fiction*, New York 1950.
MUIR, EDWIN, *The Structure of the Novel*, London 1928.
PEPER, JÜRGEN, *Bewusstseinslagen des Erzählens und erzählte Wirklichkeiten*, Leiden 1966.
POUILLON, JEAN, *Temps et Roman*, Paris 1946.
RABAN, JONATHAN, *The Technique of Modern Fiction*, London 1968.
RABINOVITZ, R., *The Reaction against Experiment in the English Novel 1950-60*, New York/London 1967.
ROMBERG, BERTIL, *Studies in the Narrative Technique of the First-Person Novel*, Lund 1962.
SARTRE, JEAN PAUL, *Situations I*, Paris 1947.
SCHOLES, ROBERT ed., *Approaches to the Novel*, San Francisco 1966.
SCHOLES, R. & KELLOGG, R., *The Nature of Narrative*, New York 1966.
SERVOTTE, H., *De Verteller in de Engelse Roman*, Hasselt 1965.
SIMON, IRÈNE, *Formes du roman anglais de Dickens à Joyce*, Liège 1949.
STANG, RICHARD, *The Theory of the Novel in England 1850-1870*, London 1959.
STANTON, R., *An Introduction to Fiction*, New York 1965.
STEVICK, PHILIP ed., *The Theory of the Novel*, New York 1967.
TANS, J. and others, *Buitenlandse letterkunde na 1945*, Utrecht/Antwerpen 1964.
TRILLING, LIONEL, *The Liberal Imagination*, New York 1950.
TROLLOPE, ANTHONY, *Autobiography*, London 1883.
TURNELL, MARTIN, *The Novel in France*, London 1950.
ULLMANN, STEPHEN, *Style in the French Novel*, Oxford 1964².
WATT, IAN, *The Rise of the Novel*, London 1957.
WEINRICH, HARALD, *Tempus; besprochene und erzählte Welt*, Stuttgart 1964.
WEST, PAUL, *The Modern Novel*, London 1963.

3. *Articles*

ELIOT, T. S., Introduction to DJUNA BARNES, *Nightwood*, New York 1961.

FREY, JOHN R., 'The Historical Present in Narrative Literature, particularly in Modern German Fiction', *The Journal of English and Germanic Philology*, XLV (1946), 43-67.

FRIEDMAN, N., 'Point of View in Fiction', *PMLA*, LXX (1955), 1160-1184.

FUNKE, OTTO, 'Zur "erlebte Rede" bei Galsworthy', *Englische Studien* XLIV (1929), 454 ff.

GIBSON, WALKER, 'Authors, Speakers, Readers and Mock Readers', *CE*, XI (1950), 265-269.

GREGORY, M., 'Old Bailey Speech in *A Tale of Two Cities*', *REL*, VI (1965), 42-55.

KAYSER, WOLFGANG, 'Wer erzählt den Roman?' in *Die Vortragsreise;* repr. in KLOTZ, *Zur Poetik des Romans*.

KUNST, J., 'De vertaalbaarheid van de Roman', *Handelingen van het negenentwintigste Nederlandse Filologencongres*, Groningen 1966, 131-133.

LEAVIS, F. R., 'Joyce and the "Revolution of the Word"', *Scrutiny*, II (1933-34), repr. in BENTLEY, ERIC, *The Importance of Scrutiny*, New York 1948.

LEES, F. N., 'George Meredith: Novelist', in *The Pelican Guide to English Literature*, vol. 6, London 1958.

MACDONALD, M., 'The Language of Fiction', *Proceedings of the Aristotelian Society*, 1954, repr. in CALDERWOOD/TOLIVER, *Perspectives on Fiction*.

PASCAL, ROY, 'Tense and Novel', *MLR*, LVII (1962), 1-12.

—, 'The Present Tense in Bunyan's *Pilgrim's Progress*', *MLR*, LX (1965), 12 ff.

QUIRK, R., 'Some Observations on the Language of Dickens', *REL*, II (1961), 19-28.

RAHV, PHILIP, 'Fiction and the Criticism of Fiction', *KR*, XVIII (1956), 276-299.

RANSOM, JOHN CROWE, 'The Understanding of Fiction', *KR*, XII (1950), 197-218.

RICKWORD, C. H., 'A Note on Fiction', *Calendar of Modern Letters*, repr. London 1966, vol. III (1926-27), 226-233.

SCHORER, MARK, 'Technique as Discovery', *Hudson Review* I (1948), repr. in ALDRIDGE, *Essays and Critiques on Modern Fiction;* CALDERWOOD & TOLIVER, *Perspectives on Fiction* and SCHOLES, *Approaches to the Novel*.

—, 'Fiction and the Analogical Matrix', *KR*, XI (1949), 539 ff., repr. in ALDRIDGE, *Essays and Critiques on Modern Fiction*.

SHANNON, EDGAR F., 'The Present Tense in *Jane Eyre*', *Nineteenth Century Fiction*, X (1955), 141 ff.

STANZEL, FRANZ, 'Episches Praeteritum, Erlebte Rede, Historisches Praesens', *Deutsche Vierteljahrsschrift für Literaturwissenschaft und Geistesgeschichte*, XXXIII (1959), 1-12. Repr. in KLOTZ, *Zur Poetik des Romans*.

STONE, HARRY, 'Dickens and Interior Monologue', *Philological Quarterly*, XXXVIII (1959), 52-65.

WATT, IAN, 'The First Paragraph of *The Ambassadors:* an Explication', *EC*, X (1960), 250-274.

C. *IRIS MURDOCH*

1. *Bibliography*

WIDMANN, R. L., 'An Iris Murdoch Checklist', *Critique: Studies in Modern Fiction*, 1968, 17-29.

2. Books

BYATT, A. S., *Degrees of Freedom; the Novels of Iris Murdoch*, London 1965.

CIRLOT, J. E., *A Dictionary of Symbols*, London 1962.

FRASER, G. S., *The Modern Writer and His World*, Pelican ed., London 1964.

GINDIN, J., *Postwar British Fiction*, Berkeley/London 1962.

JUNG, C. G., *Symbole der Wandlung*, Zürich 1952.

—, *Von den Wurzeln des Bewusstseins*, Zürich 1954.

KARL, FREDERICK R., *A Reader's Guide to the Contemporary English Novel*, New York 1962.

KERMODE, FRANK, *The Sense of an Ending: Studies in the Theory of Fiction*, London/New York 1967.

MEHTA, VED, *The Fly and the Flybottle*, New York 1962.

MURDOCH, IRIS, *Sartre, Romantic Rationalist*, Cambridge 1953.

RABAN, JONATHAN, *The Technique of Modern Fiction*, London 1968.

RABINOVITZ, R., *Iris Murdoch*, Columbia Essays on Modern Writers, New York/London 1968.

RIPPIER, J. S., *Some Postwar English Novelists*, Frankfurt/Main 1965.

WOLFE, PETER, *Philosophical Themes in the Novels of Iris Murdoch*, unpublished Ph.D. thesis, see *Dissertation Abstracts* XXVI, December 1965, 3357-3358.

—, *The Disciplined Heart*, Columbia Mo., 1966.

3. Articles

BALDANZA, FRANK, 'Iris Murdoch and the Theory of Personality', *Criticism*, VII (1965), 176-189.

DICK, BERNARD F., 'The Novels of Iris Murdoch; a Formula for Enchantment', *Bucknell Review*, XIV (1966), 66-68.

HALL, JAMES, 'Blurring the Will: the Growth of Iris Murdoch', *Journal of English Literary History*, XXXII (1965), 256-273.

HALL, WILLIAM, '"The Third Way": the Novels of Iris Murdoch', *Dalhousie Review*, XLVI (1966-67), 306-318.

HOFFMAN, F. J., 'Iris Murdoch: The Reality of Persons', *Critique: Studies in Modern Fiction*, VII (1964-65), pp.48 ff.

MARTIN, GRAHAM, 'Iris Murdoch and the Symbolist Novel', *The British Journal of Aesthetics*, V (1965), 296-300.

MURDOCH, IRIS, 'The Novelist as Metaphysician', *The Listener* 16.3.1950.

—, 'The Existentialist Hero', *The Listener* 23.3.1950.

—, 'The Sublime and the Good', *Chicago Review*, XIII (1959), 42 ff.

—, 'A House of Theory', *Partisan Review*, XXVI (1959), 17-31.

—, 'The Sublime and the Beautiful Revisited', *The Yale Review*, XLIX (1959-60), 247-271.

—, 'Against Dryness, a Polemical Sketch', *Encounter*, January 1961, 16-20.

—, 'The Idea of Perfection', *The Yale Review* LIII (1963-64), 342-380.

—, 'The Darkness of Practical Reason', *Encounter*, July 1966, 46-50.

—, 'The Sovereignty of Good over Other Concepts', The Leslie Stephen Lecture 1967, Cambridge 1967.

SOUVAGE, J., 'The Novels of Iris Murdoch', *Studia Germanica Gandensia*, IV (1962), 225-252.

—, 'Symbol as Narrative Device: an Interpretation of Iris Murdoch's *The Bell*', *ES*, XLIII (1962), 81-96.

VAN O'CONNOR, W., 'Iris Murdoch: the Formal and the Contingent', *Critique: Studies in Modern Fiction*, III (1960), 34-46.

WEATHERHEAD, A. K., 'Backgrounds with Figures in Iris Murdoch', *Texas Studies in Literature and Language*, X (1968-69), 635-648.

WHITSIDE, G., 'The Novels of Iris Murdoch', *Critique: Studies in Modern Fiction*, VII (1964-65), 43 ff.

4. *Reviews of* The Italian Girl

ANON., *The Times Literary Supplement*, 10.9.1964.

DAWSON, S. W., *EC*, XVI (1966), 330-335.

DICK, KAY, *The Spectator*, 11.9.1964.

FURBANK, P. N., *Encounter*, November 1964.

JANEWAY, ELIZABETH, *The New York Times Book Review*, 13.9.1964.

SALVESEN, C., *The New Statesman*, 11.9.1964.

WALL, STEPHEN, *The Listener*, 10.9.1964.

WHITTINGTON-EGAN, R., *Books and Bookmen*, October 1964.

Appendix

The first chapter of *The Italian Girl* by Iris Murdoch, reprinted from the first edition, London, Chatto & Windus 1964.
The figures in the margin correspond to the original page-numbers.

A MOONLIGHT ENGRAVING

p.11. I PRESSED the door gently. It had always been left open at night in the old days. When I became quite certain that it was locked, I stepped back into the moonlight and looked up at the house. Although it was barely midnight, there was not a light showing. They were all abed and asleep. I felt a resentment against them. I had expected a vigil, for her, and for me.

I moved through a soft tide of groundsel and small thistles to try the two front casements, but they were both firm and a greater blackness breathed at me from within. Calling out or throwing stones at windows in such a silence, these were abhorrent things. Yet to wait quietly in the light of the moon, a solitary excluded man, an intruder, this was abhorrent too. I walked a little, with dewy steps, and my shadow, thin and darkest blue, detached itself from the bulk of the house and stealthily followed. At the side it was all dark too and protected by such a dense jungle of ash saplings and young elder trees that it would have been impossible to reach a window, even had there been one unlatched. I measured, by the growth of these rank neglected plants, how long it was since I had last been in the north: it must be all of six years.

p.12. It had been foolish, entirely foolish, to come. I ought to have come earlier when she was ill, earlier when she wanted me and wrote in letters which for anger and guilt I could scarcely bear to read, come, come, come. To have come then would have made sense in the light of the last abstract consideration I had for her: after all she was my mother. But to come now that she was dead, to come merely to bury her, to stand in her dead presence with those half-strangers, my brother and my sister-in-law, this was senseless, a mere self-punishment.

I returned across the lawn, following my own tracks in the dew. The clouded moon had spread a luminous transparent limb across the sky, and showed me the silhouettes of the great trees which surrounded the house. It was still the skyline I knew best in the world. I felt for a moment almost tempted to go away, to try the door once again and then to go, like the mysterious traveller of the poem. "Tell them I came and no one answered". I looked again at the familiar shapes of the trees and shivered at the sudden proximity of my childhood. These were the old June smells, the wet midsummer night

155

smells, the sound of the river and the distant waterfall. An owl hooted, slowly, deliberately, casting out one inside the other his expanding rings of sound. That too I remembered.

The thought that I might go away and leave them all there asleep made me pause with a sort of elation. There was an air of vengeance about it. That would

p.13. be to leave them forever, since if I went away now I was sure I would never return. Indeed, whatever happened I would probably never, after this one time, return. My mother's existence here had been the reason for my not coming. Now her non-existence would provide an even stronger reason.

I must have been standing there for some time in a sad reverie when I saw what for a weird second looked like a reflection of myself. I had so vividly, I now realised, pictured myself as a dark figure upon that silver expanse that when I saw, emerged into the dim light in front of me, another such figure I thought it could only be me. I shivered, first with this weird intuition, and the next moment with a more ordinary nervousness of this second night intruder. I knew at once from the outline of the man that it was not my brother Otto. Otto and I are both very big men, but Otto is bigger, although his stooping six foot three may pass for no more than my upright six foot one. The figure that now slowly advanced towards me was small and slim.

Although I am not especially a coward I have always been afraid of the dark and of things that happen in the dark: and this night illumination was worse than darkness. The sense that I was also frightening the other man simply made me more alarmed. In a horrible silence I moved slowly towards him until we were near enough to catch a glint from each other's eyes.

A soft voice said, "Ah—you must be the brother."

p.14. "Yes. Who are you?"

"I am your brother's apprentice. My name is David Levkin. For a moment you frightened me. Are you locked out?"

"Yes." I hated saying this to him, and suddenly all my old love for the place, my old patriotism for it, filled me with pain. I was locked out. It was monstrous.

"Don't worry. I'll let you in. They are all gone to bed."

He moved across the lawn to the shadow of the house and I followed him. The moonlight fell in streaks through the overgrown lattice of the porch, weighed down with honeysuckle, and revealed the fumbling hand and the key. Then the door gave softly to show the thick waiting blackness of the house, and I followed the boy out of the honeysuckle fragrance into the old stuffy foxy darkness of the hall. The door closed and he turned on a light and we looked at each other.

I recalled now that my sister-in-law Isabel, the news-giver of the family, had written to me some time ago about a new apprentice. Otto's apprentices were something of a sad tale and a cause of scandal always to my mother. With unerring care he had attracted to himself a notable sequence of juvenile delinquents, each one worse than the last. I scanned the boy, but could not for the moment recall anything Isabel had said about him. He seemed about twenty. He did not look English. He

p.15. was slim and long-necked, with big prominent lips and a lot of very straight brown hair. His nose was wide with big suspicious nostrils and he eyed me now with narrow eyes, very doubtfully, his lips apart. Then he smiled, and as the eyes almost vanished the cheeks broadened out in great wreaths of welcome. "So you have come."

The locution might have been impertinent or merely foreign. I could not see his face properly. My mother, intensely mean with money, had always insisted on using the weakest possible electric light bulbs, so that there was scarcely more to be seen within than by the light of the moon. It was a weak, dirty, weary sort of dimness. I wished to be rid of him, and said, "Thank you. I can look after myself now".

"I do not sleep in the house." He said it solemnly and now with a perceptible foreignness. "You will know where to go?"

"Yes, thank you. I can always wake my brother."

"He does not sleep in the house now either."

I felt unable to discuss this. I felt suddenly utterly tired and ill-used. "Well, goodnight, and thank you for letting me in."

"Goodnight." He was gone, dissolving in the pale, uncertain, yellow light, and the door was closing. I turned and began to go slowly up the stairs with my suitcase.

At the top of the stairs I paused as the familiar pattern of the house seemed to enter into my body

p.16. magnetically: Otto's room, my room, my father's room, my mother's room. I turned toward my own room, where I assumed a bed would have been made up for me; and then I paused. I had not yet really conceived of her as dead. I had thought about journeys and times, about the cremation which was to take place tomorrow, about the nature of the ceremony, about Otto, even about the property, but not about her. My thoughts, my feelings about her belonged to some other dimension of time, belonged to before whatever it was that had happened to her twenty-four or thirty-six hours ago. The sense of her mortality invaded me now, and it became inevitable that I should enter her room.

The dim electric light revealed the big landing, the oak chest and the fern which never grew but never died either, the fine but entirely threadbare Shiraz rug, the picture which might have been by Constable but wasn't which my father had got in a sale at a price for which my mother never forgave him: and the closed silent doors of the rooms. Before the sick feeling should make me feel positively faint I went to my mother's door and quickly opened it and turned on the light within.

I had not expected her face to be uncovered. I closed the door behind me and leaned back against it with a violently beating heart. She lay, raised up rather high upon the pillows, her eyes closed and her hair undone. She could not have been sleeping, though it would have been hard to say quite how

p.17. this was evident. Her face was yellowish white and narrowed, shrunk already away from life, altogether smaller. But her long hair which had been bronze once, now a dark brown striped with grey, seemed vital still, as if the terrible news had not yet come to it. It seemed even to move a little at my entrance, perhaps in a slight draught from the door. Her dead face had an expression which I had known upon it in life, a sort of soft crazed expression, like a Grünewald Saint Antony, a look of elated madness and suffering.

My mother's name was Lydia, and she had always insisted that we call her by this name. This had displeased my father, but he did not cross her in this or indeed in anything else. My mother's affections had early turned away from her husband and focused with rapacious violence upon her sons, with whom she had had, as it were, a series of love-affairs, transferring the centre of her affection to and fro between us: so that our childhood passed in an alternate frenzy of jealousy and of suffocation. In my first memories she was in love with Otto, who is my senior by two years. When I was six she loved me passionately, and again when I was ten, and again in my later years at school; and perhaps later too, and most fiercely of all, when she felt me slipping from her grasp. It was when it was at last clear to her that I had escaped, that I had run away and would not come back, that she turned her emotions on to her last love, her granddaughter Flora, Otto and Isabel's only child. She would often say that no one but she could control the little girl. It was true; Lydia had seen to it that it was true.

p.18.

She was a small woman. She had been so proud, when we were at art school, of her two huge, talented sons. I can recall her walking between us and looking up at each in turn with a proud possessive leer, while we stared ahead and affected not to notice. She was, in some way, a great spirit; all that power, with some turn of the screw, might have organised some notable empire. There was nothing of the artist in her. Yet with this she was a timid woman, convinced of the hostility of the world and incapable of crossing a hotel lounge without believing that everyone there was staring at her and talking maliciously about her.

Isabel had put up but little fight. She lost Otto almost at once and withdrew herself into a sad sarcastic remoteness. Almost the last serious talk I had had with my brother, many years ago now, had been when I implored him, on his marriage, to get away from Lydia. I can recall the paralysed look with which he said that it was impossible. Shortly after that I departed myself. It was perhaps the spectacle of Lydia's ruthlessness to Isabel which finally sickened me and made me feel for my mother at last the positive hatred which was a necessity for my escape. Yet Lydia never destroyed Isabel: Isabel was strong too in her own way, another ruined person, but strong.

p.19.

It was scarcely credible that all that power had simply ceased to be, that the machine worked no longer. My father had passed from us almost unnoticed, we believed in his death long before it came. Yet my father had not been a nonentity. When he was the young and famous John Narraway, Narraway the socialist, the free-thinker, the artist, the craftsman, the saint, the exponent of the simple life, the redeemer of toil, he must have impressed my mother, he must indeed have been an impressive person, a talented and perhaps a fine person. Yet my early memories are not of my father, but of my mother one day saying to us: your father is not a good man, he is merely a timid man with unworldly tastes. We felt for him a faint contempt and later pity. He never beat us. It was Lydia who did that. He passed on to us only, in some measure, his talents. He had been a sculptor, a painter, an engraver, a stone mason. He left us behind, two lesser men, Otto the stone mason and I, Edmund, the engraver.

I looked at what lay before me with a horror which was not love or pity or sadness, but was more like fear. Of course I had never really escaped from Lydia. Lydia had got inside me, into the depths of my being, there was no abyss and no darkness where she was not. She was my self-contempt. To say that I hated her for it was too flimsy a saying: only those will understand

158

who have suffered this sort of possession by another. And now the weird thought that I had survived her did not increase my being, but I felt in her presence mutilated and mortal, as if her strength, exercised from *there*, could even now destroy me. I looked with fascination upon the live, still burnished hair and upon the white, already shrunken face. Leaving the room, I switched the light off and it seemed very strange to leave her there in the dark.

I moved softly across the landing to my own door. The house creaked about me as if in recognition, the inarticulate greeting of some primitive dog-like house-ghost. I had no thought of waking Otto now. The closed doors breathed a stupefaction of slumber; and I wanted desperately to sleep myself, as if to appease with that semblance of death the angry defeated spirit. I reached my own door and opened it wide, and then stopped in my tracks. The moon shone clearly on to my bed and revealed the form of a young girl with long glistening hair.

For a moment it seemed like a hallucination, something hollow and incompletely perceived, some conjuration of a tired or frightened mind. Then the form stirred slightly and turned, the bright hair falling on to an almost bare shoulder. I started back and closed the door in a shock of guilty terror. This was a magic of exclusion which was too strong for me. A moment later, like an evil spirit put to flight, I was stumbling away down the stairs.

A woman's voice above me softly spoke my name. I paused now and looked up. A face was looking at

me over the bannisters, a face which I dimly, partly, recognised. Then I realised that it was only my old nurse, the Italian girl. We had had in the house, ever since we were small children, a series of Italian nursery-maids; whether one had led to another or whether this was a foible of my mother's I never remember discovering. But one result had been that my brother and myself, with no natural gift for languages, spoke fluent Italian. The post had become, in a manner, traditional, so that I had always had, as it were, two mothers, my own mother and the Italian girl. Looking up now at the remembered face, I felt a sort of temporal giddiness and could not for a moment make out which one this was, while a series of Giulias and Gemmas and Vittorias and Carlottas moved and merged dreamlike in my mind. "Maggie."

Her name was Maria Magistretti, but we had always called her Maggie. I came back up the stairs.

"Maggie, thank you. Yes, I see. Of course, Flora is in my room. You've put me in Father's old room? Yes, that's fine."

As I whispered, she pushed open the door of my father's room and I followed her into the bleak lighted interior.

I had never known her to wear anything but black. She stood there now, a small dark figure, gesturing towards the narrow bed, her long bun of black hair trailing down her back like a waxen pigtail. With her pale, framed face, in the solemnity

of the hour, she seemed like an attendant nun: one expected to hear the clink of a rosary and a murmured *Ave*. She looked to me ageless, weary: the last of the Italian girls, left as it were stranded by the growing up of her two charges. She must have been, when she came, but little older than the boys she was to look after; but some trick of fate had left her behind ever since in that northern house. Otto claimed he remembered being wheeled by Maggie in his pram, but this was certainly a false memory: some previous Carlotta, some Vittoria, merged here with her image; they were indeed all, in our minds, so merged and generalised that it seemed as if there had always ever been only one Italian girl.

"A hot-water bottle in the bed? How kind of you, Maggie. No, not a meal, I've eaten, thank you. Just bed. It's at eleven tomorrow, isn't it? Thank you, goodnight." With this came to me some old comforting breath of childhood; warm beds, prompt meals, clean linen: these things the Italian girl had provided.

I stood alone in the faded pretty room. The patchwork bed-cover was turned back for me. I looked about. A lot of my father's pictures hung in this room, placed there by Lydia who had, after his death, collected them from elsewhere in the house to make of this place a sort of museum, a mausoleum. It was as if she had, in the end, enclosed him in a narrow space. I looked at the pale water-colours which had once seemed the equal of Cotman and the mannered engravings which had once seemed the equal of Bewick; and there emanated from them all a special and limited sense of the past. They looked to me, for the first time, dated, old-fashioned, insipid. I felt his absence then with a quick pathos, his presence as a sad reproachful ghost: and it was suddenly as if after all it was he who had just died.

p.23.